AF352585

A Prairie Season

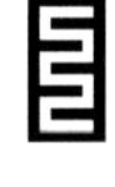

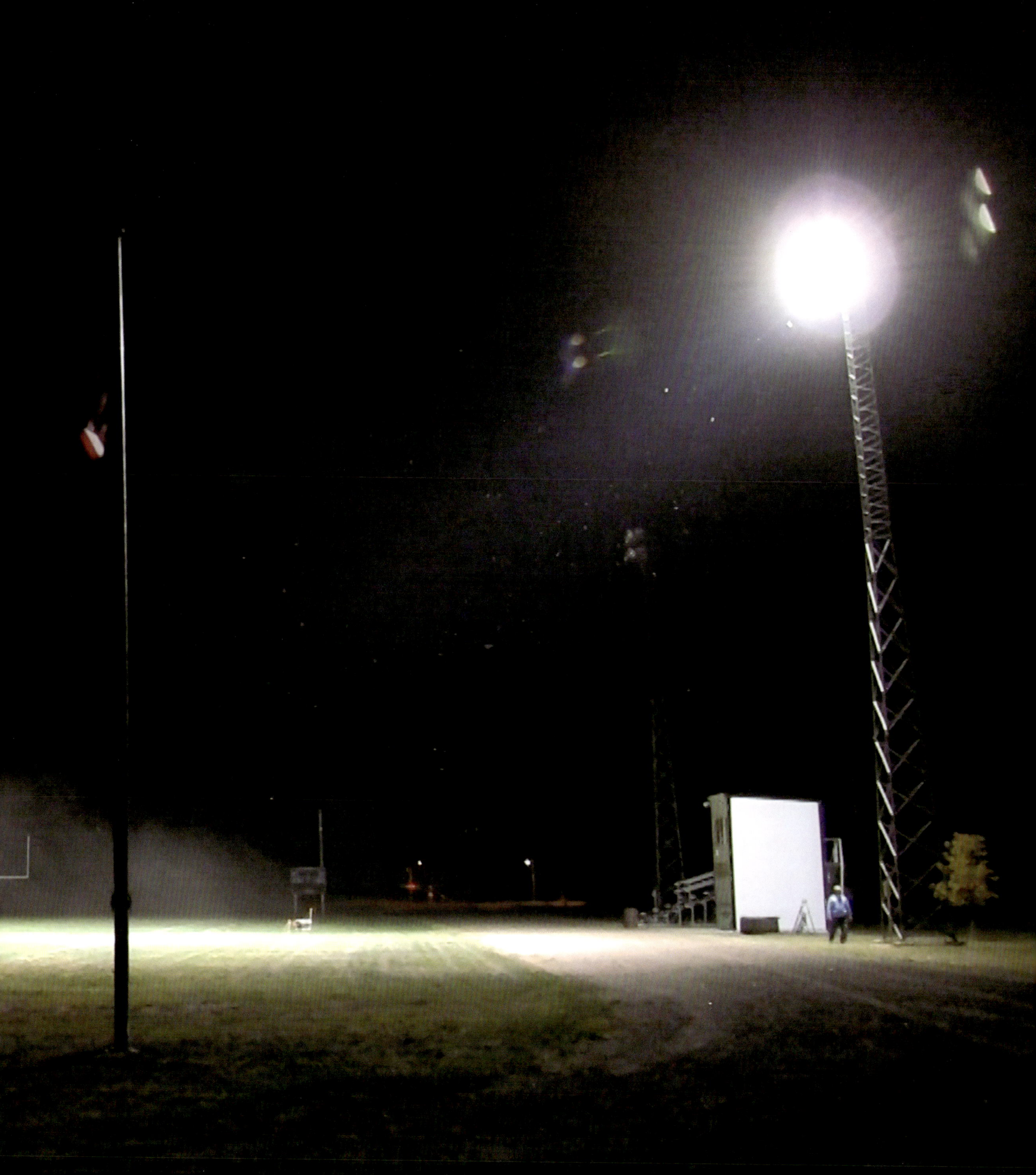

Flood Editions, Chicago

William Wylie

A Prairie Season

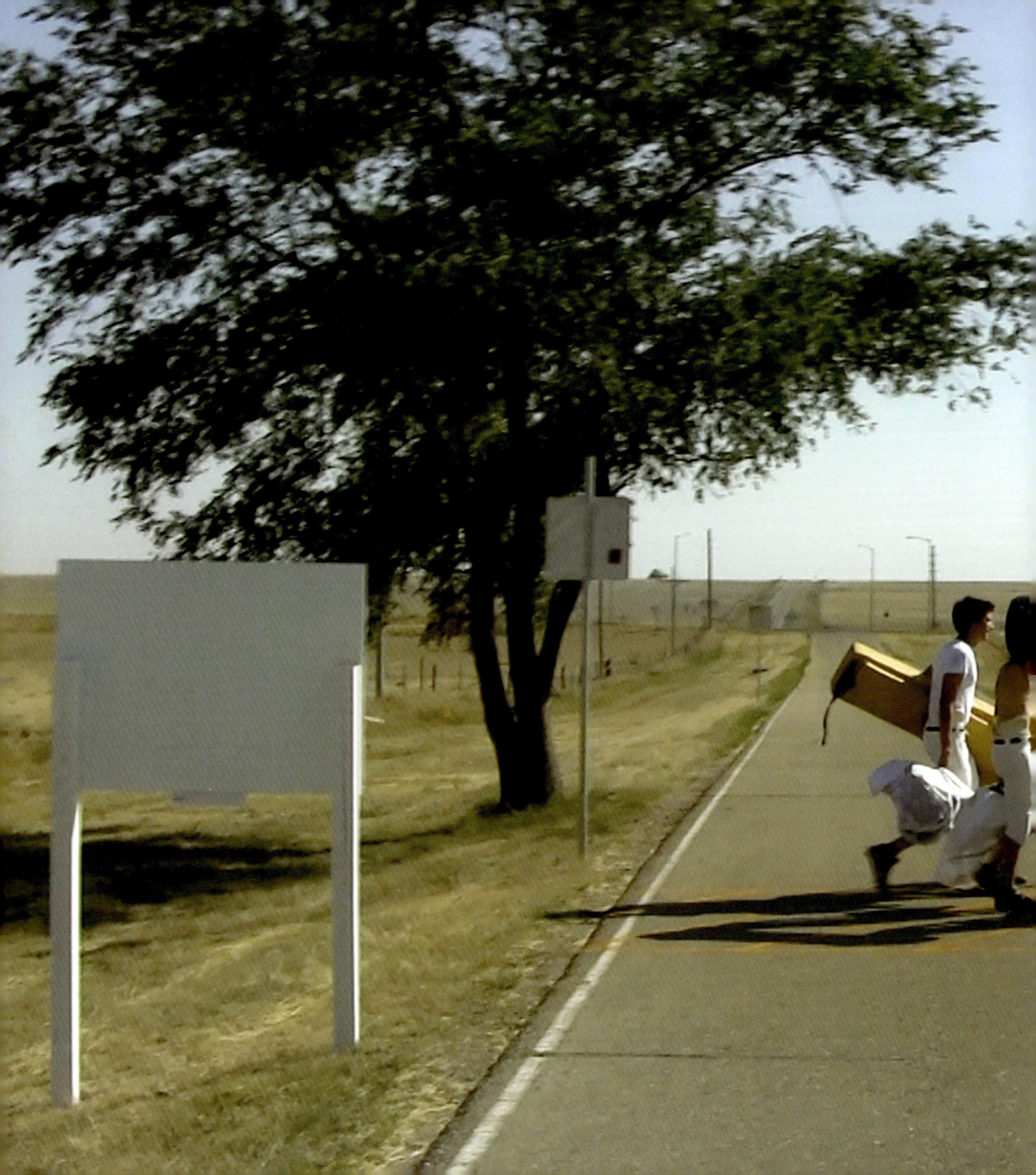

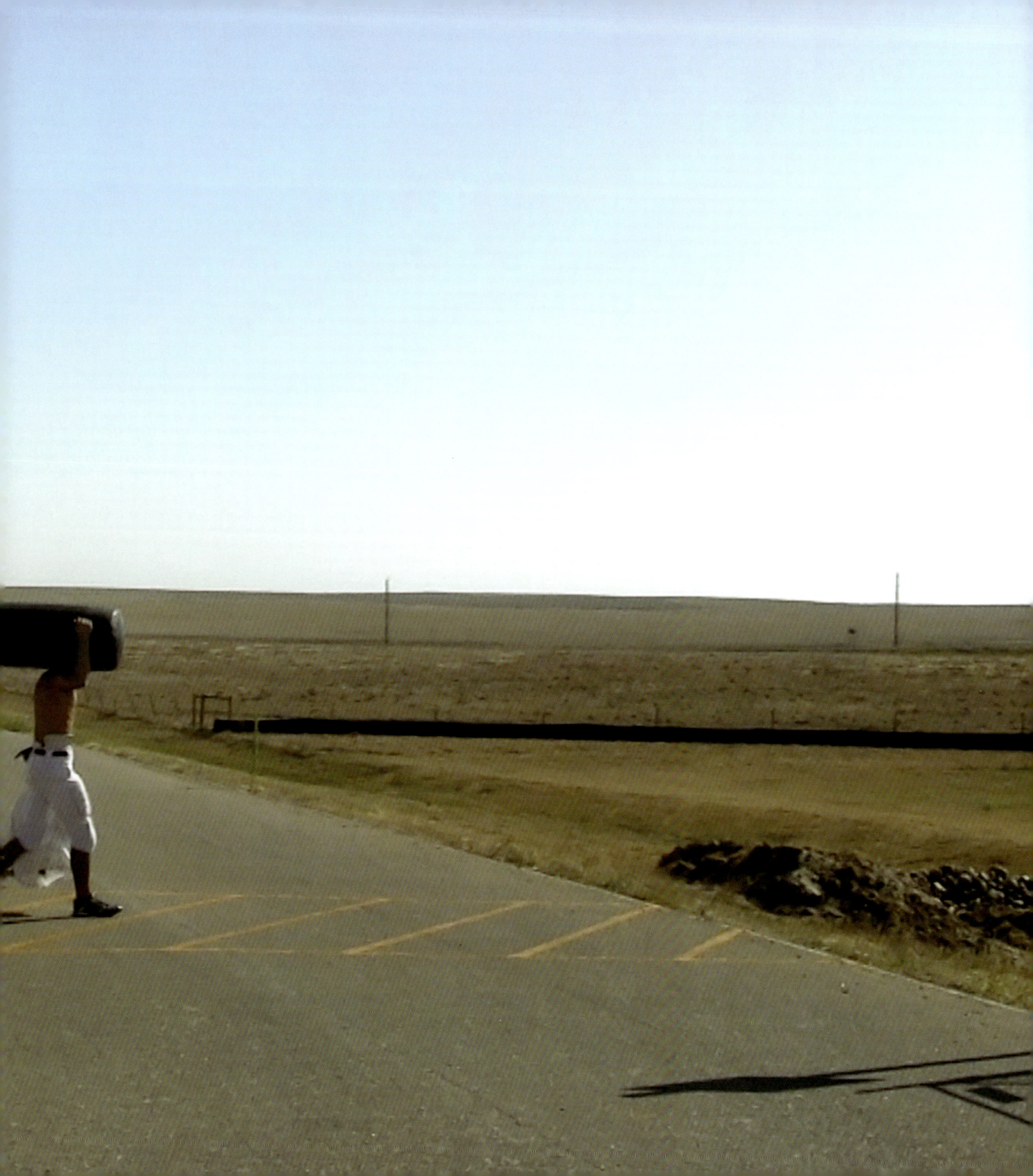

The Place

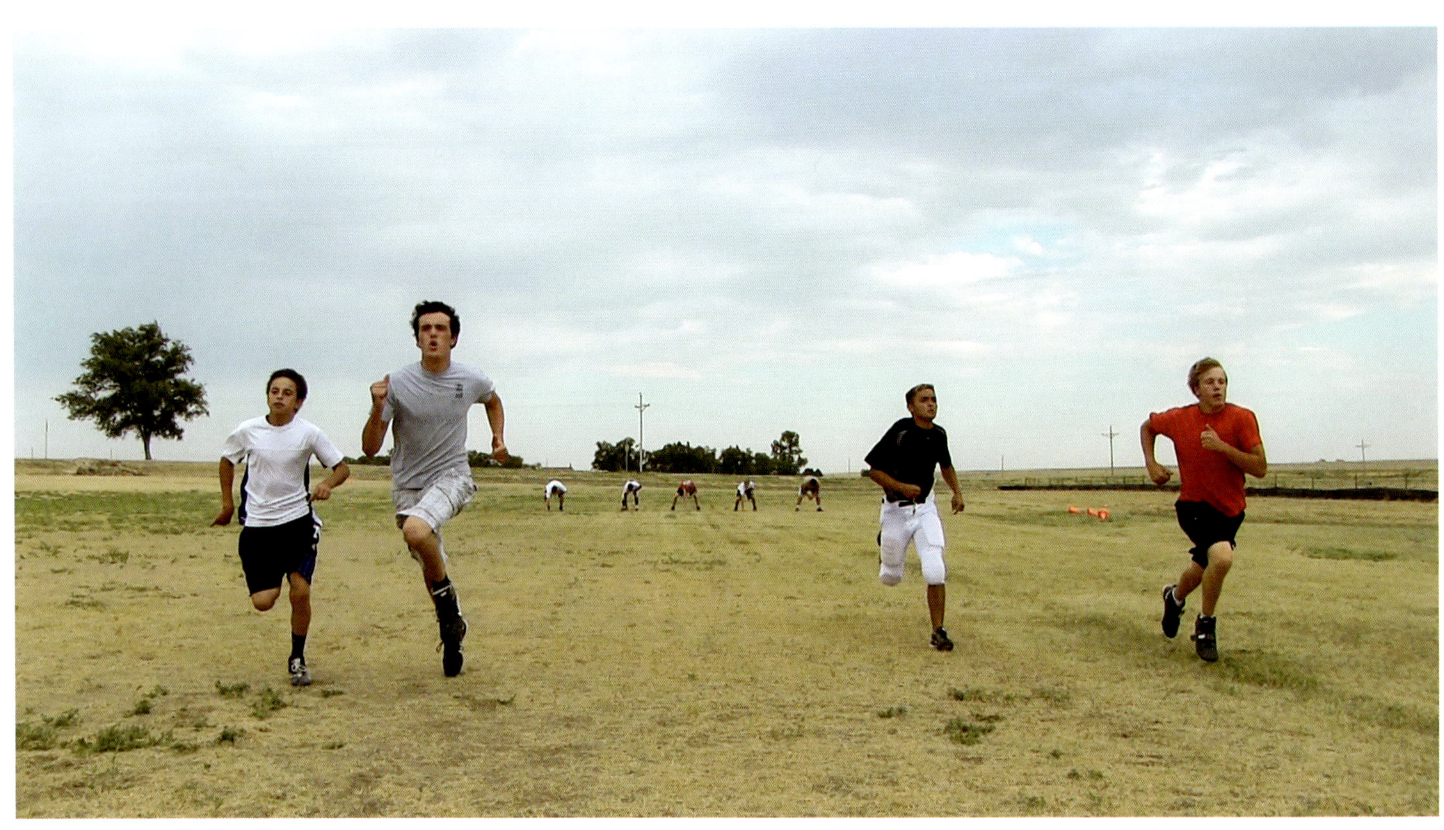

From a distance at night, across the flat earth, Prairie School's football field appears as no more than a glowing light on the horizon. I first encountered it that way, driving east on Highway 14 as the sun set behind the peaks of the Front Range in late summer. As darkness enveloped the prairie and what remained of the small township of New Raymer, I could see the intense green patch of a field illuminated by lights off in the void. I had read about a unique style of football played at rural schools in the area, so I pulled off down a side road to stretch and have a closer look.

The eastern Colorado plains are among the most sparsely populated areas in the continental U.S., and for me that emptiness is part of their appeal. This sense of emptiness also drew the attention of the federal government, who, in the 1960s, located over fifty Minuteman III nuclear-missile silos in the area to act as a "nuclear sponge," or potential targets, in case of a nuclear attack.

All was still as I walked out to the gravel track that ran around the field. I could hear the electric buzz of the high-intensity lights up on the towers and the semis a mile away, barreling east towards Sterling. After the brutally hot day, the cool and crisp air was welcome relief. I greeted a man who had come out to check on some newly laid sod. It was during our conversation that an idea began to take shape: I would return the next year and document the entire Prairie School football season. On Friday nights in fall, with a moon rising over the plains, surrounded by all that space, and the families and teachers and ranchers and roughnecks gathered in the bleachers under the lights to watch a game, there might not be any better place to be.

A Nebraskan coach, Stephen Epler, developed the six-man game in 1934, as an alternative for smaller high schools struggling to field teams during the Great Depression. By 1951, six-man football had been adopted by 2,463 schools in all but two states. Currently, for a school to play in the Colorado six-man league, it must have a population of less than 75 students. At present, only 30 schools qualify.

Teams play on a smaller than normal football field, 80 × 40 yards, which accounts for the pace of the game and some rule changes. A first down requires 15 yards instead of 10, and all players, even the center, can be downfield receivers. Because preventing a kick from being blocked is difficult, a successful field goal counts for four points, and a kick after a touchdown counts for two points, while an extra point scored by a pass or run is only one point. Games have a quick tempo and are usually high scoring, which sometimes necessitates implementation of the slaughter or mercy rule. If an opponent achieves a lead of 45 points or more in the second half, officials simply let the clock run, no matter what happens on the field.

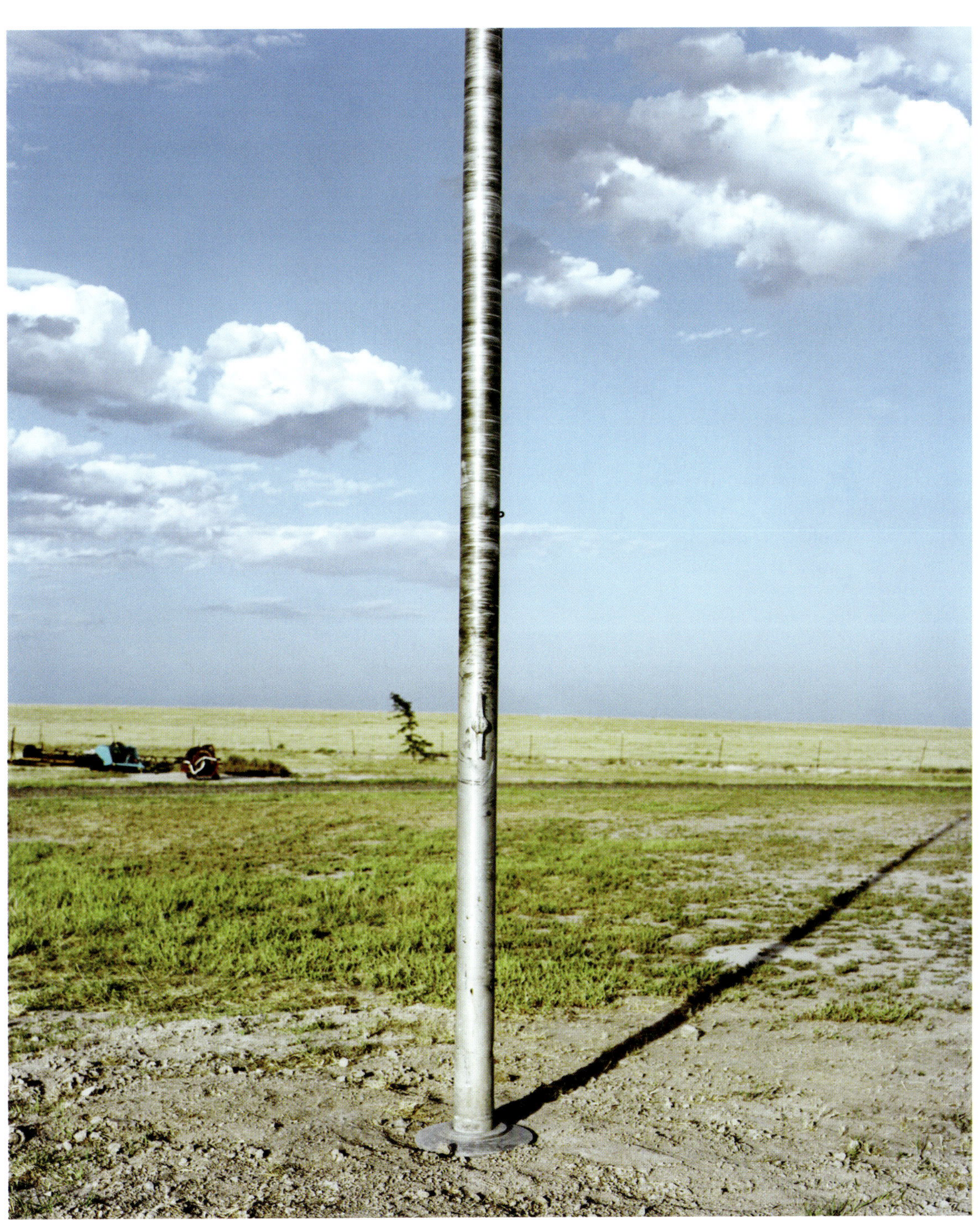

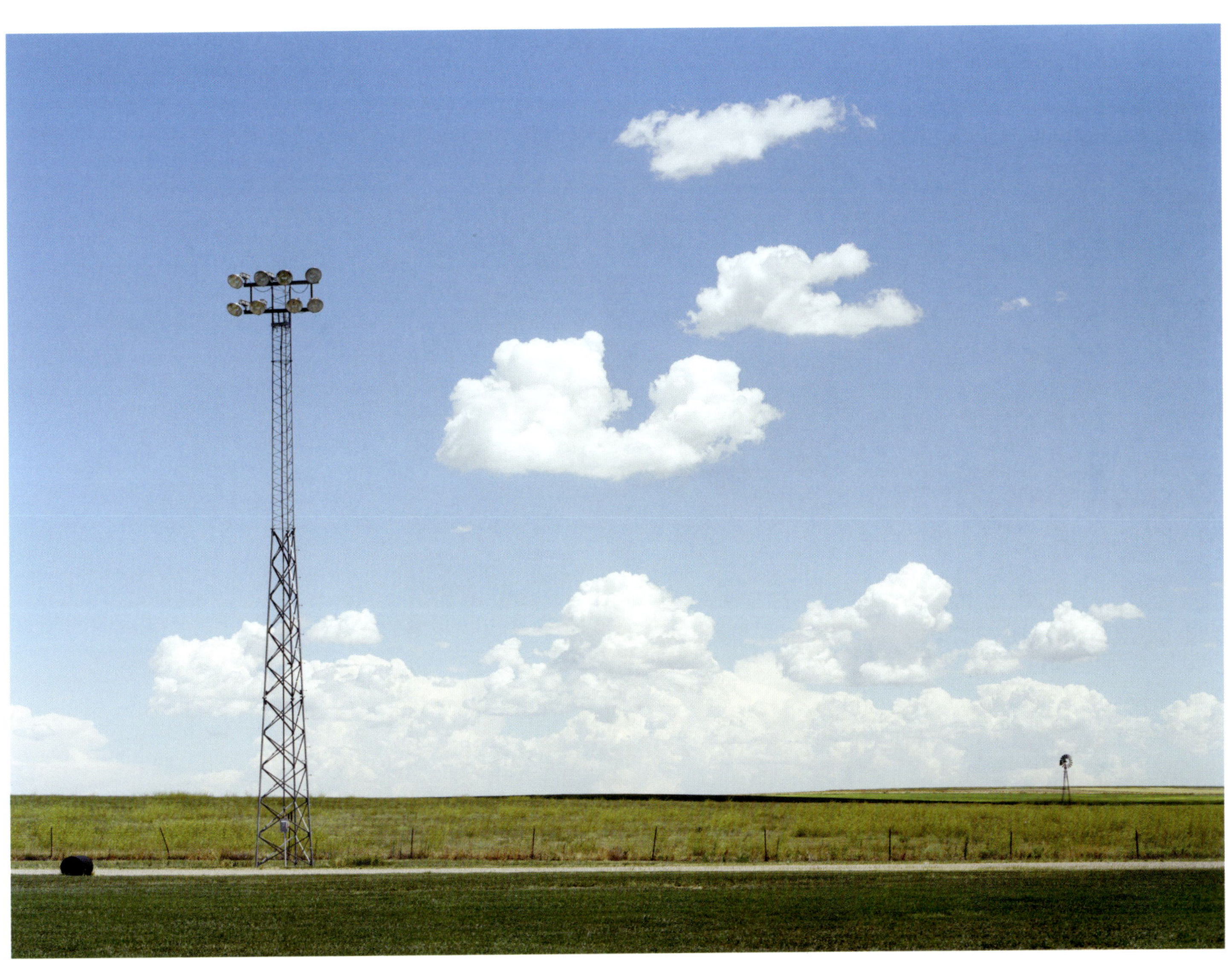

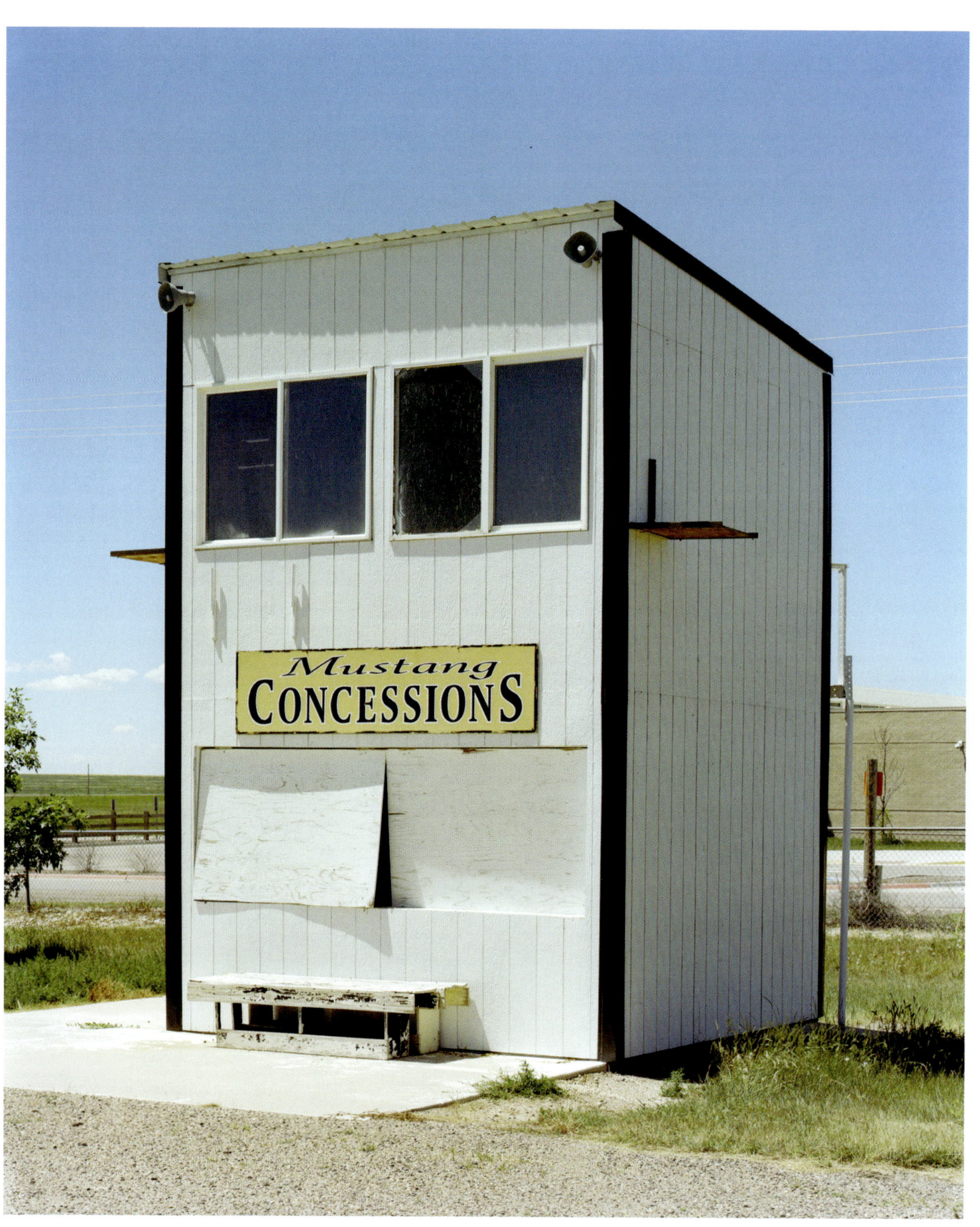

Mustang
CONCESSIONS

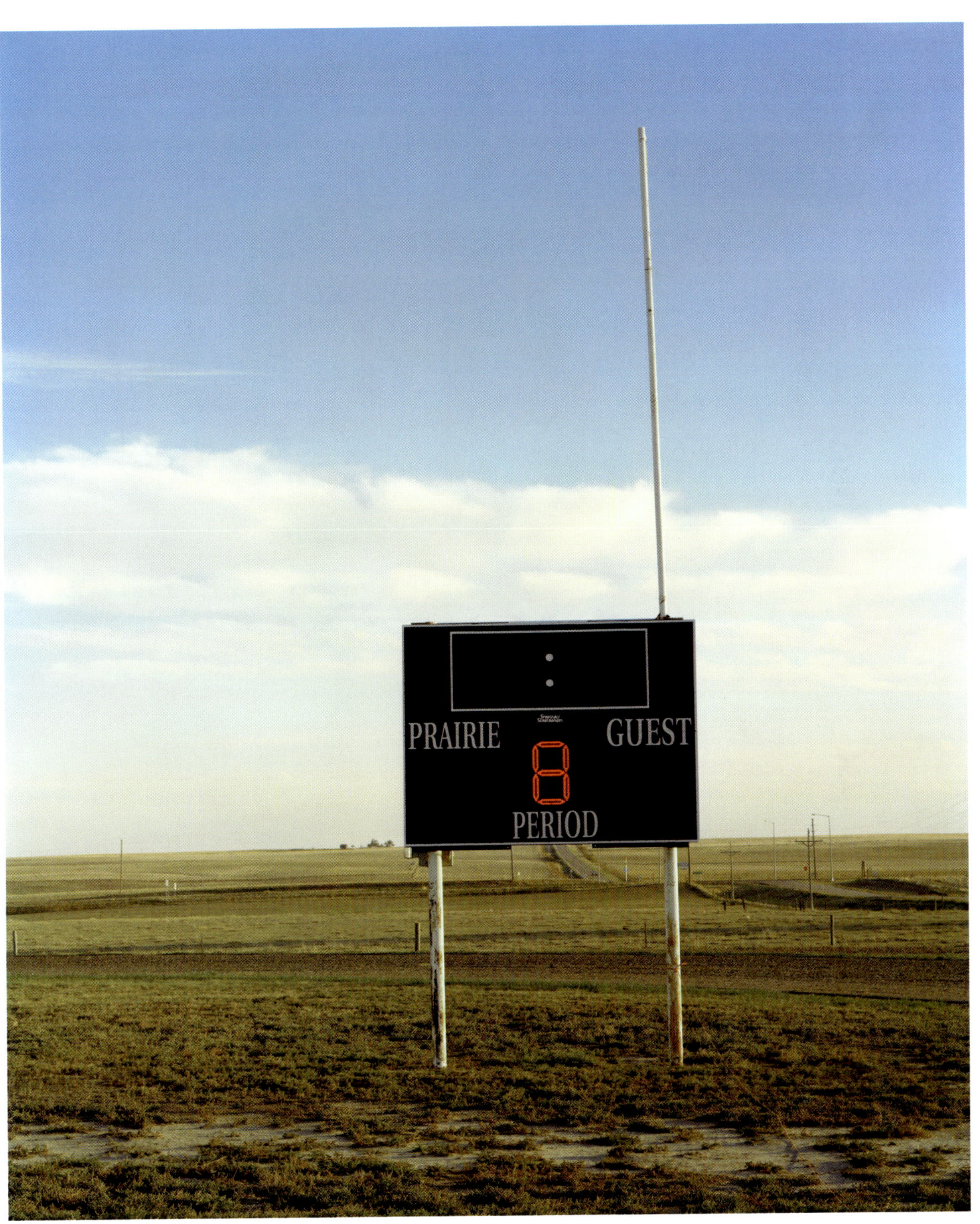

PRAIRIE
GUEST
PERIOD

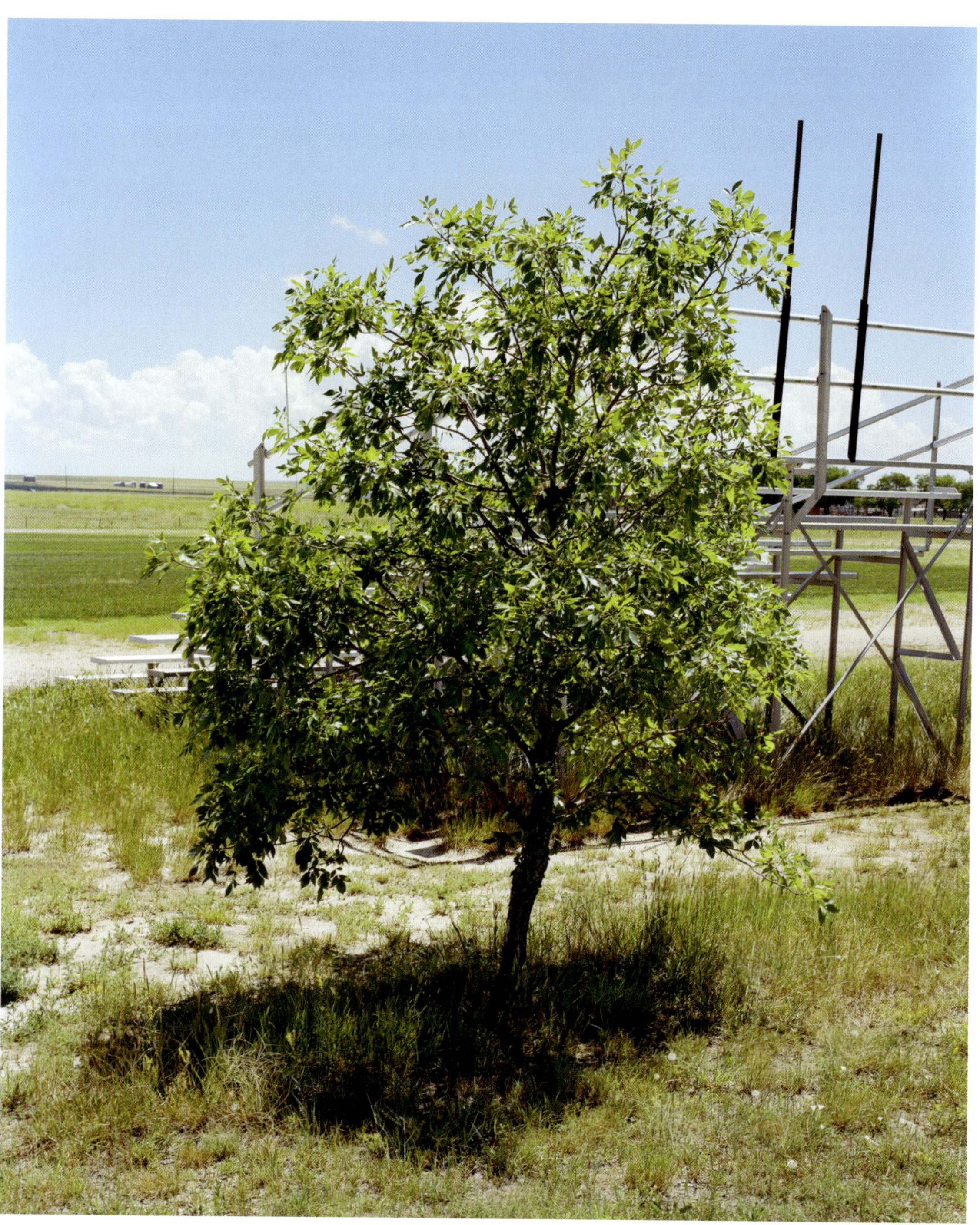

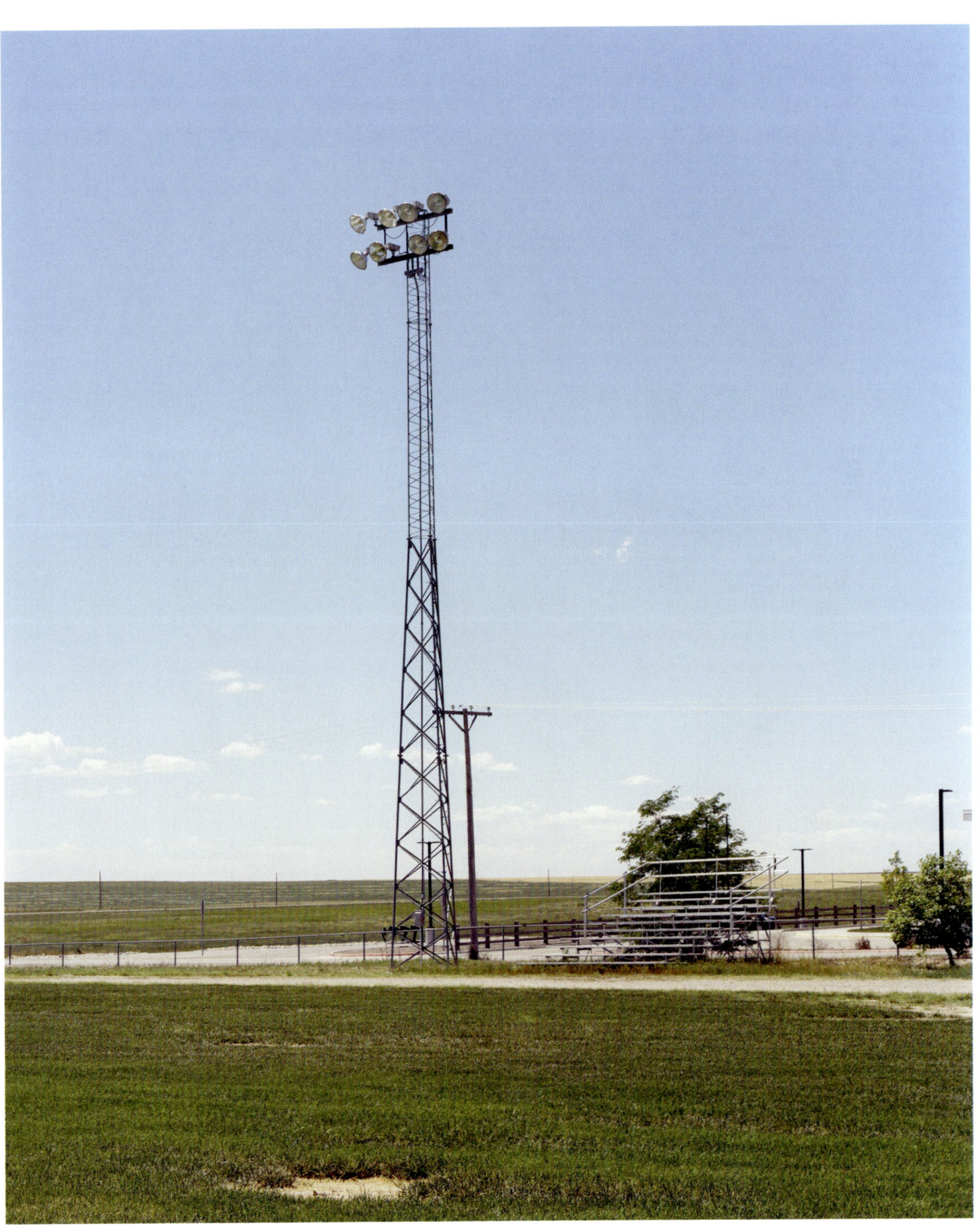

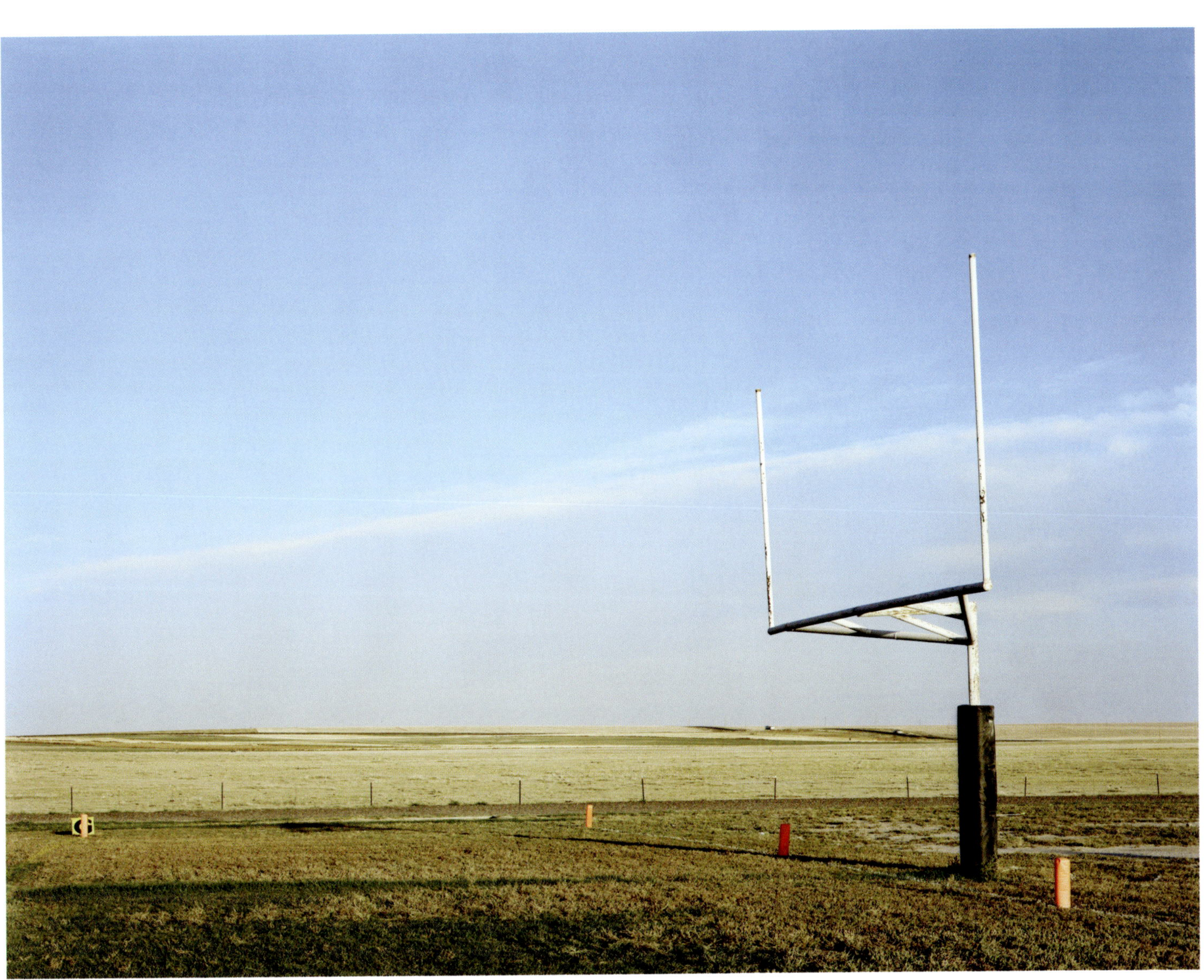

The Team

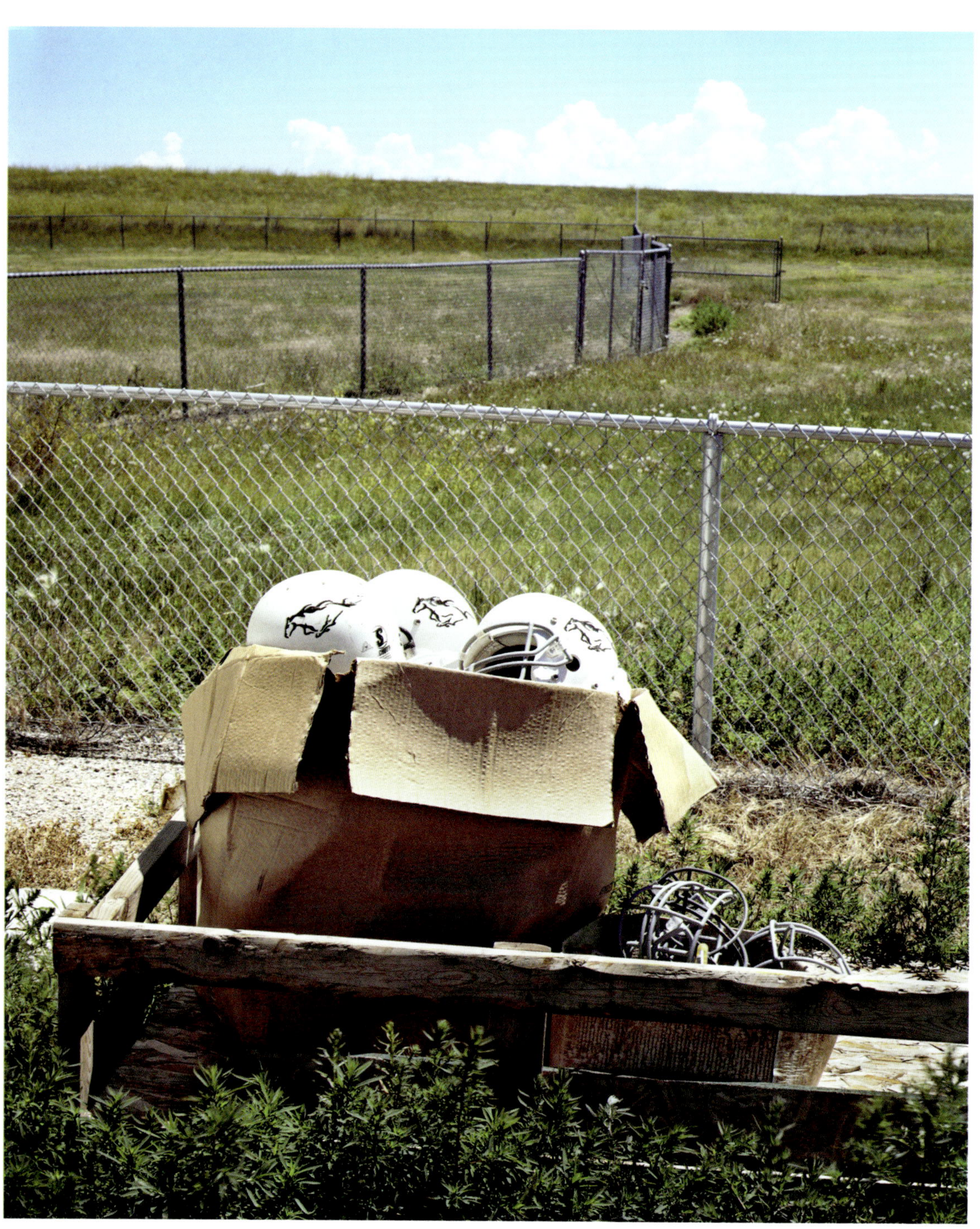

I met head coach Glenn Carlson in the Prairie School parking lot on a hot August afternoon the following year. The construction of a new building had moved the Mustangs' practice field away from the lush grassy patch next to the old gymnasium to a dusty, dried-out bit of scrub closer to the two-lane highway. There, a lone Russian olive tree, too small to create much in the way of shade, grew in the ditch beside the driveway to the school. Over the next three months that tree became something of a focal point in my photographs and videos.

For the first week before classes started, the team held two practices per day. Beginning at 6:00 am to avoid the summer heat, the players worked on conditioning and agility until breaking for an early lunch. Around noon, the coach called them back to the field for a few hours of work developing plays before the daily afternoon thunderstorms set in. The regular season began in late August and consisted of eight games over as many weeks against a set of division opponents, some as far away as a four-hour drive. Cross-division games followed, to determine who advanced to the state playoffs. The Mustangs team had fifteen players: one freshman, six sophomores, five juniors, and three seniors. They ranged in size from 5′3″ and 120 lbs. to 6′3″ and 210 lbs.

To make those early practices, I left Fort Collins at 4:30 a.m. and headed straight east. Passing Pawnee Station around 5:45, as truckers and ranchers were stopping for breakfast, I could see safety lights flashing on the huge wind turbines out in the National Grasslands. To the north, the twin Pawnee Buttes caught the first rays of sunlight. In the school parking lot, the team members arrived in their own pickup trucks or their parents' cars. From the center point of the practice field the flat, open space radiated out to the horizon line. Meadowlarks called back and forth from the fenceposts. The rising sun threw the long shadows of players across the field and filtered through the dust kicked up by the warm-up run. Antelope and cattle, grazing in the surrounding grassland, watched the practice unfold for a while but soon lost interest and disappeared into the expanse.

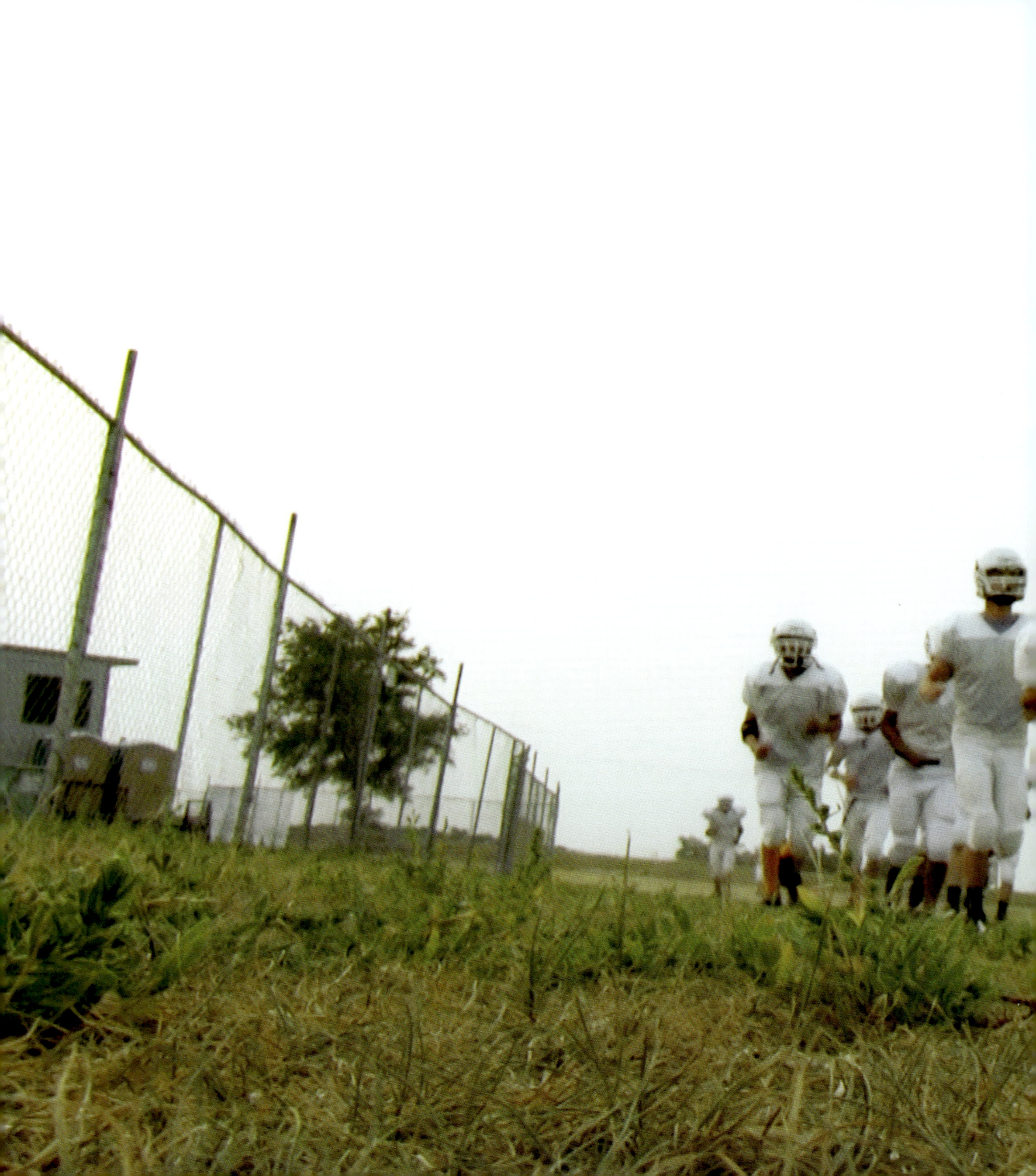

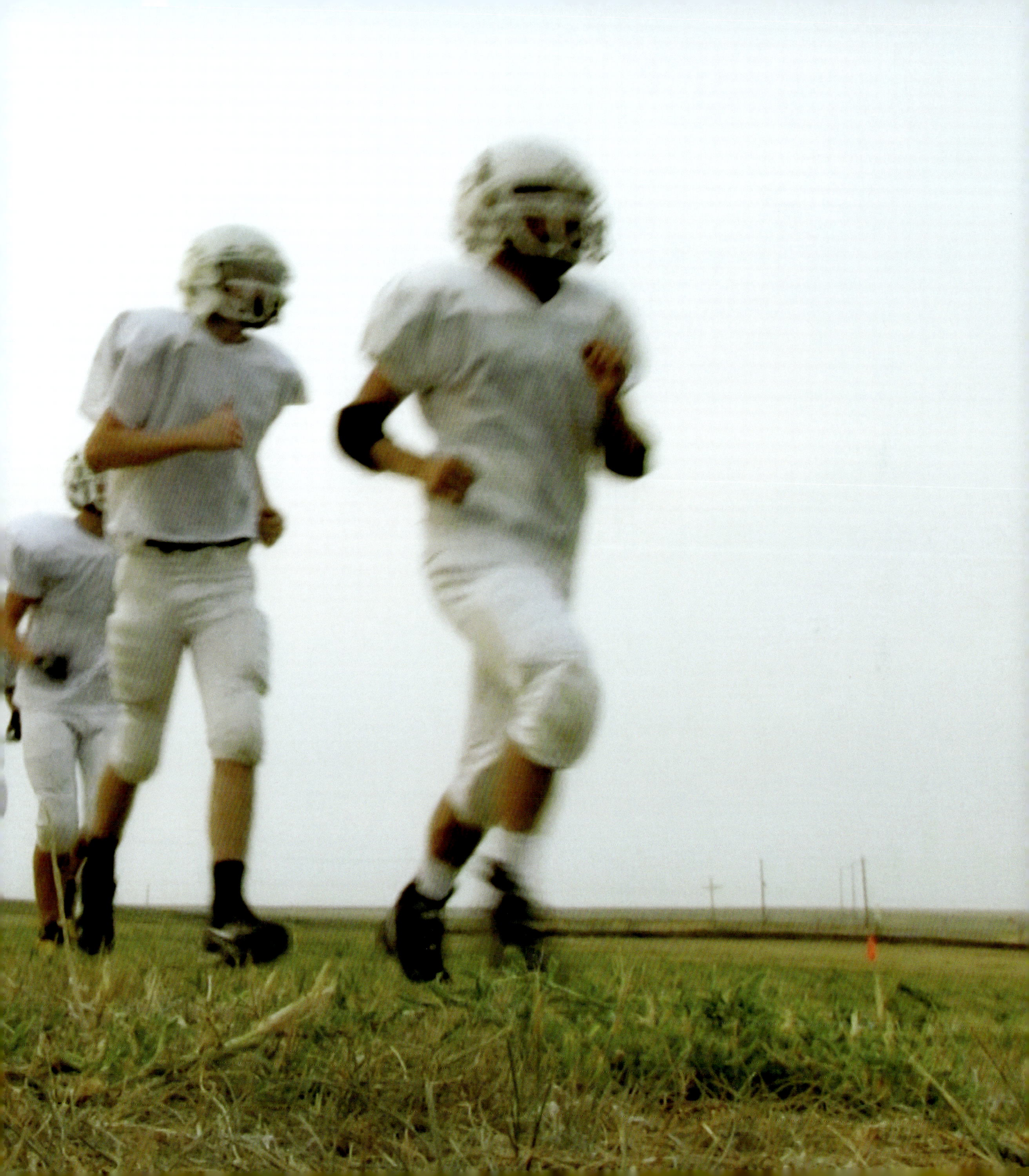

In the afternoon, the wind picked up. The clips on the flagpole began slapping a repetitive ping as the halyard rope flipped back and forth, and the metal siding on the concession stand thumped. Great cumulus clouds built up to fill the expanse of the wide sky, while their shadows, sometimes miles across, raced over the ridges and ravines. Some days, the formations were ominous, indicating a major front approaching and the possibility of tornadoes. But more often, the sweet, earthy smell of sage arrived on the wind ahead of the rain, and the streaks of virga hanging in the distance brought a calm sense of inevitability to the final conditioning sprints of the day.

When classes officially began, practice became an after-school activity and my work fell into a new pattern. As I waited near the field each day for the team to assemble, the final bell would ring, and buses and cars filled with pre-k through eighth graders would head home. High schoolers had two activities: football for the boys and volleyball for the girls. Looking to the west, I could see all the way to the Continental Divide, from the snow-capped Indian Peaks in the south to the Medicine Bows in Wyoming. To the east, all I could see was wide-open space. I'd finish my thermos of coffee, check my equipment, and slip into the flow of the team.

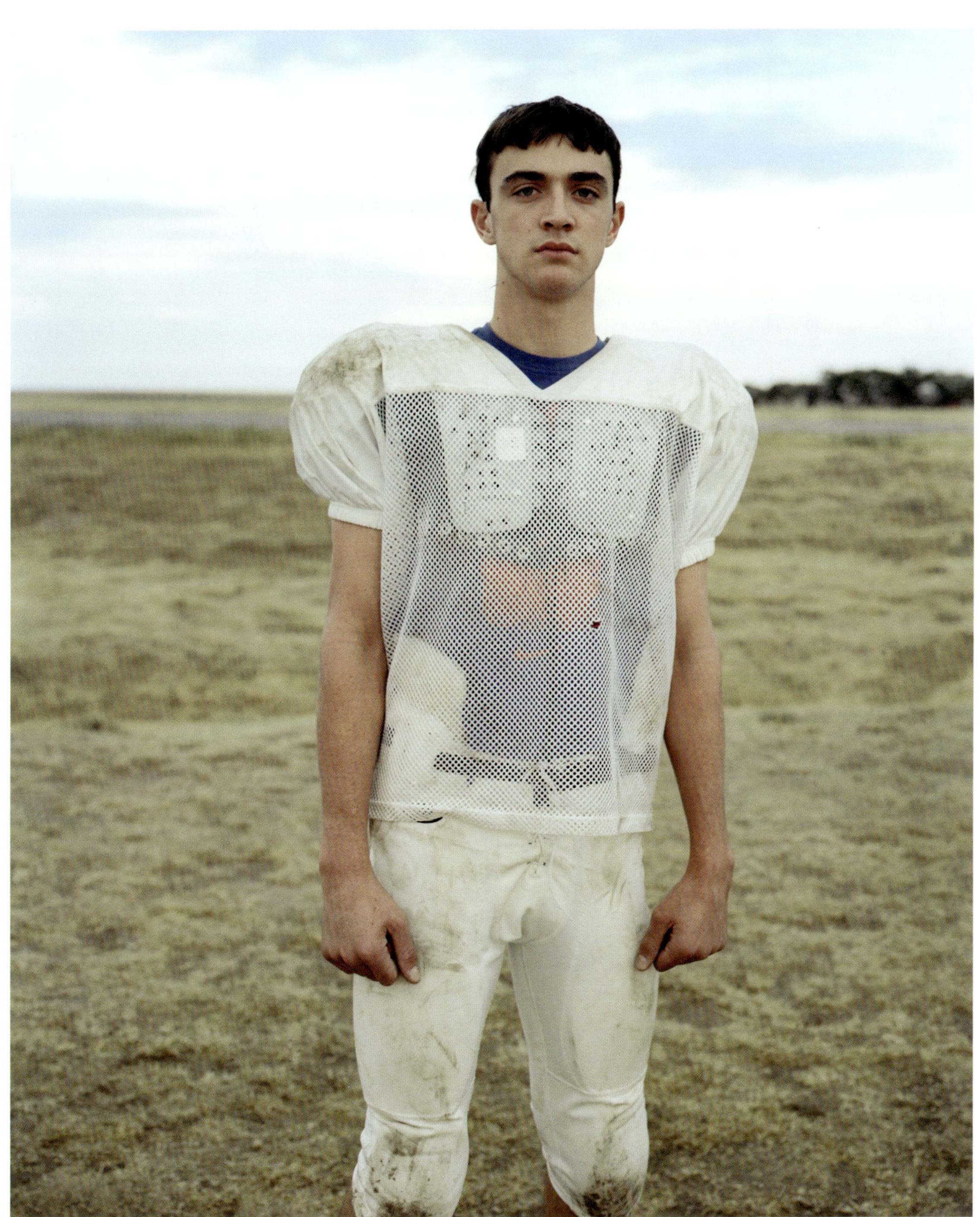

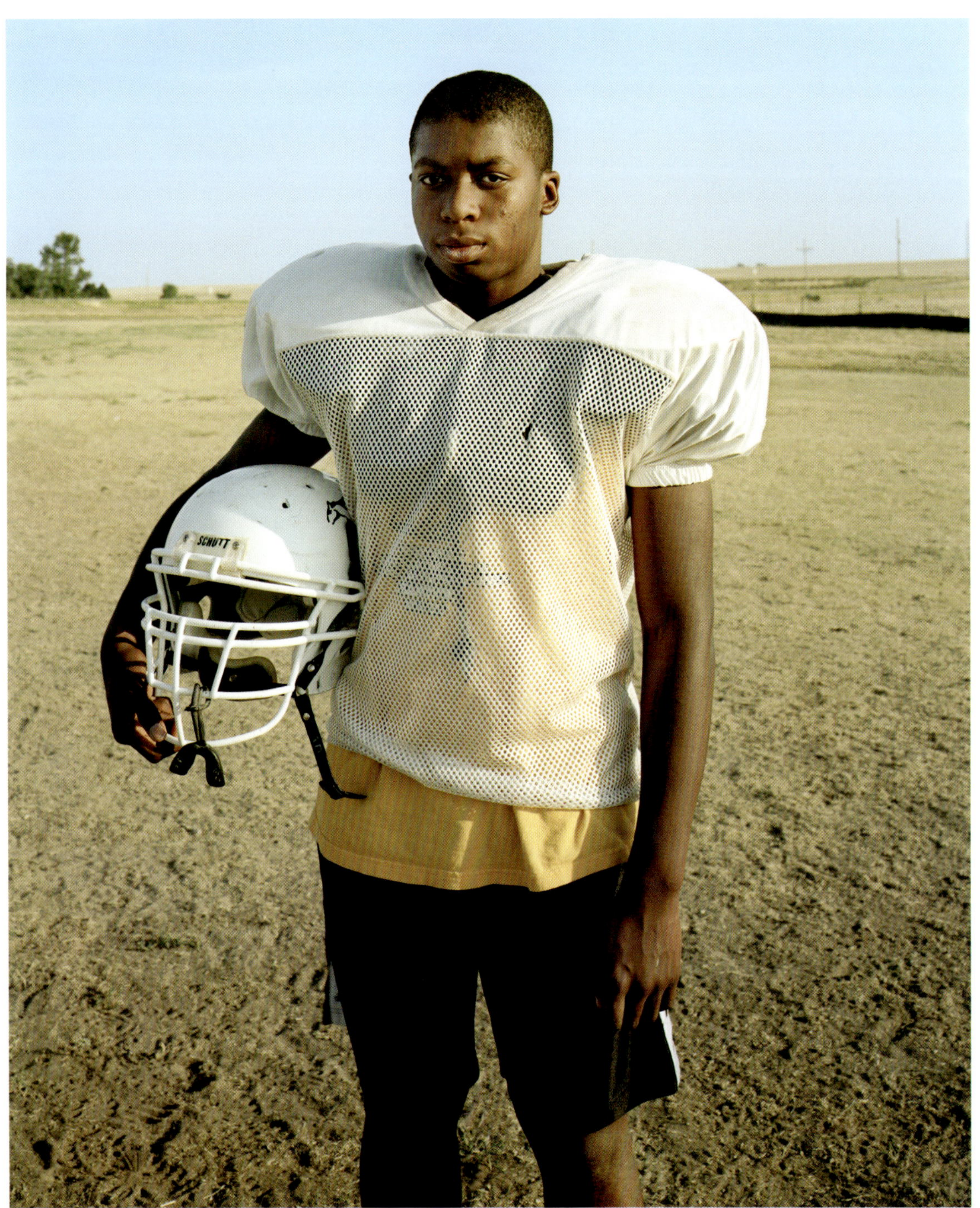

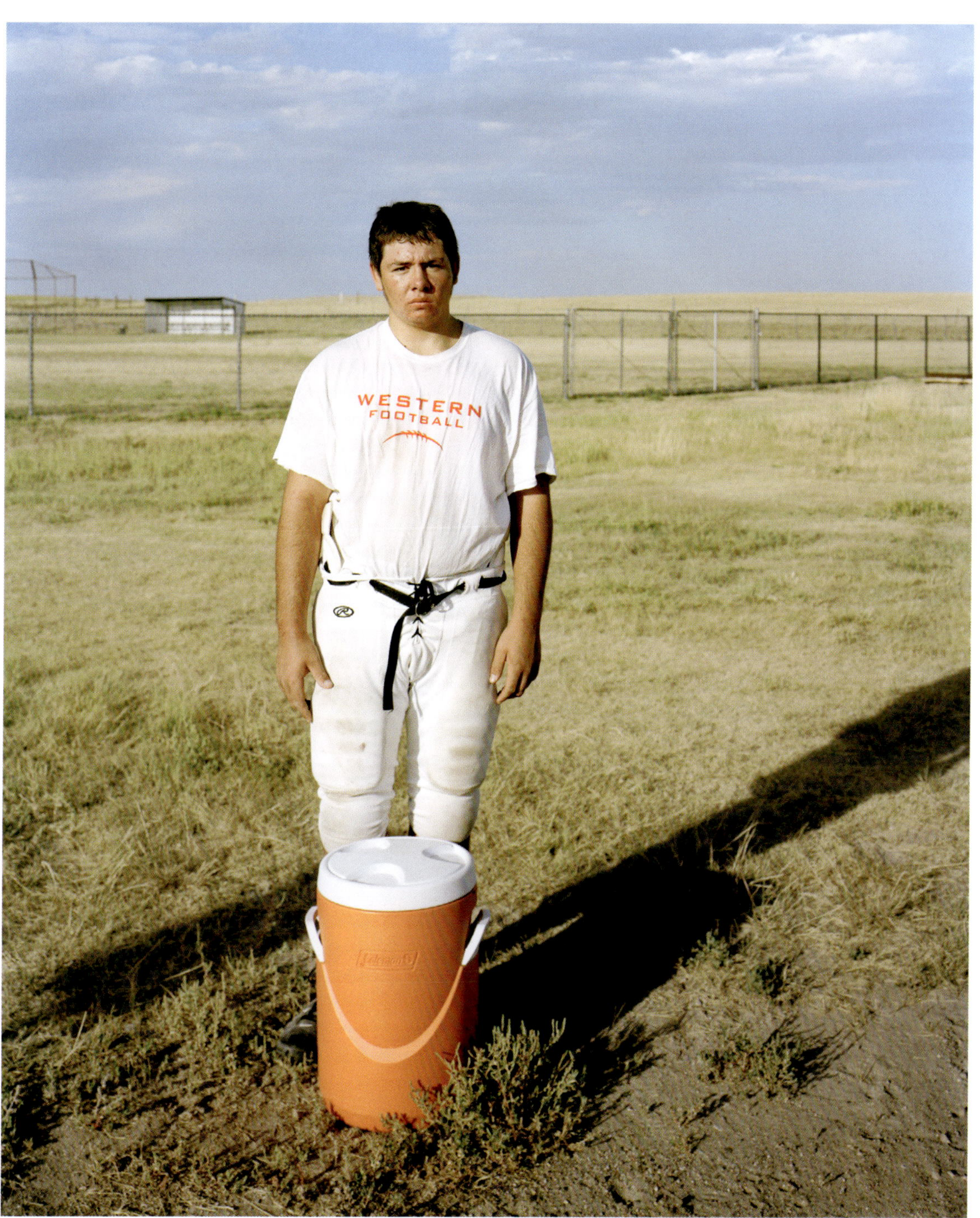

WESTERN
FOOTBALL

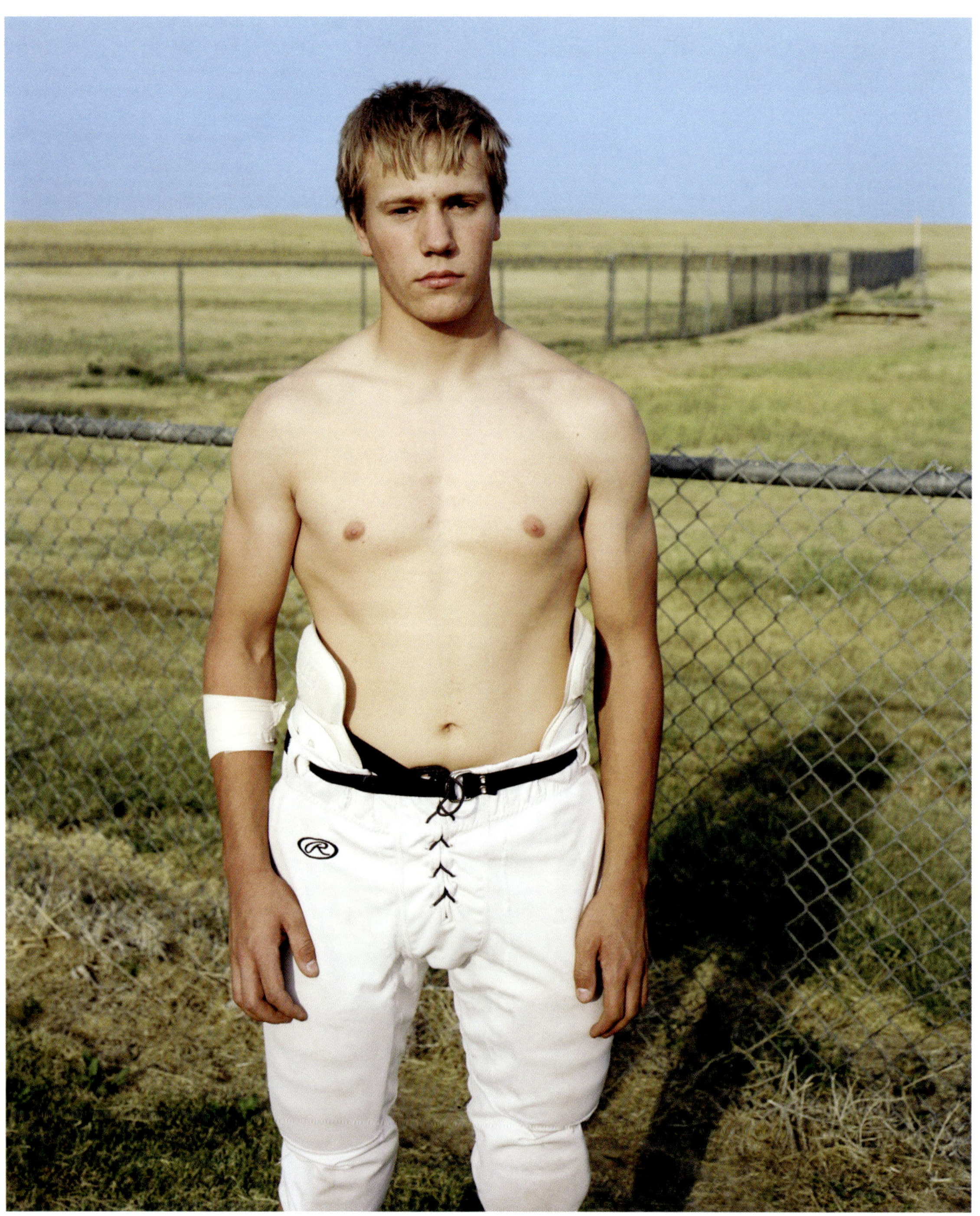

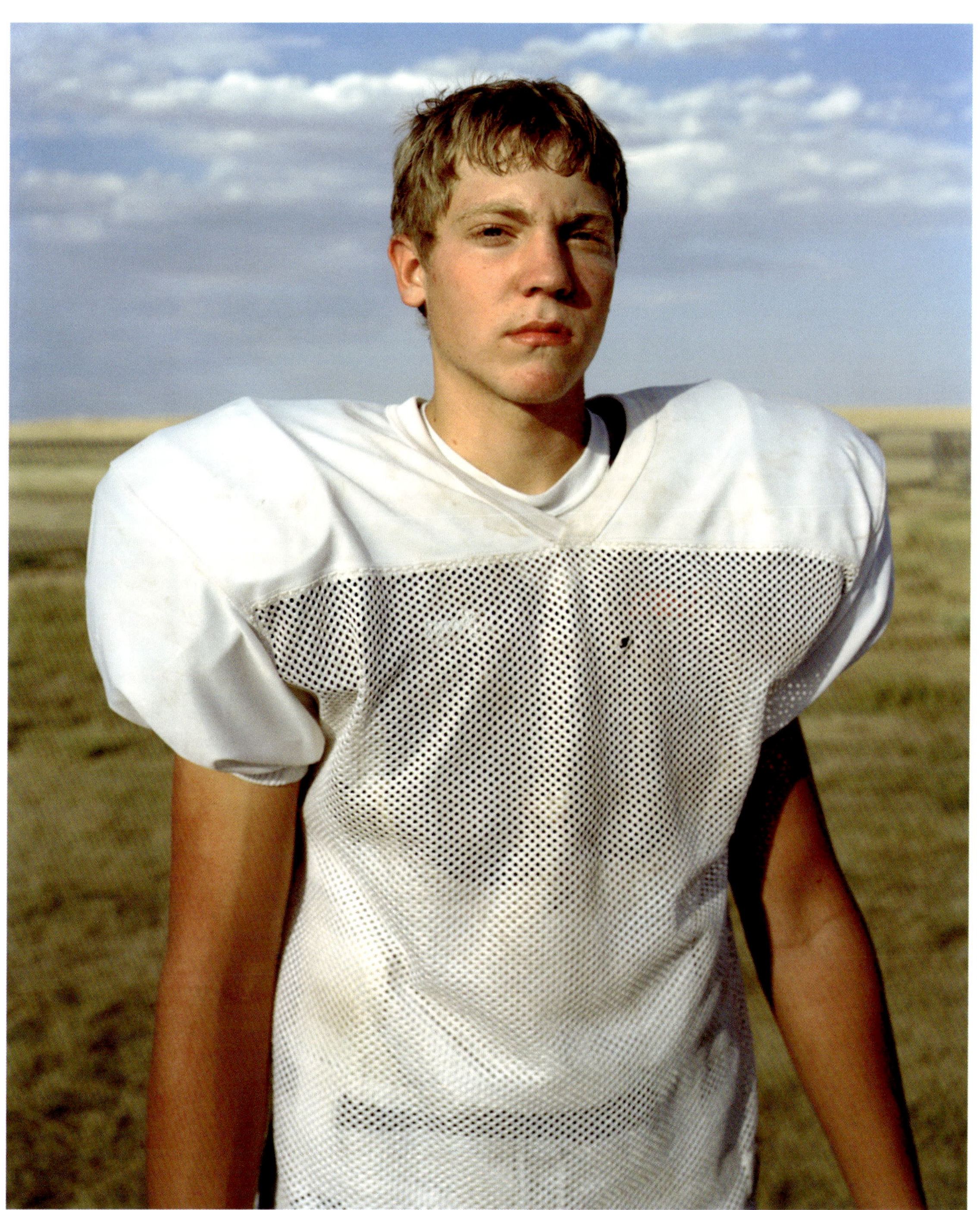

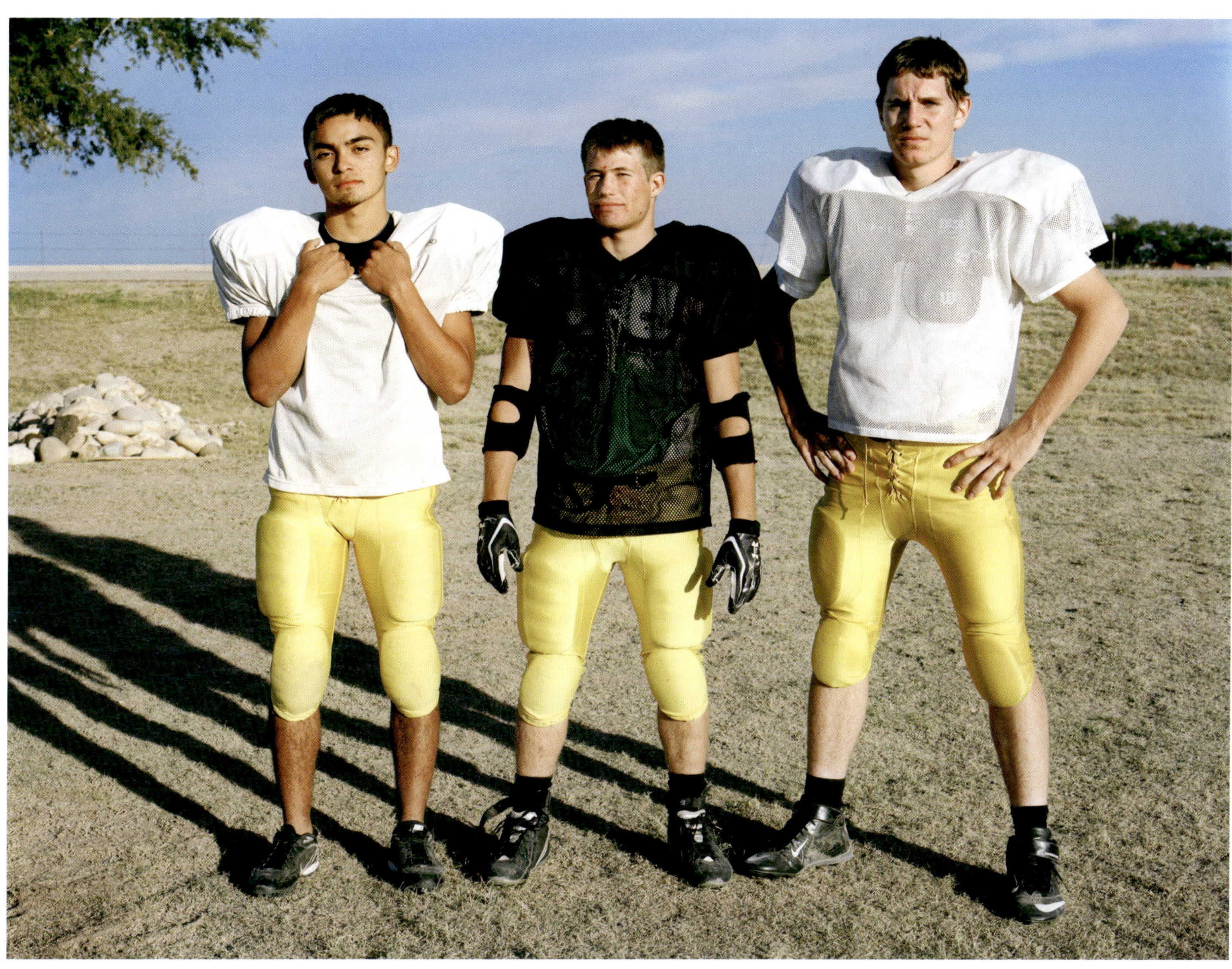

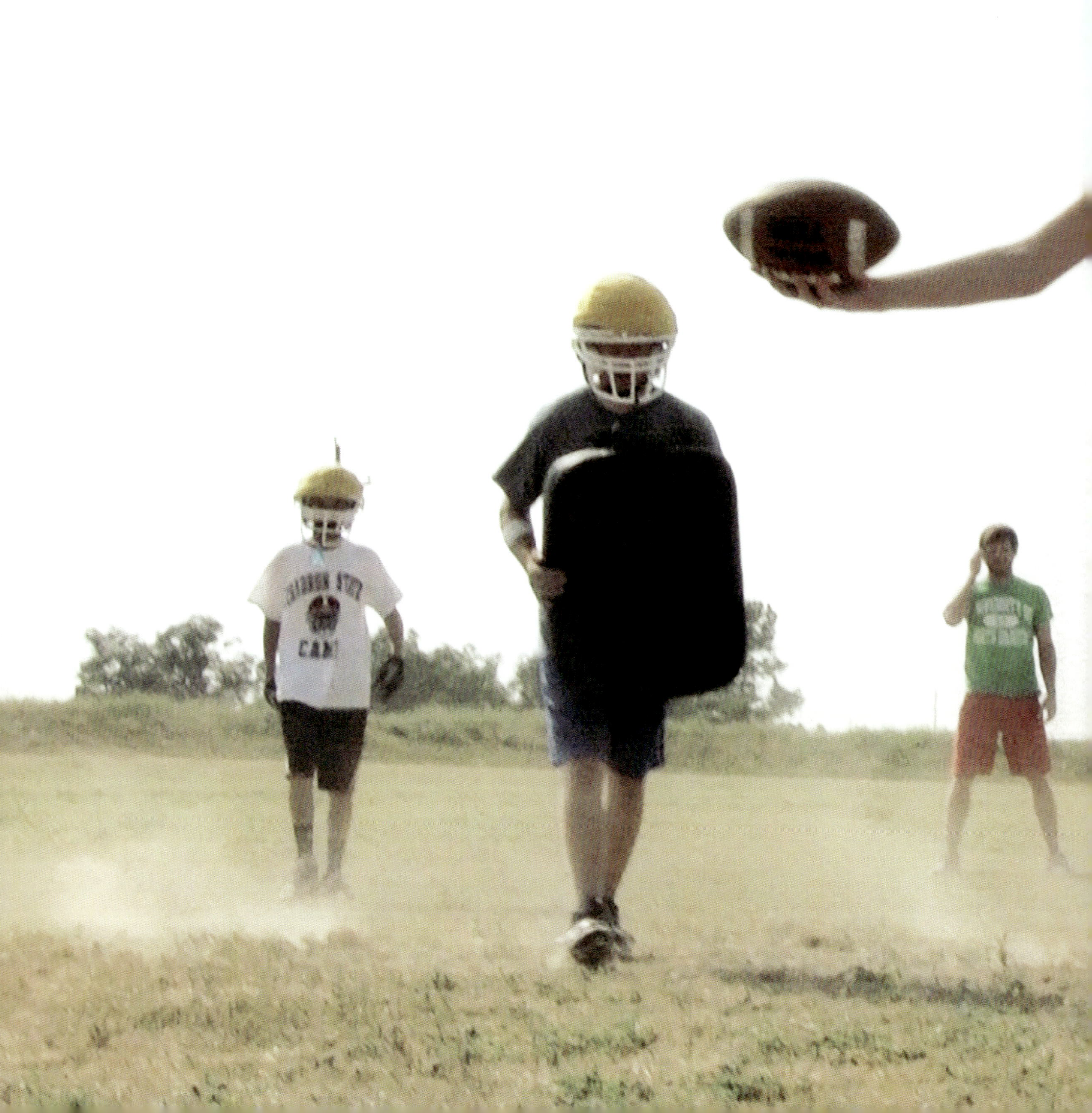

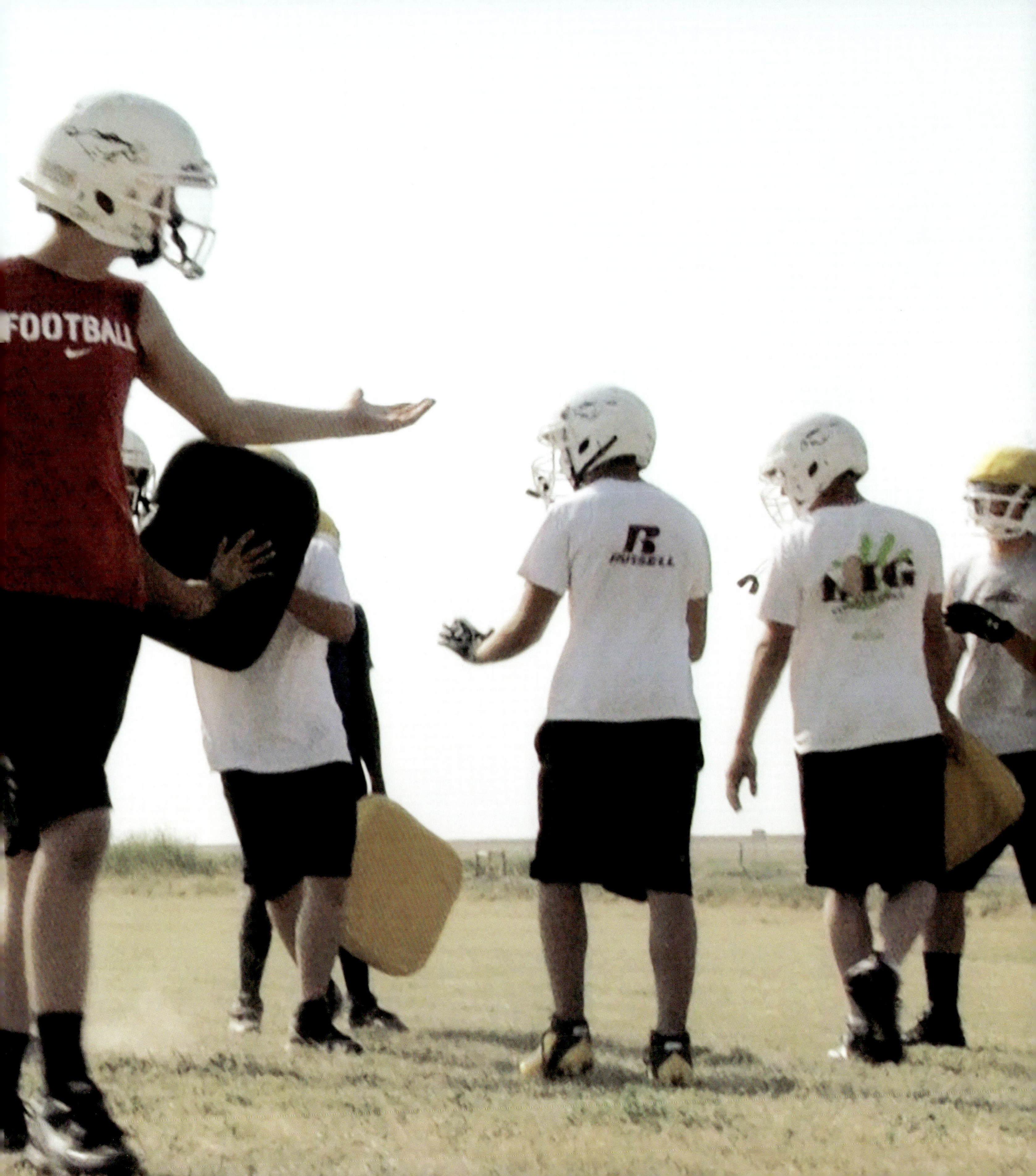

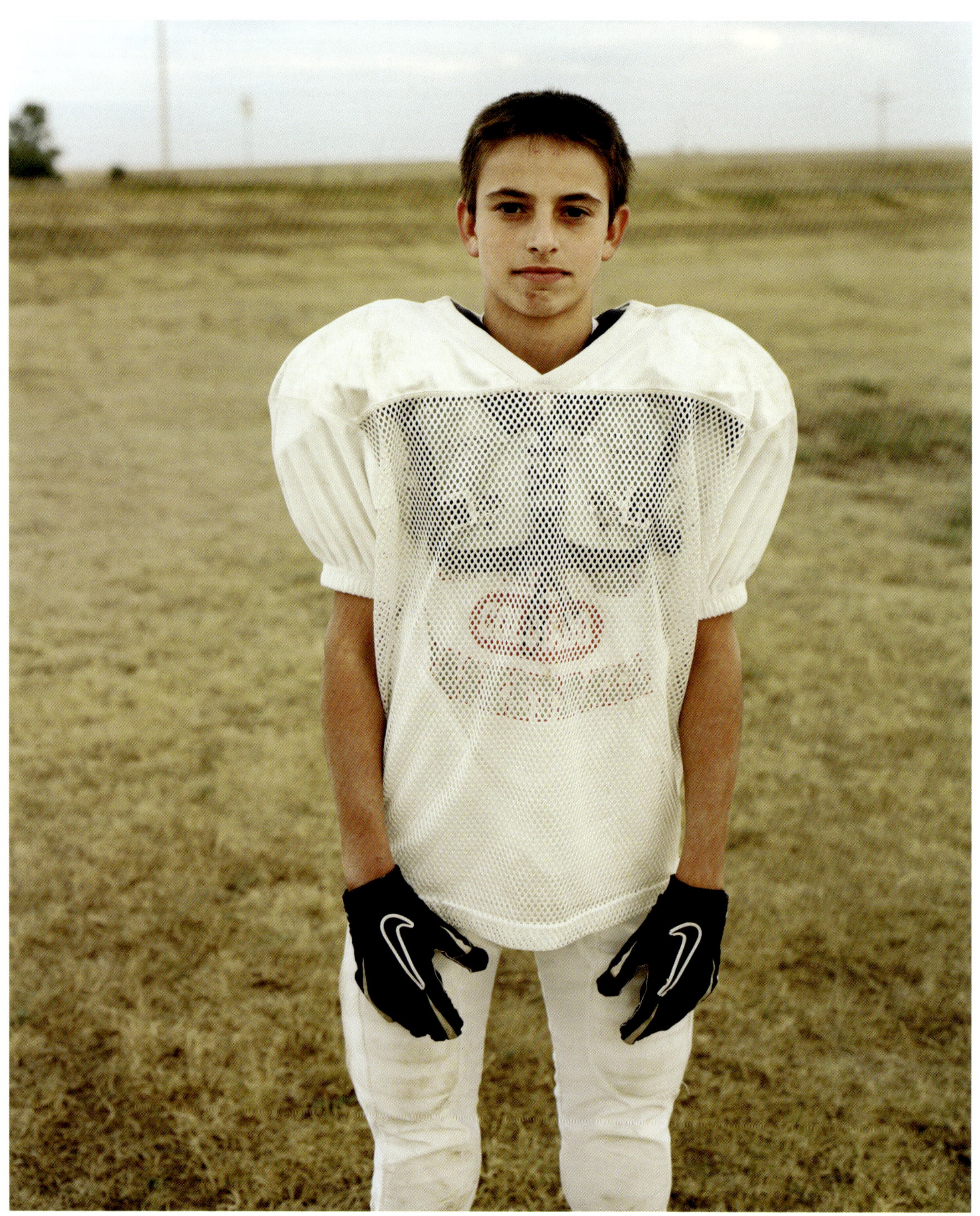

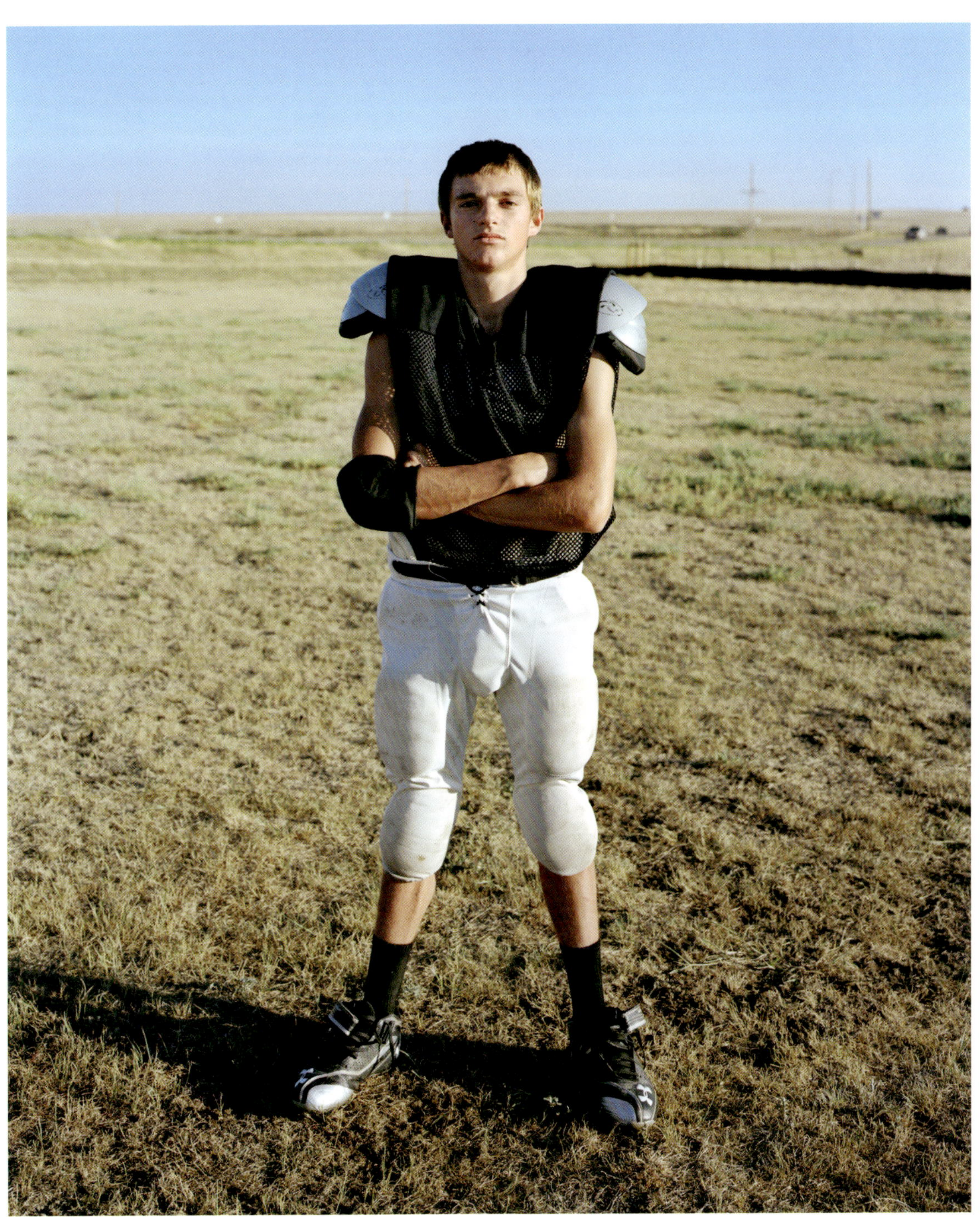

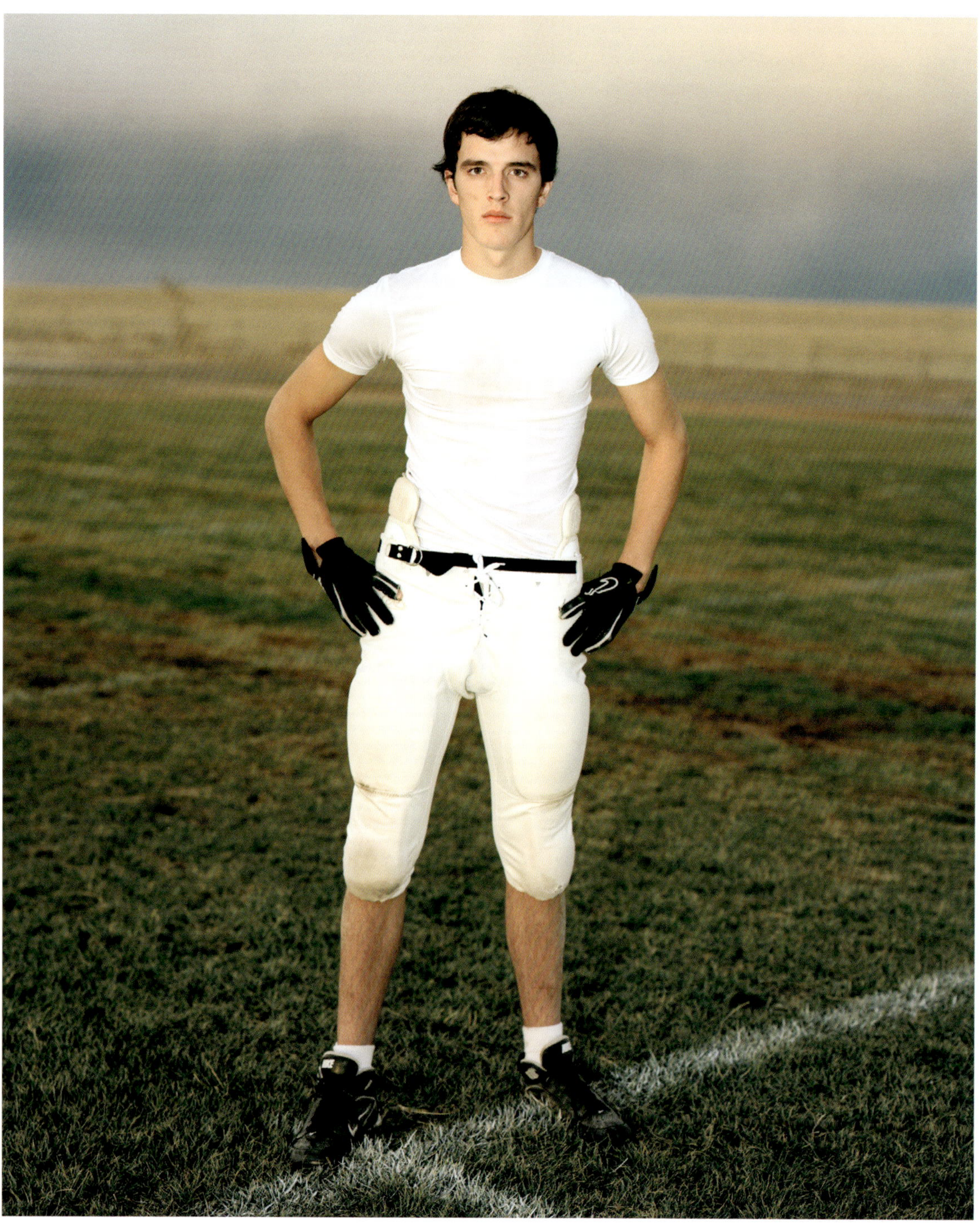

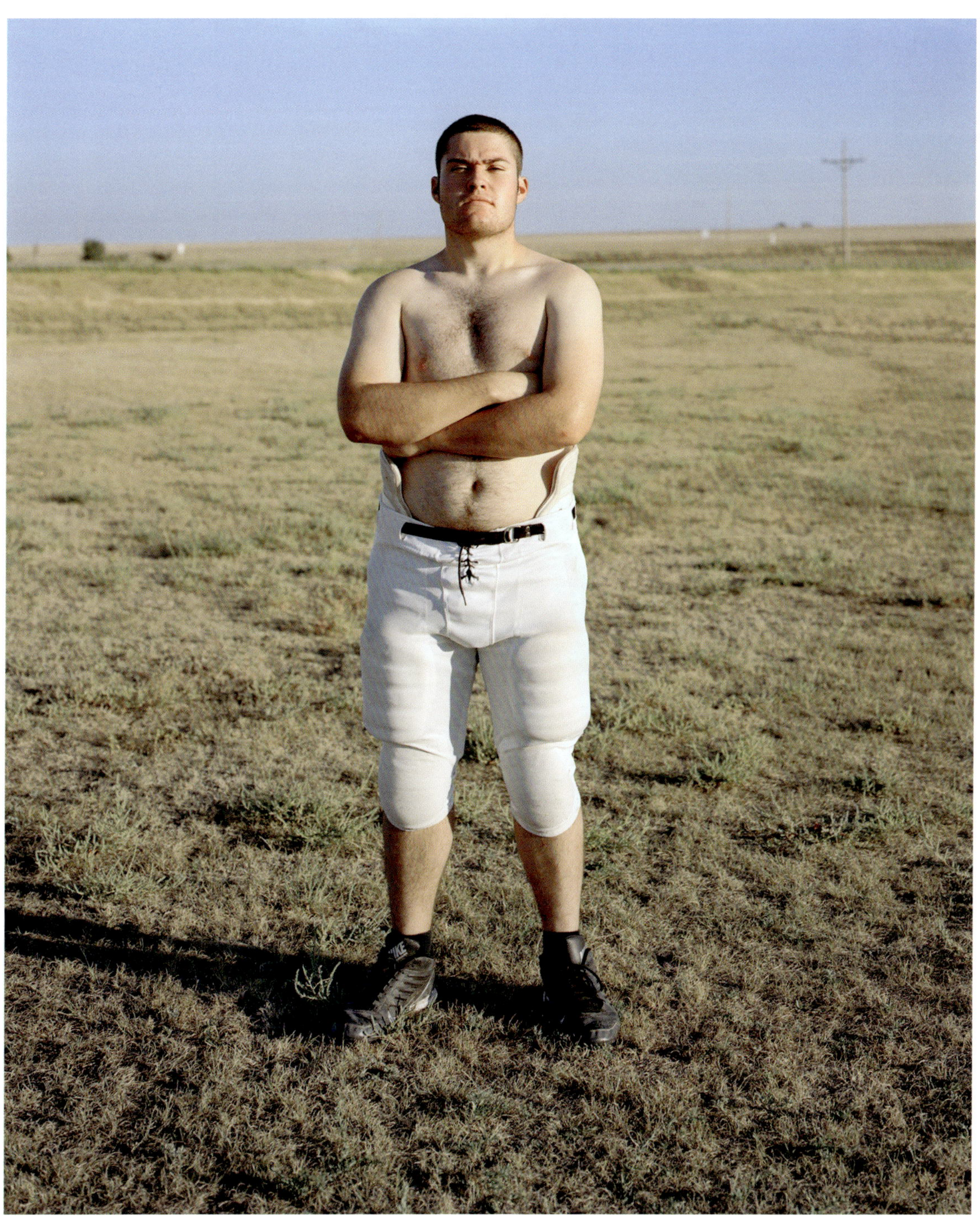

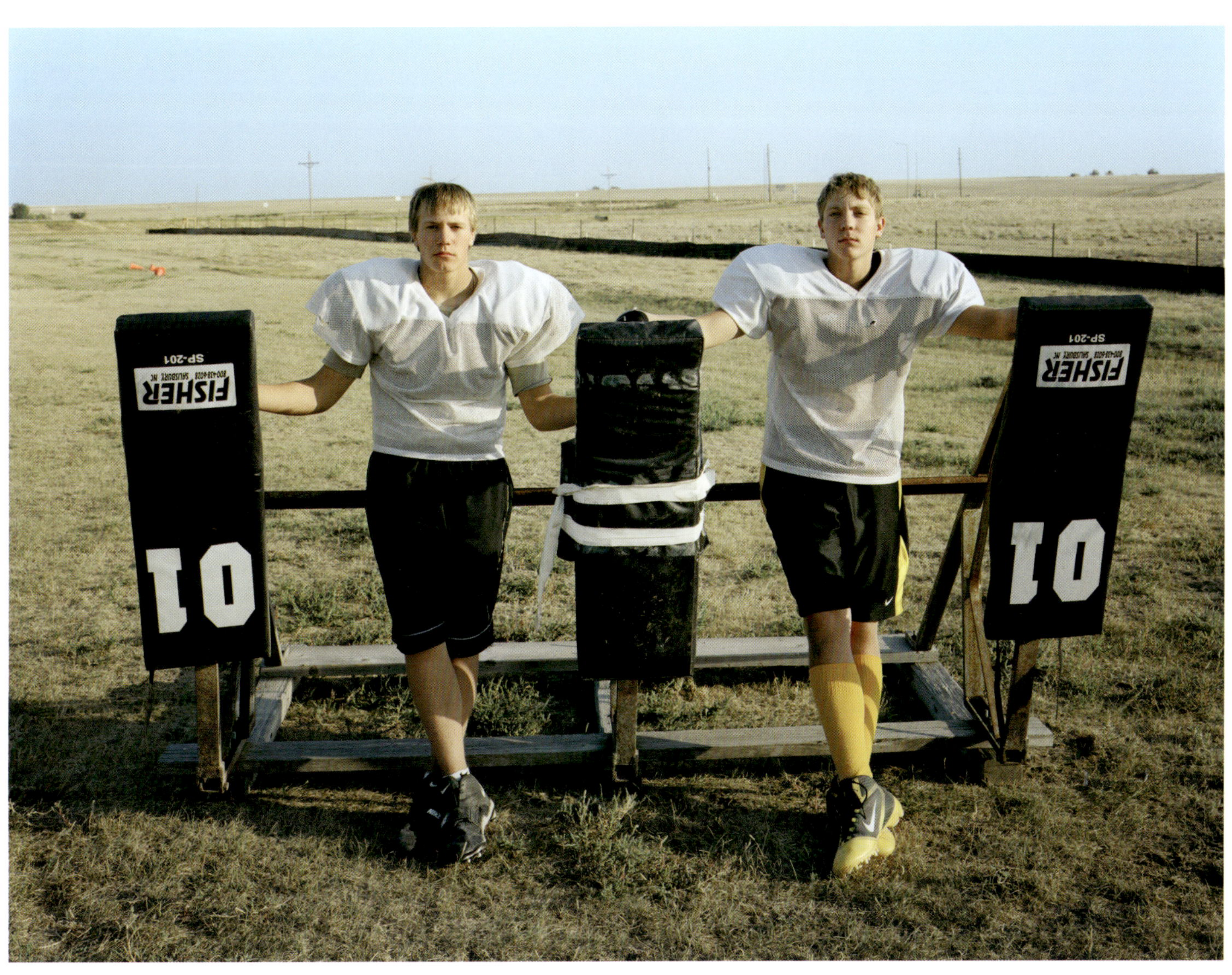

FISHER
SP-201
SALISBURY, NC
800-438-6028
10
FISHER
SP-201
SALISBURY, NC
800-438-6028
10

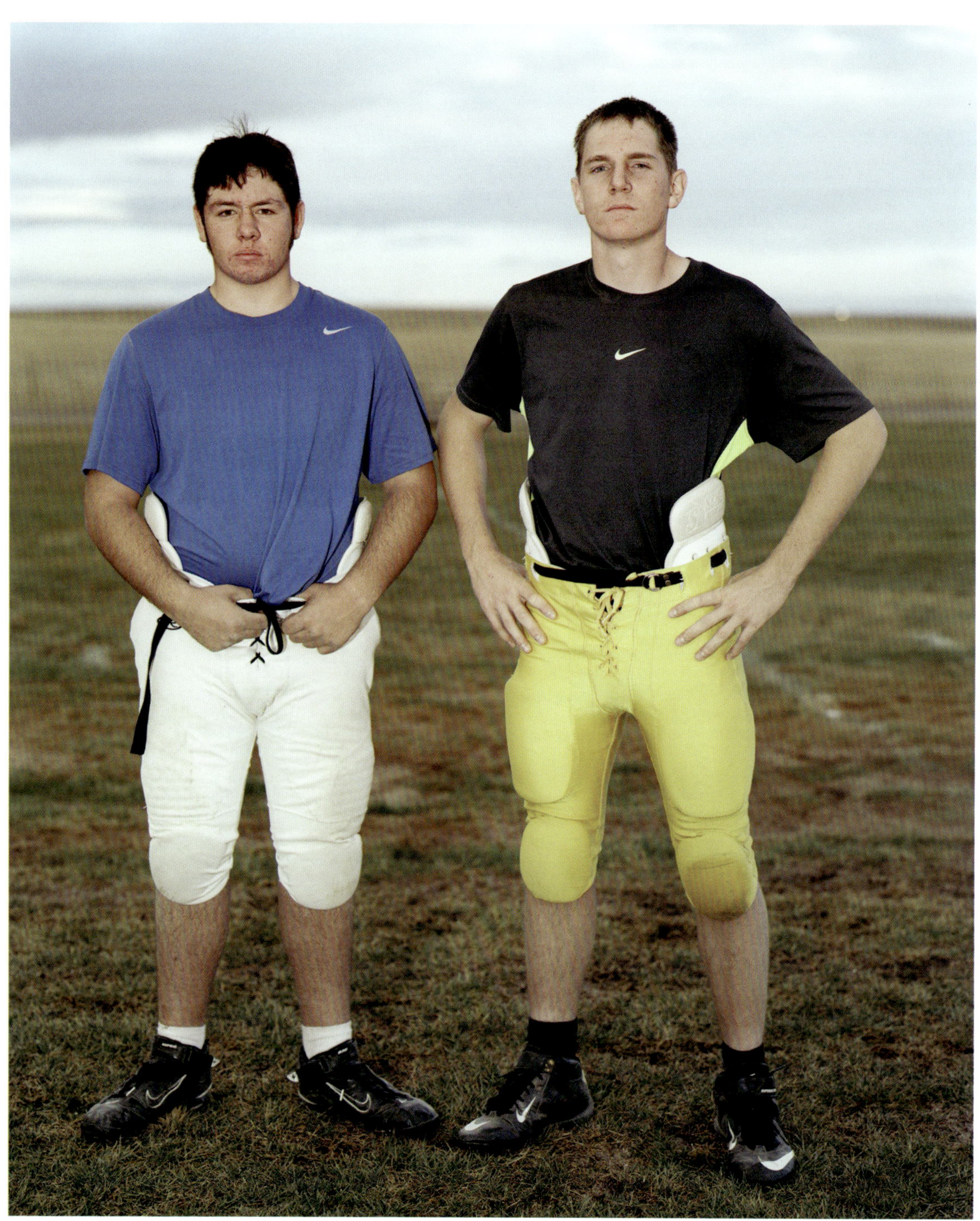

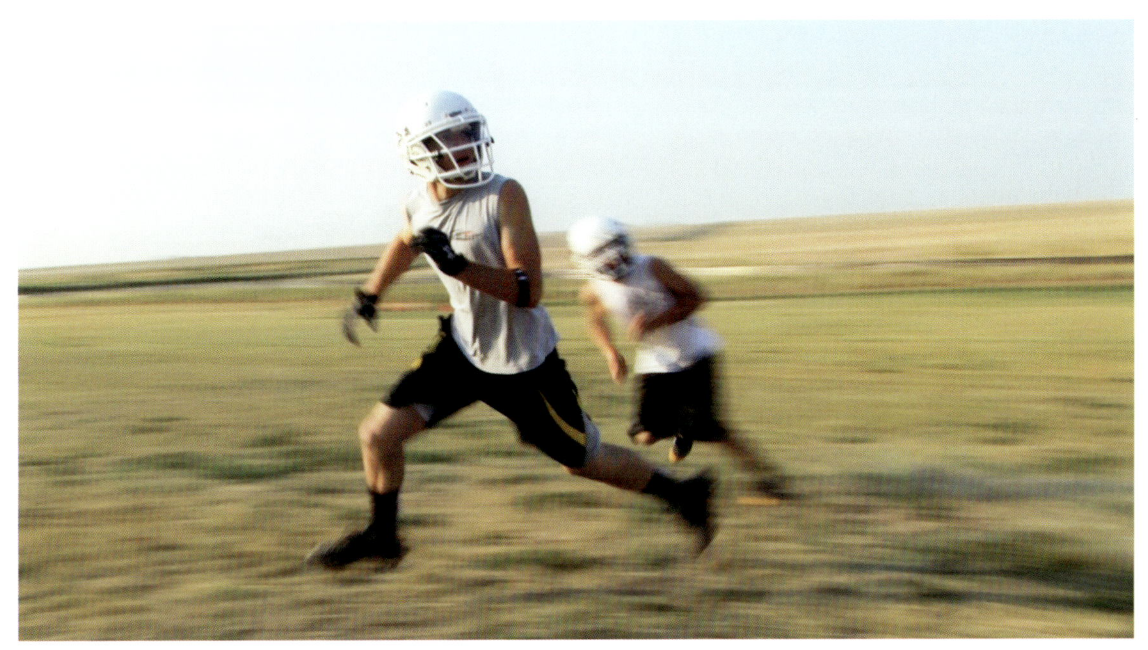

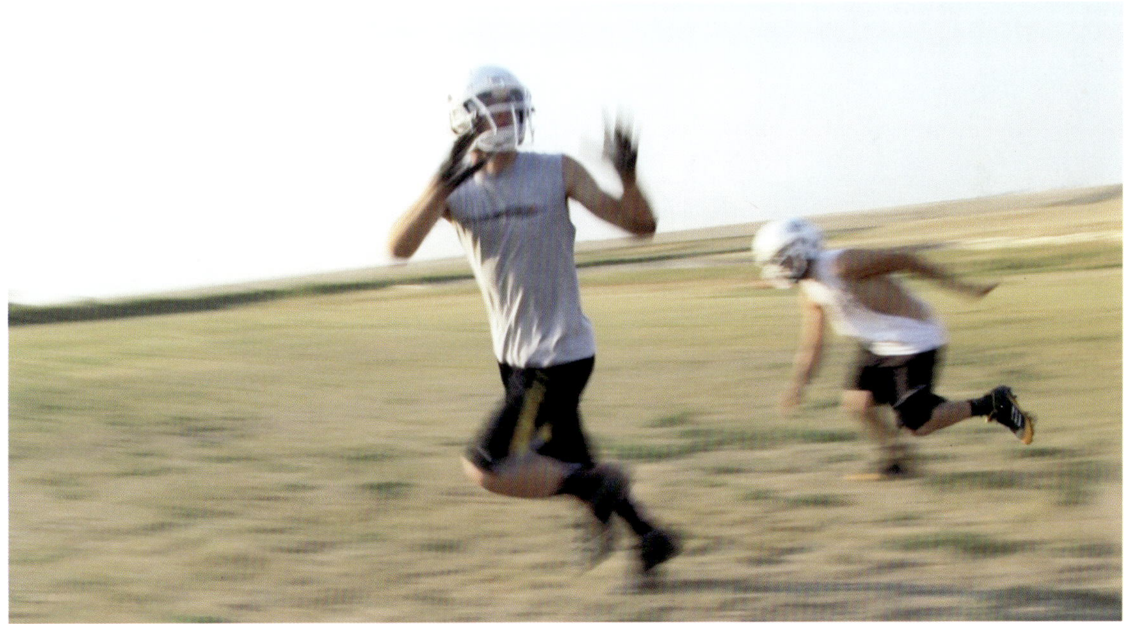

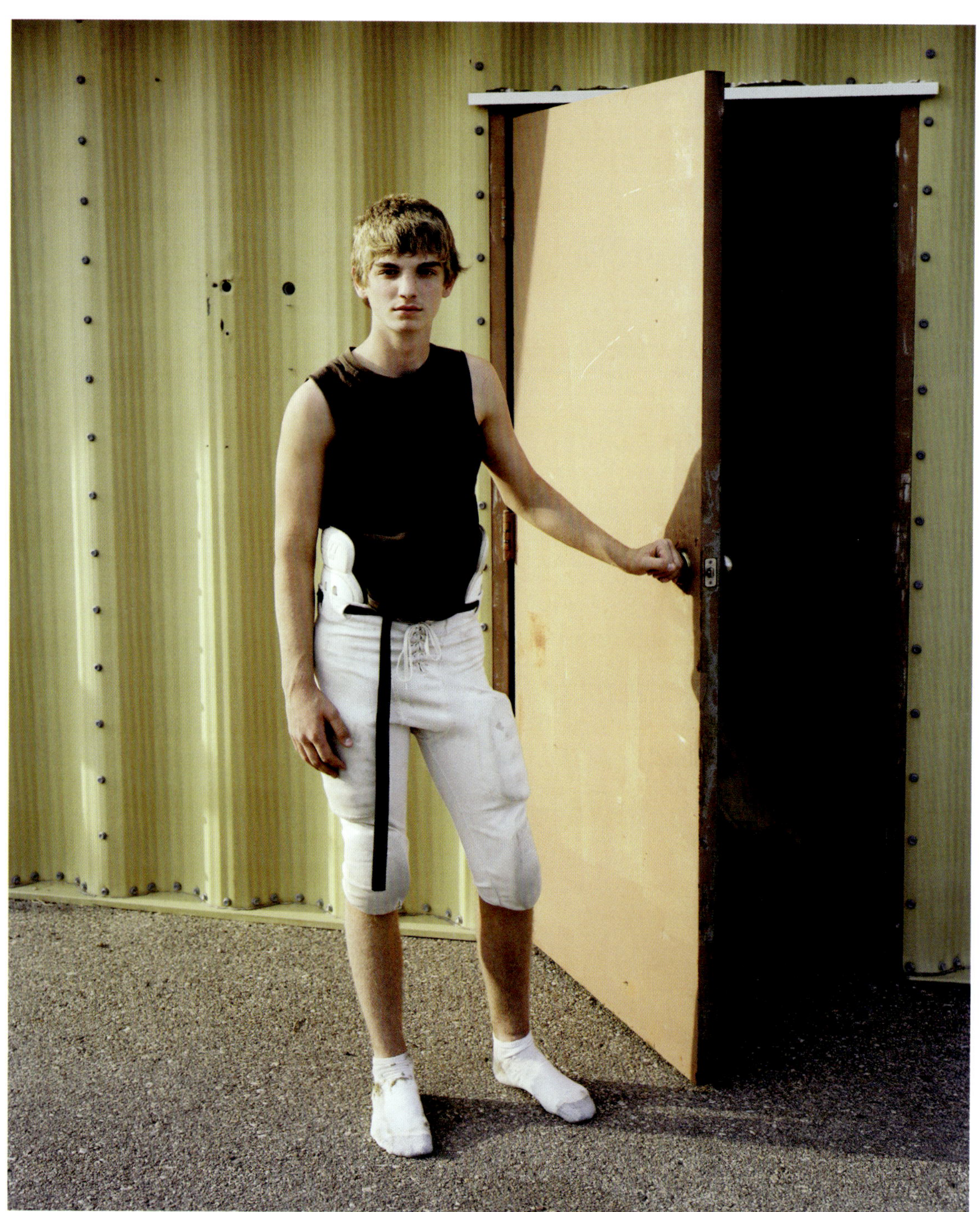

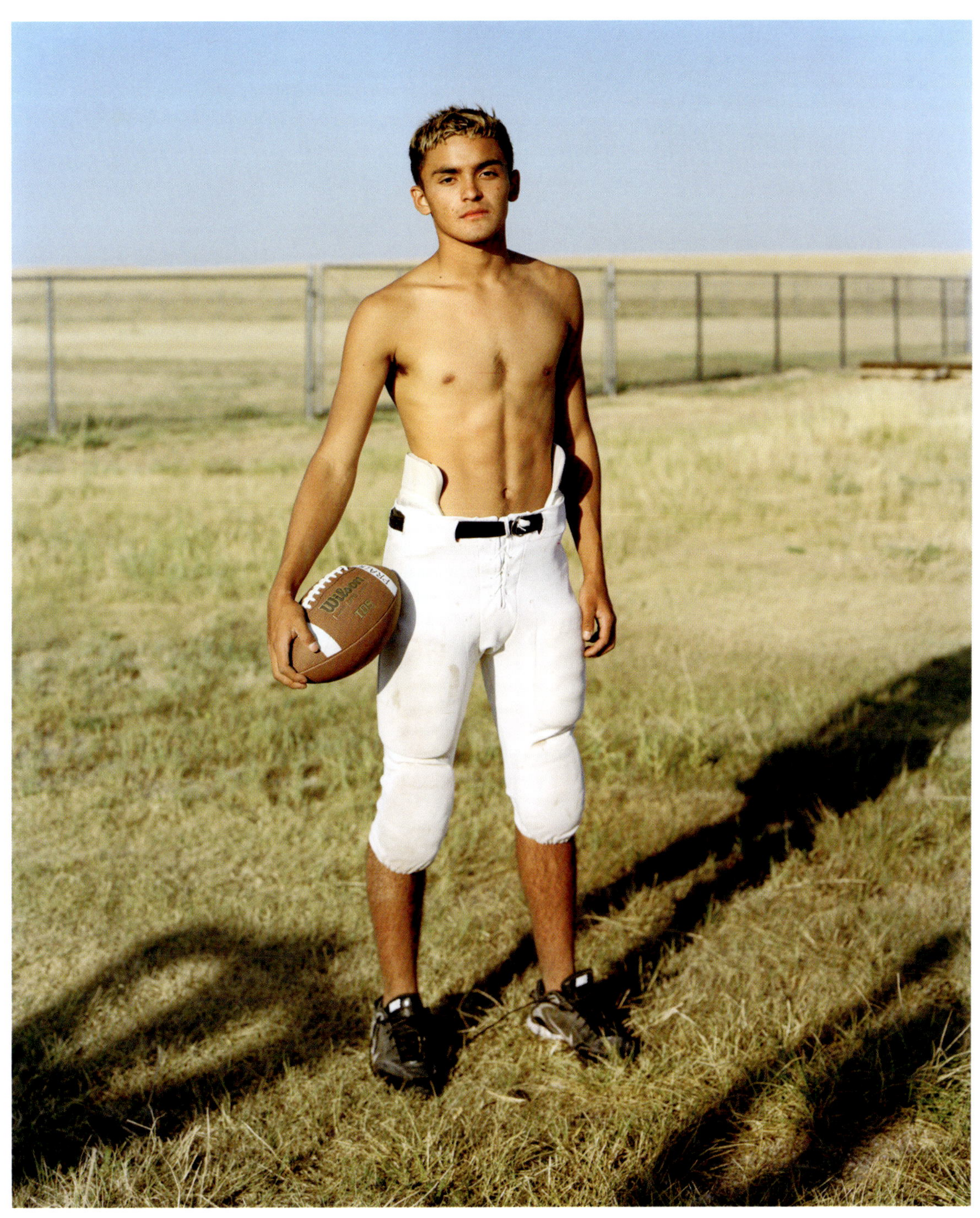

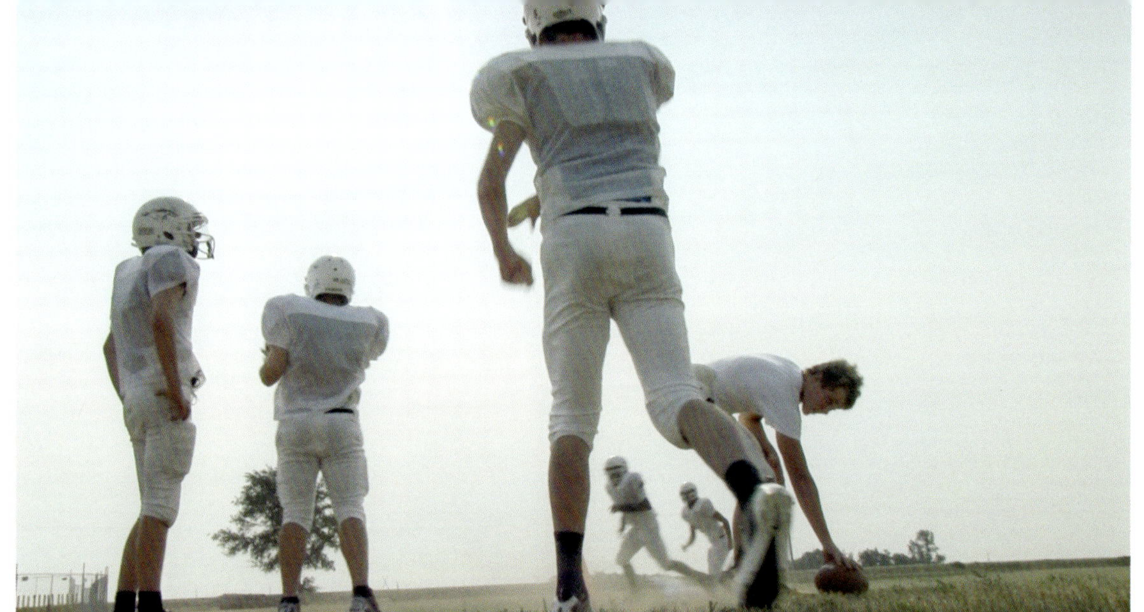

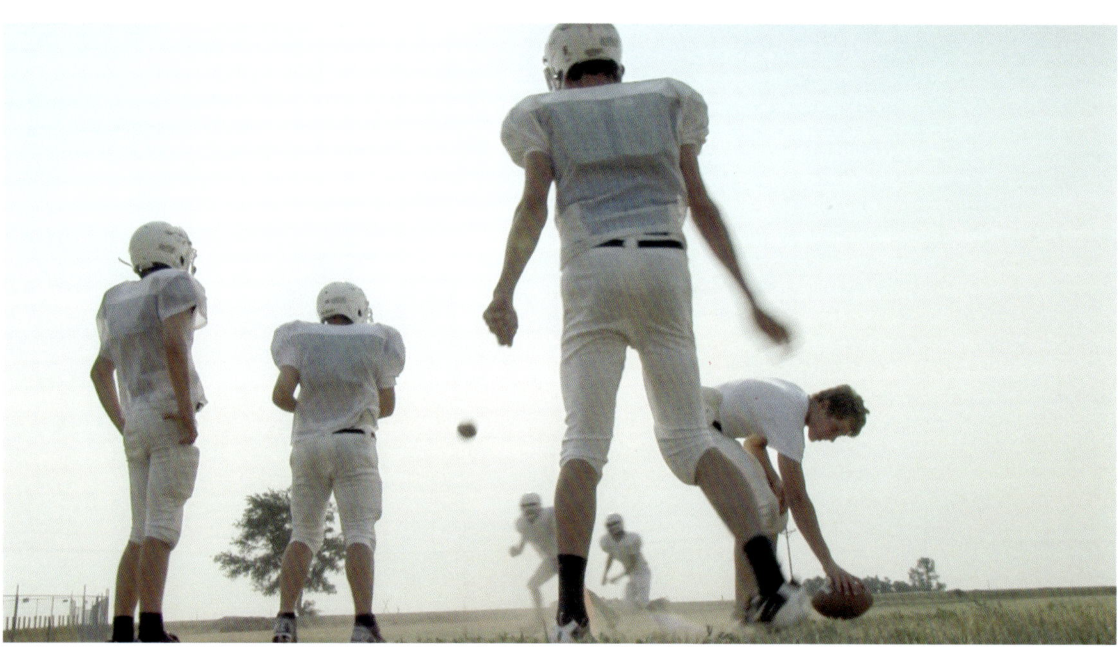

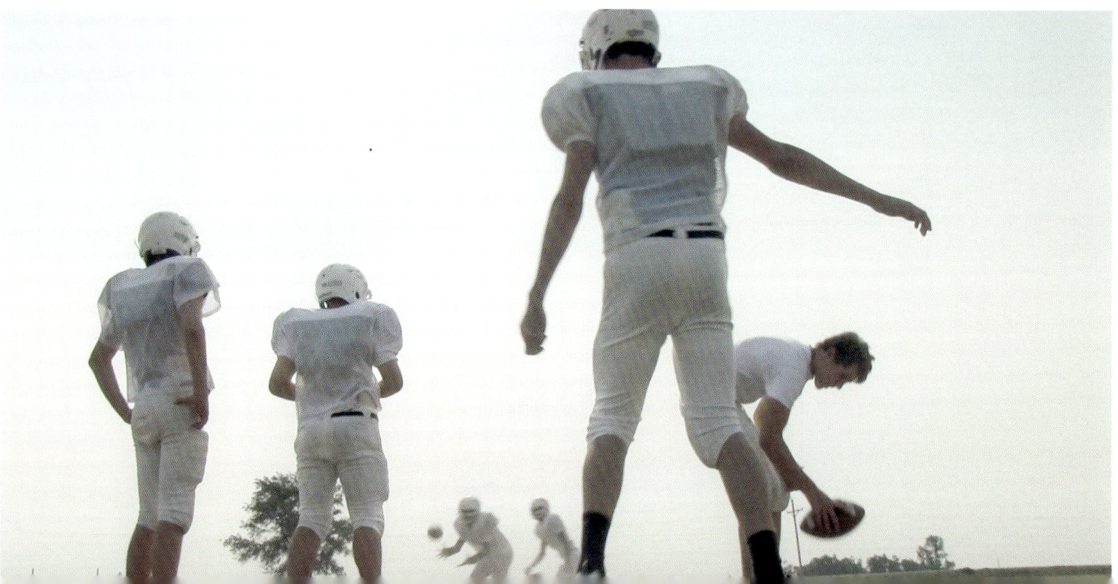

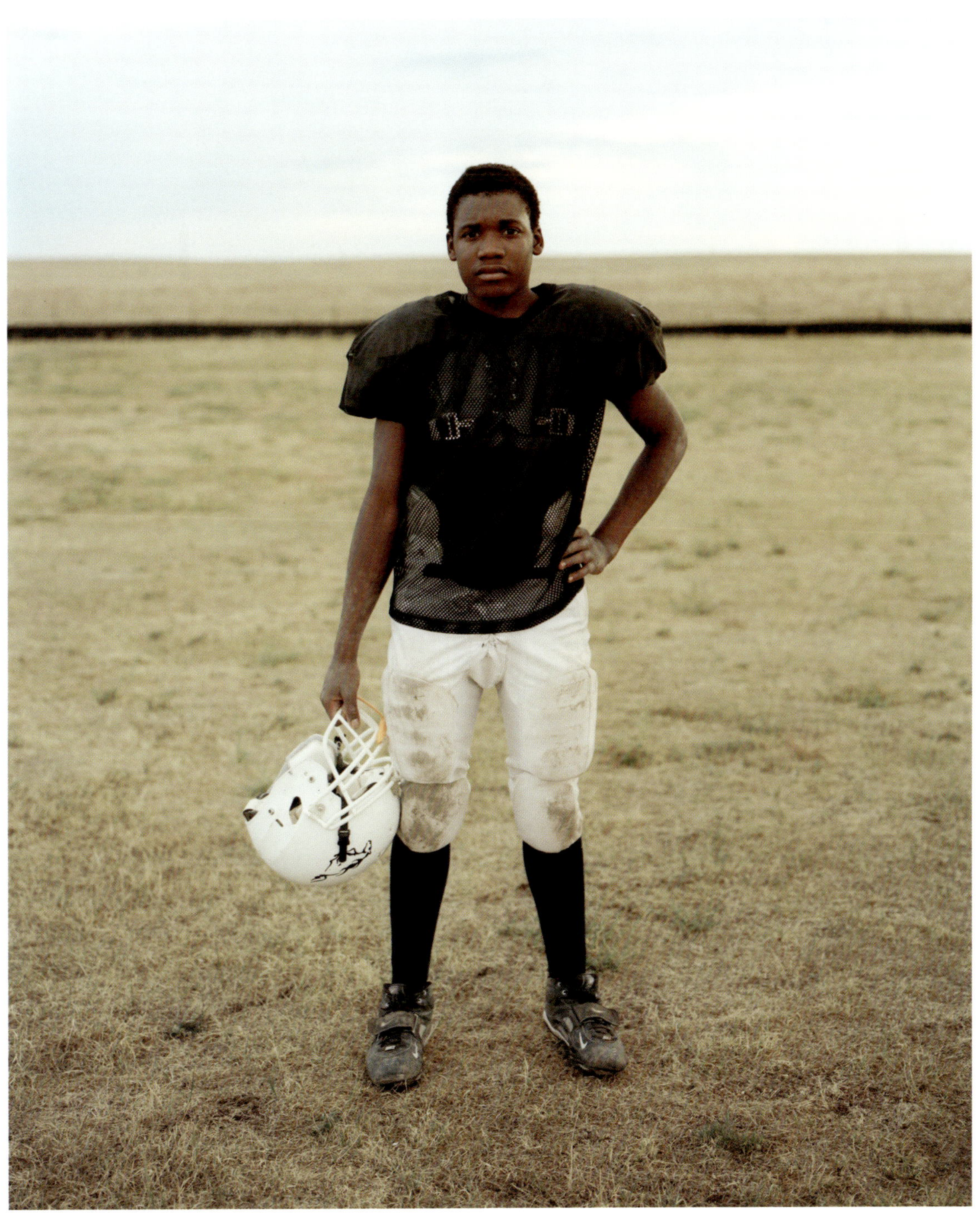

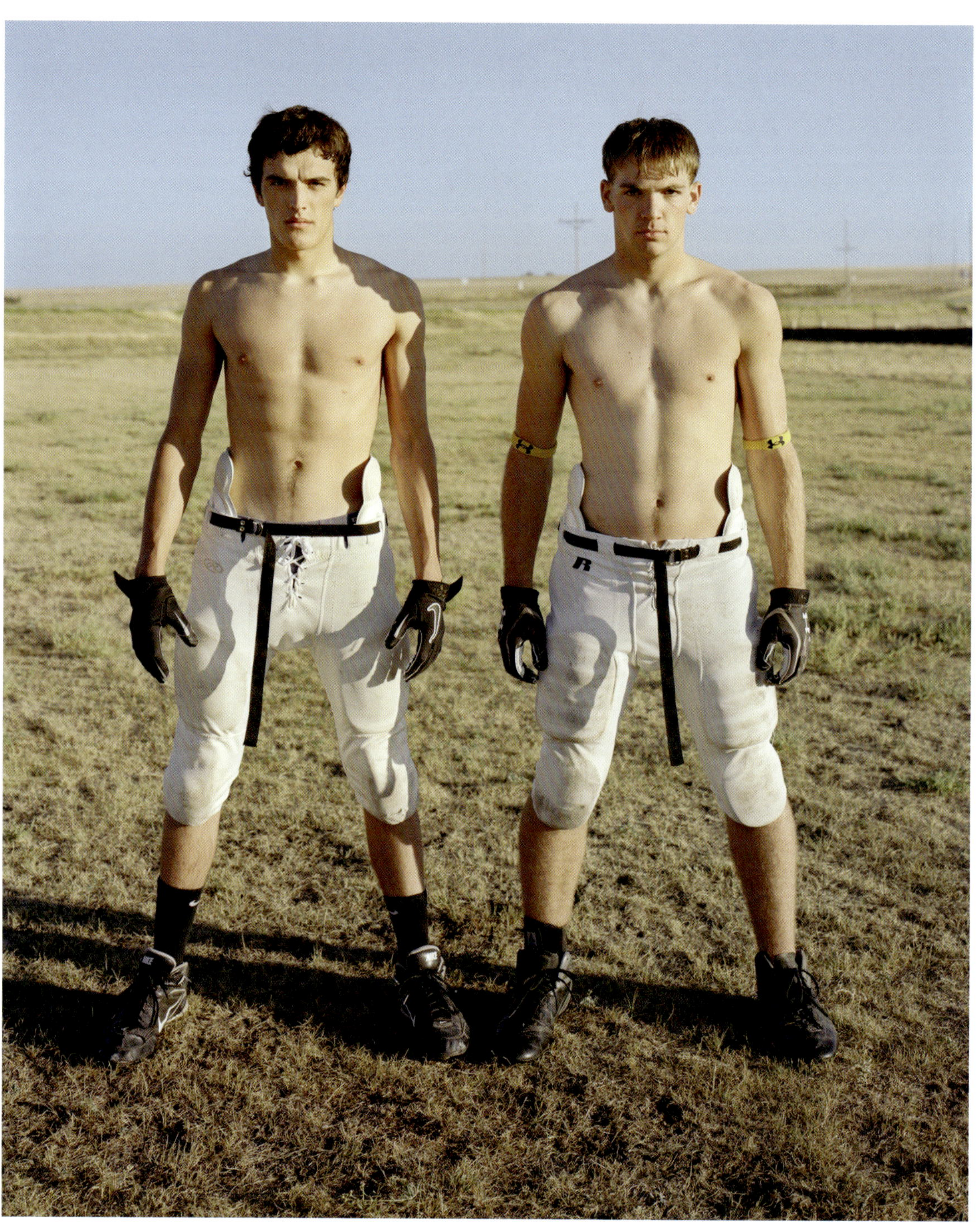

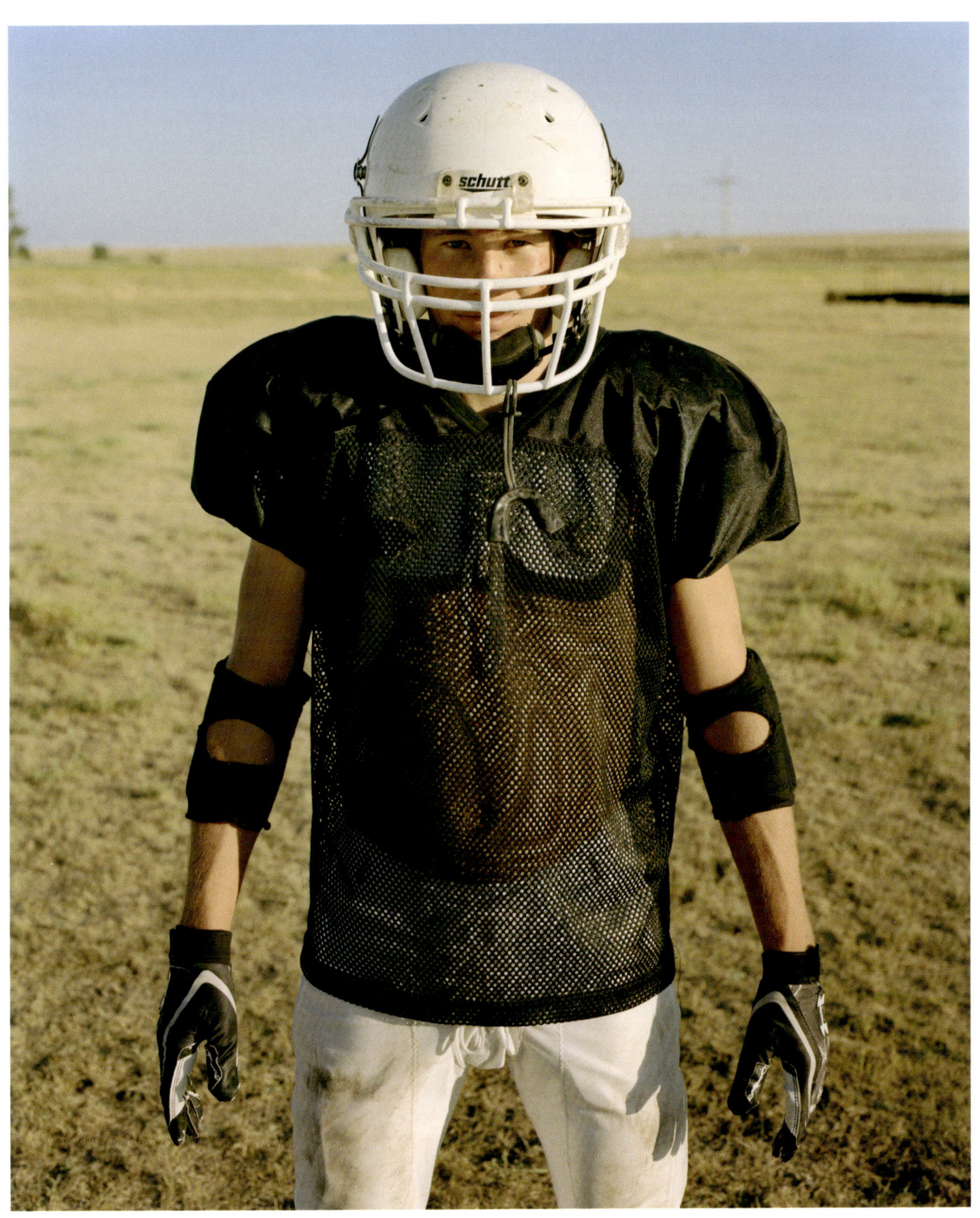

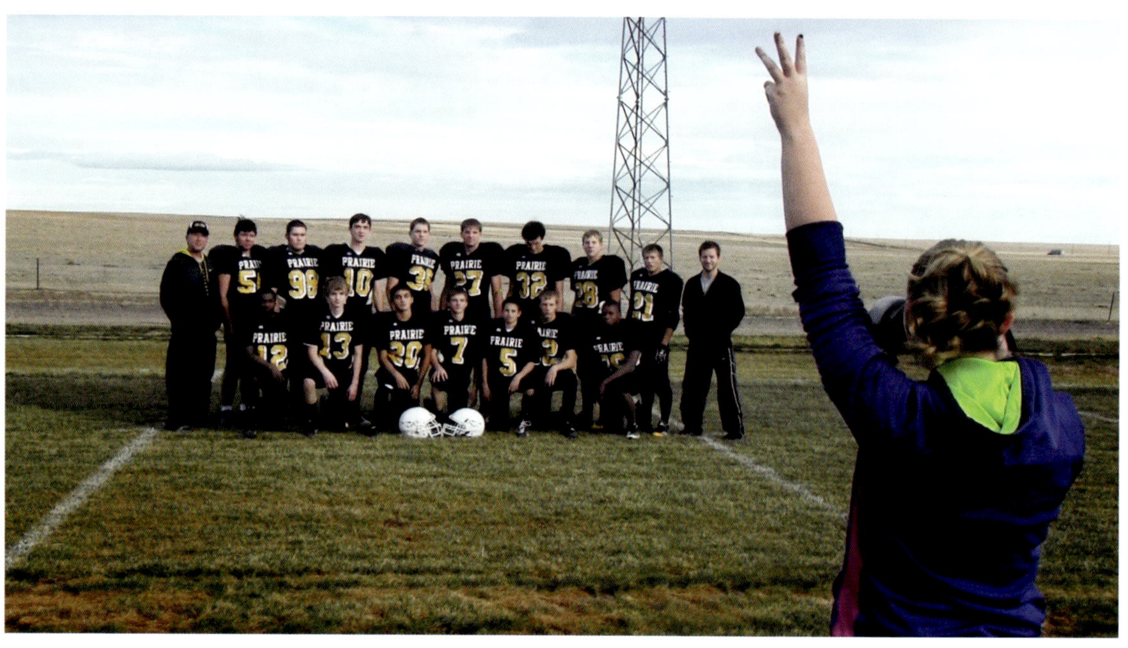

PICTURED

Ross Stump

Ian Fauconier

Trae White

Seth Gapter

Brice Funk

Mychal Godinez, Dustin Warboys, and Michael Kaiser

Austin Littlefield

T. J. Hubbard

Braden Stump

Bill Johnson

Seth Gapter and Brice Funk

Trae White and Michael Kaiser

Zachariah Hastings

Mychal Godinez

Eric Williams

Braden Stump and Tyler Carmen

Dustin Warboys

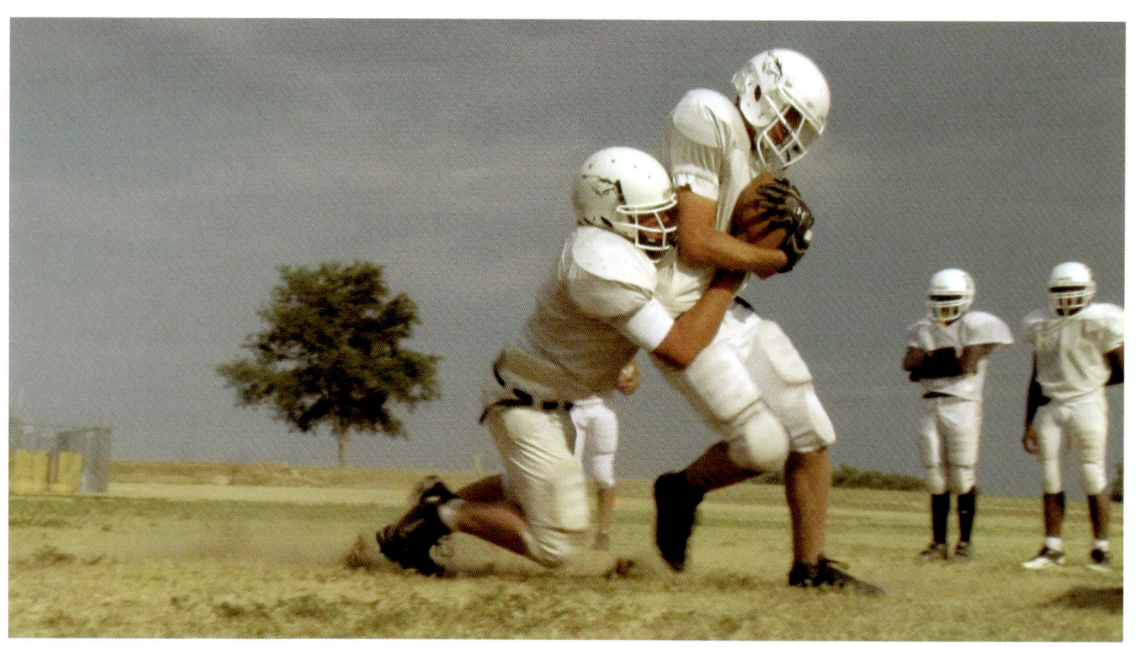

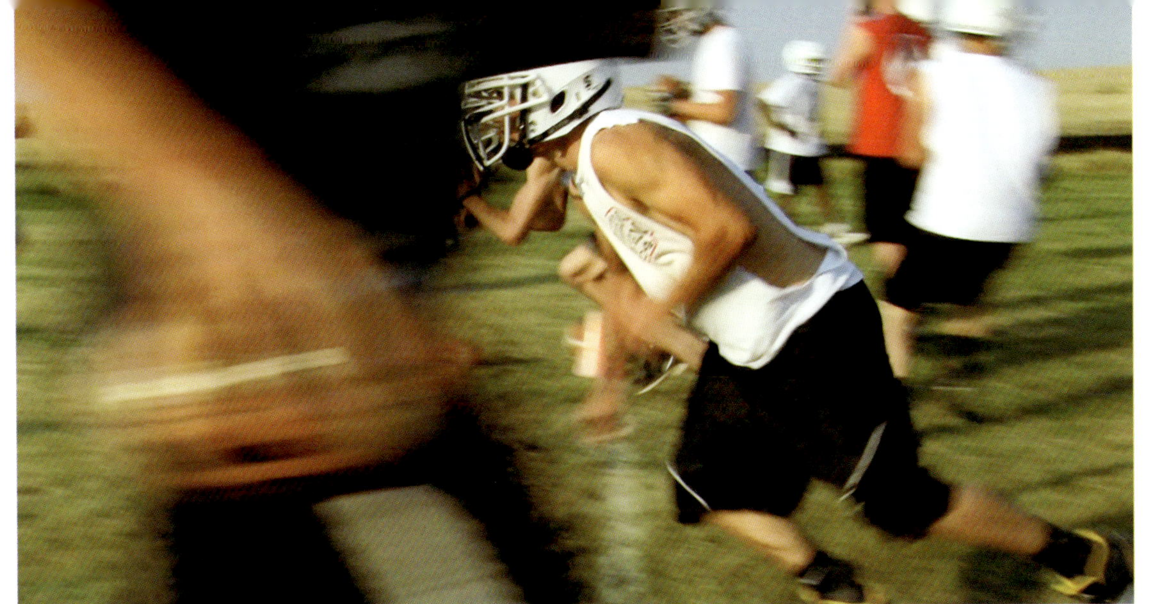

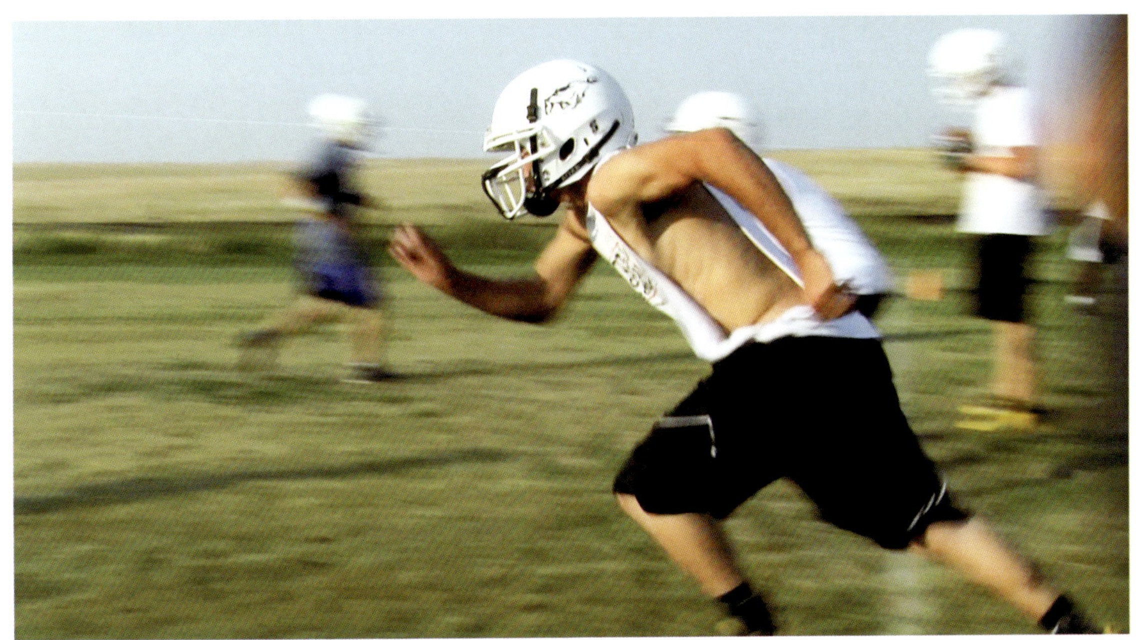

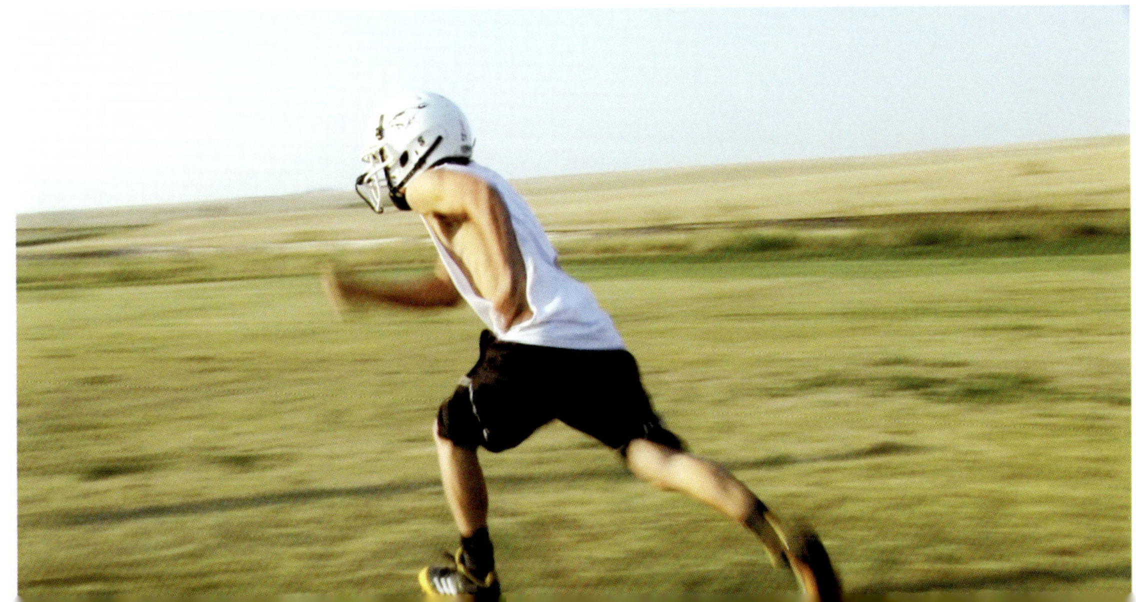

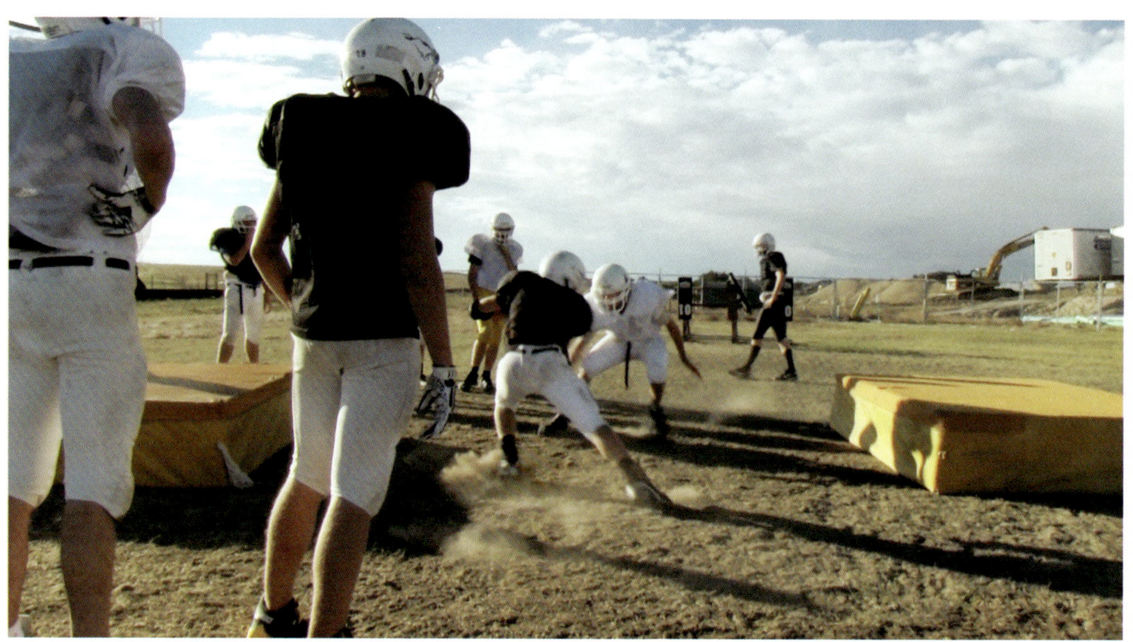

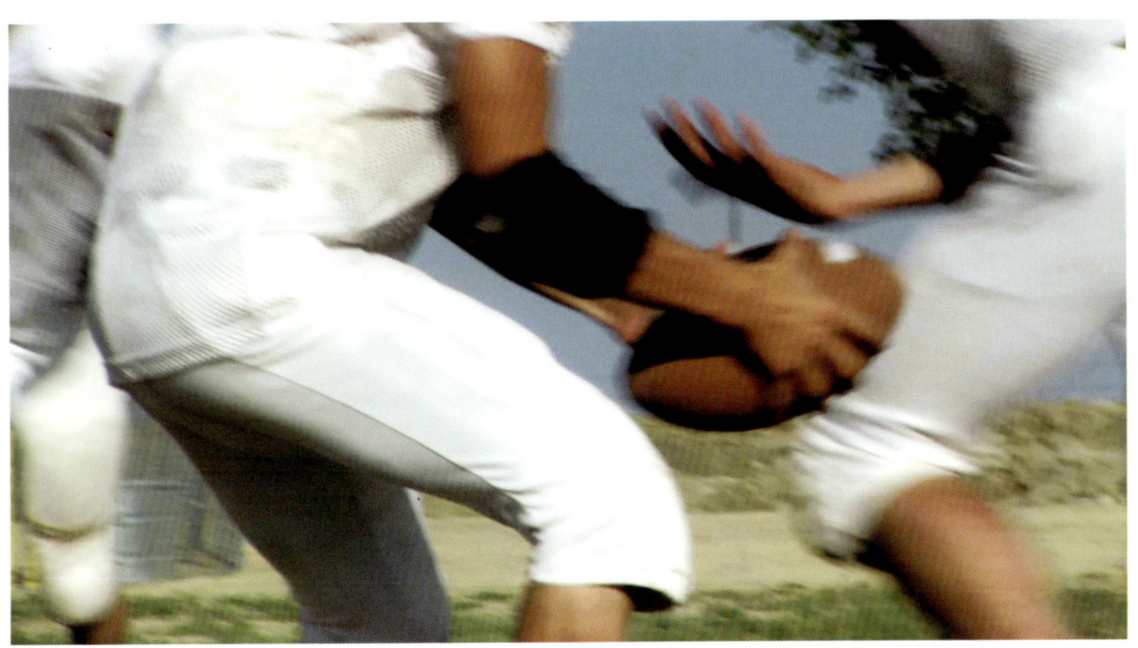

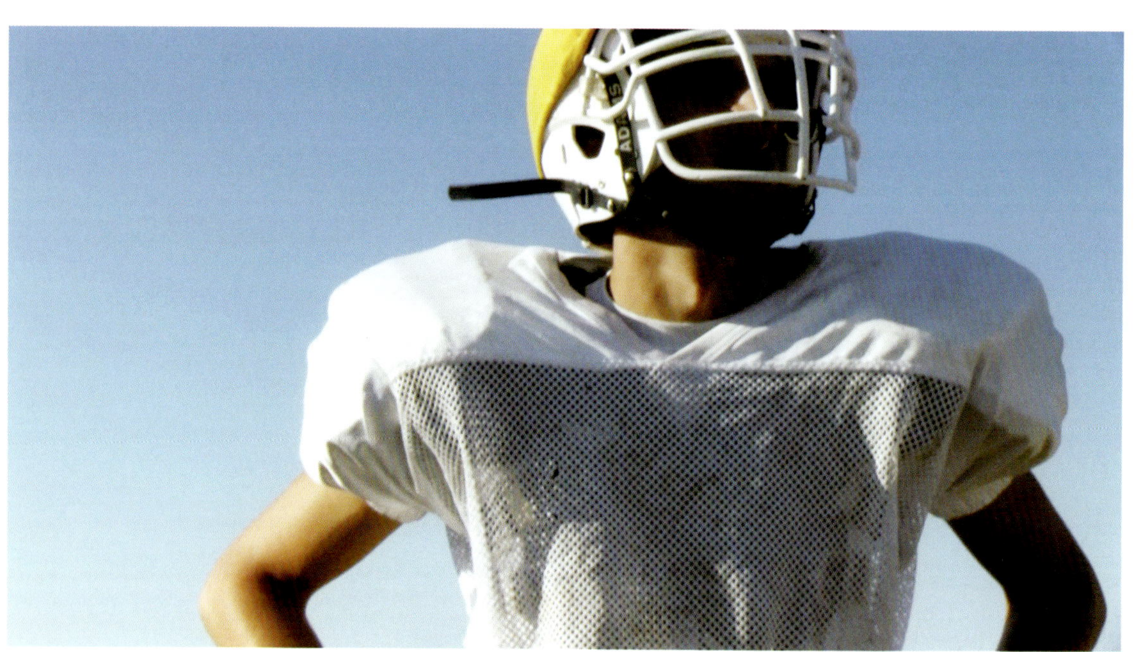

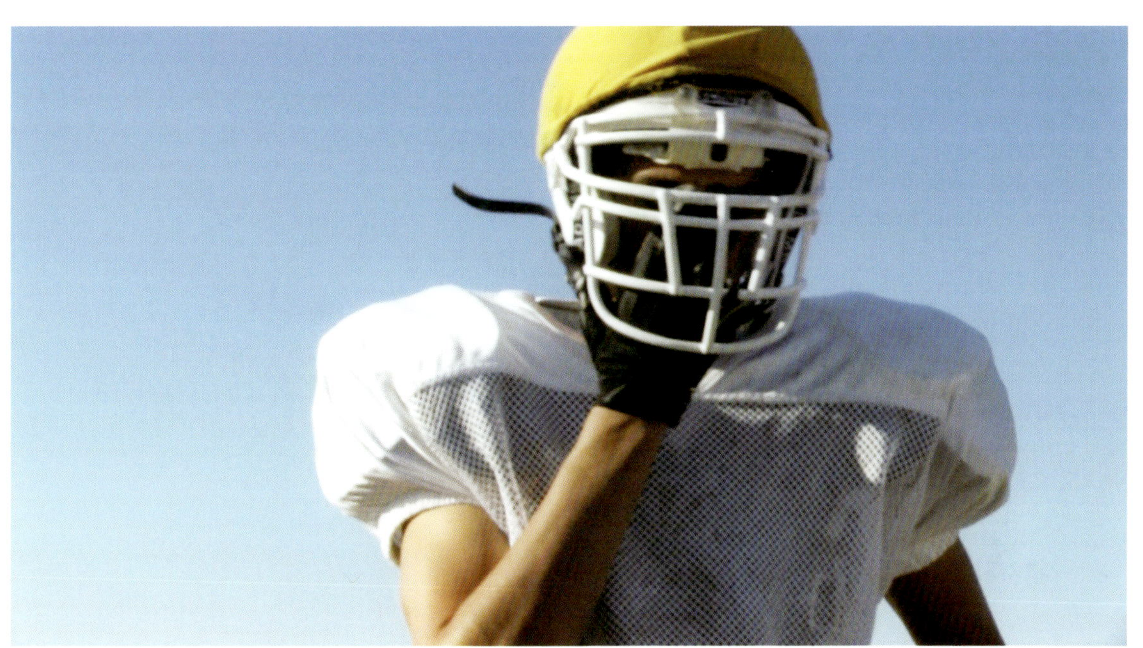

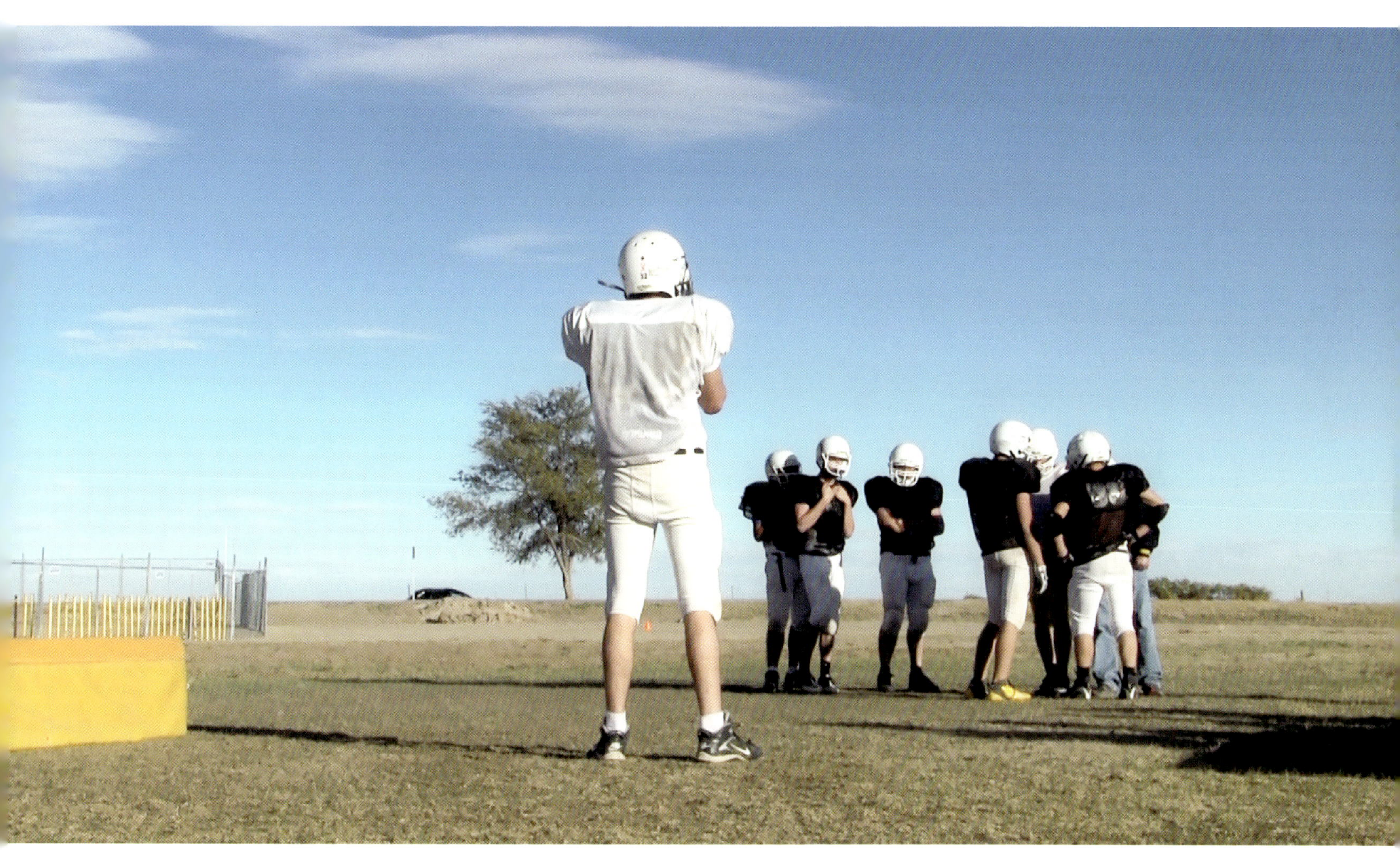

The
Season

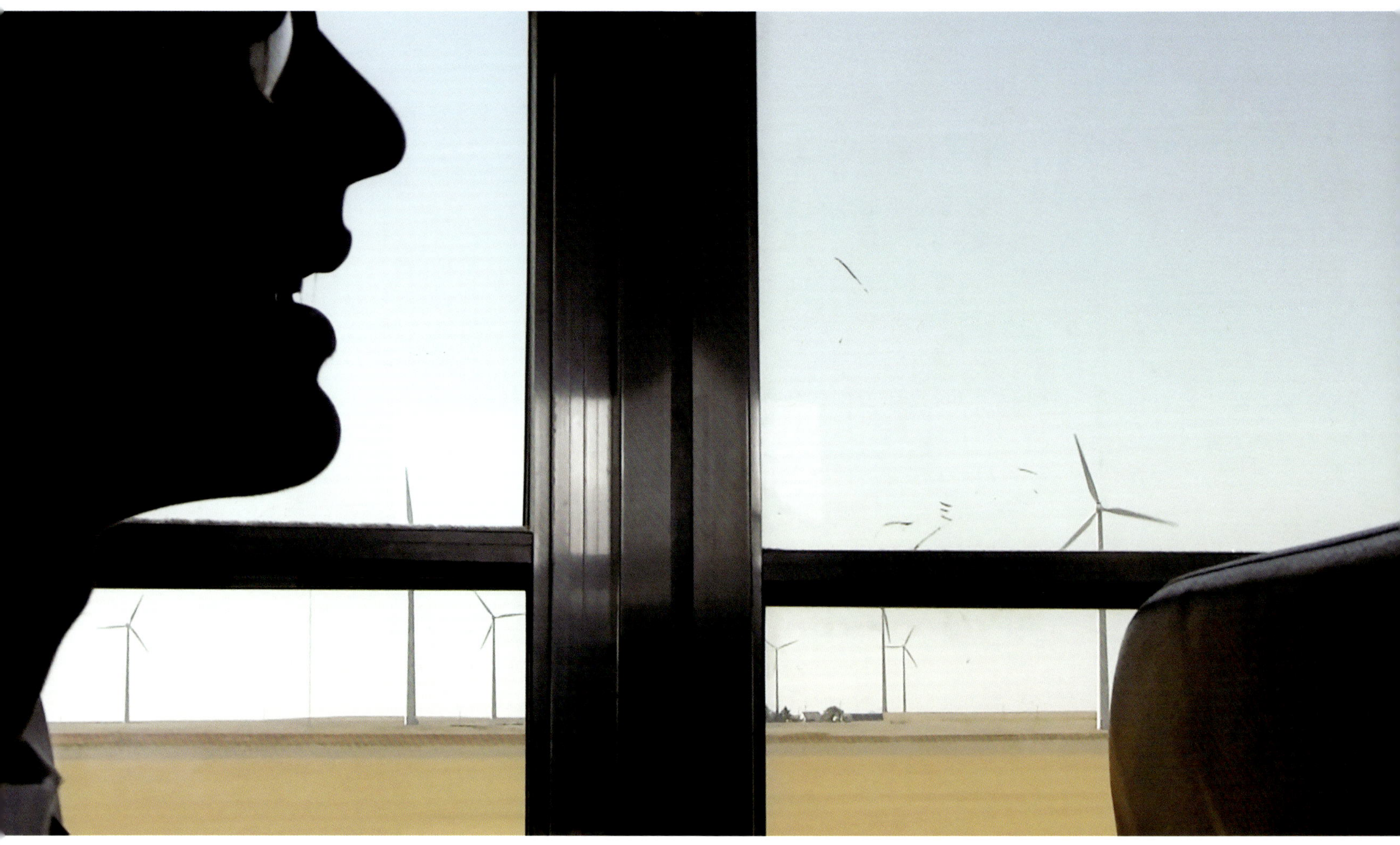

PEETZ BULLDOGS

In the first game of the season, Prairie School faced off against Peetz, a small township of about 200 people almost to the Nebraska border. On the bus, most of the team slept or listened to music through headphones. Bill Johnson read a novel; Brice Funk talked about his girlfriends.

Peetz sits in the middle of a huge wind farm, and games there unfold against the slow churning movement and low hum of giant turbines. After weeks of practice on hard dirt and stubby, blue gramma prairie grass, the Mustangs finally got a chance to play on the soft, forgiving pad of a well-watered field. As Peetz and Prairie warmed up, the setting sun threw a spectacular display of color across the sky. Then the lights came on.

At first, Prairie seemed over-confident; players lost their cool and made mistakes. Peetz wasn't supposed to be a good team this year, but the guys were big and quick. At the end of the first half, the game was tied 22–22.

The second half proceeded much the same way, with a score for one team squared by an equal count for the other. Then, with only 3:48 left in the game, the Mustangs sliced out a touchdown on a long pass from Ross Stump to Mychal Godinez. When they missed the extra point attempt it left the score an exposed 48–42, Prairie. They recovered their onside kick and held the ball for almost three minutes but came up short on fourth-and-16. Peetz got the ball back at midfield with almost a minute left in the game. The Bulldogs first play was a long sweep run that Prairie barely managed to stop. Then, the Mustangs intercepted a Hail Mary pass with 11 seconds left. Game over!

What had been a sundry group of boys, tossing a football around a backyard field, had become a real team. Many players had good games, but the standout was Dustin Warboys, the 5′8″ senior running back. He had scored five touchdowns, rushed for 191 yards, and seemed to be in on every tackle. In the parking lot, around 10 p.m., as the exhausted players got on the bus for home, Warboys mentioned he was heading off to cut hay on the family ranch.

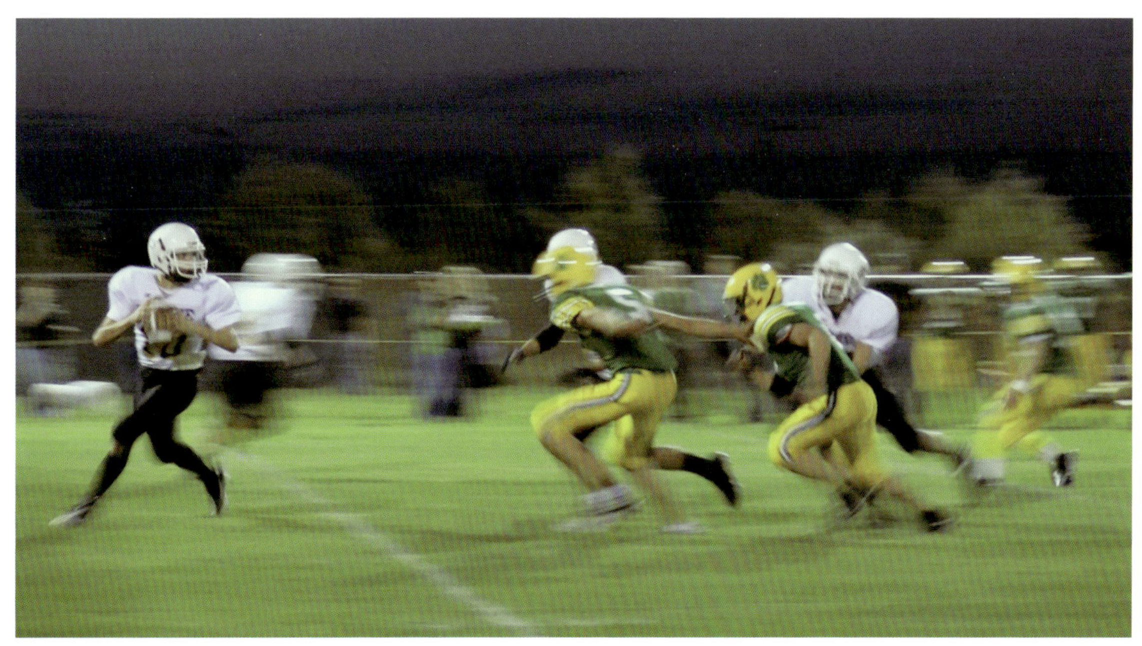

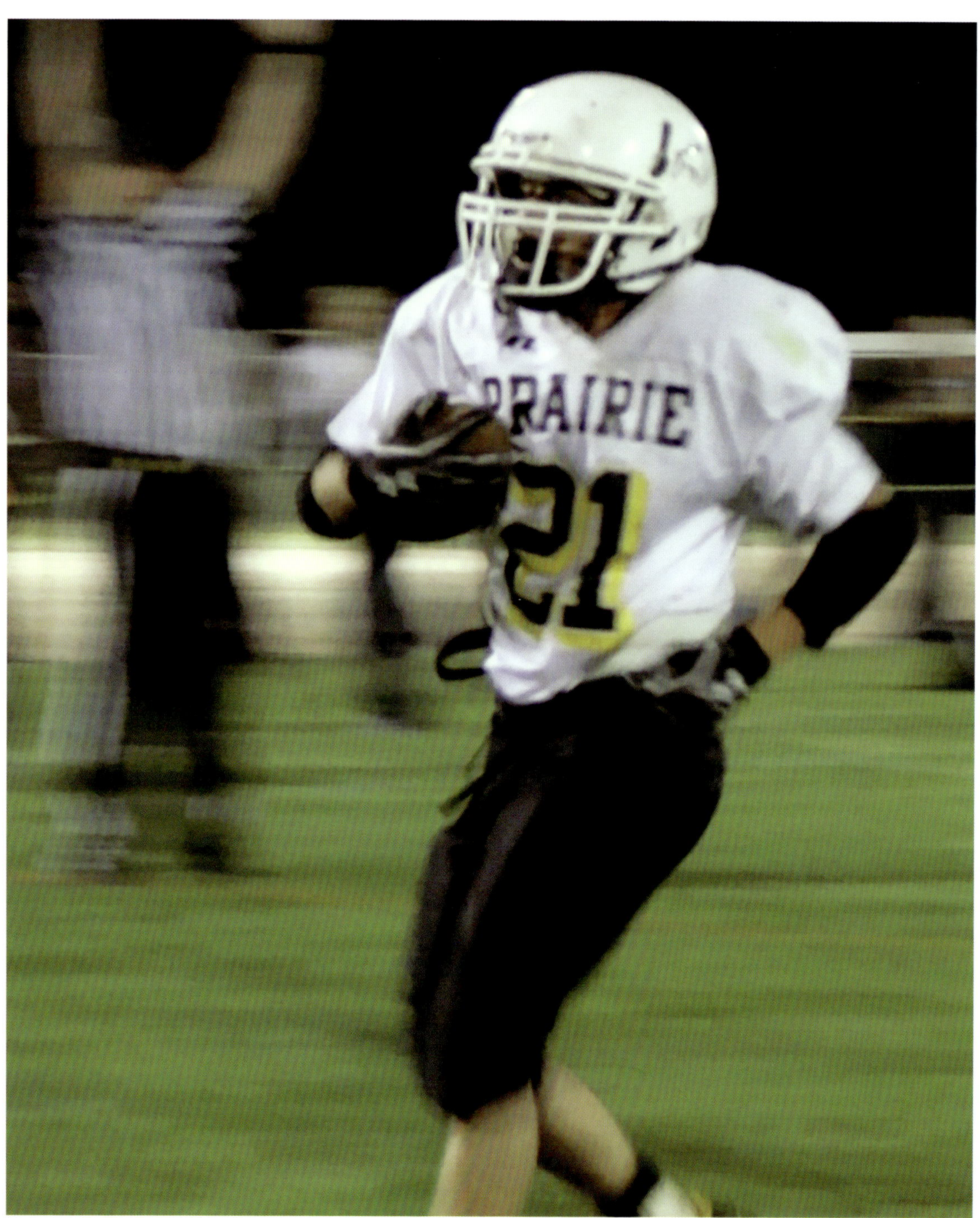
PRAIRIE
21

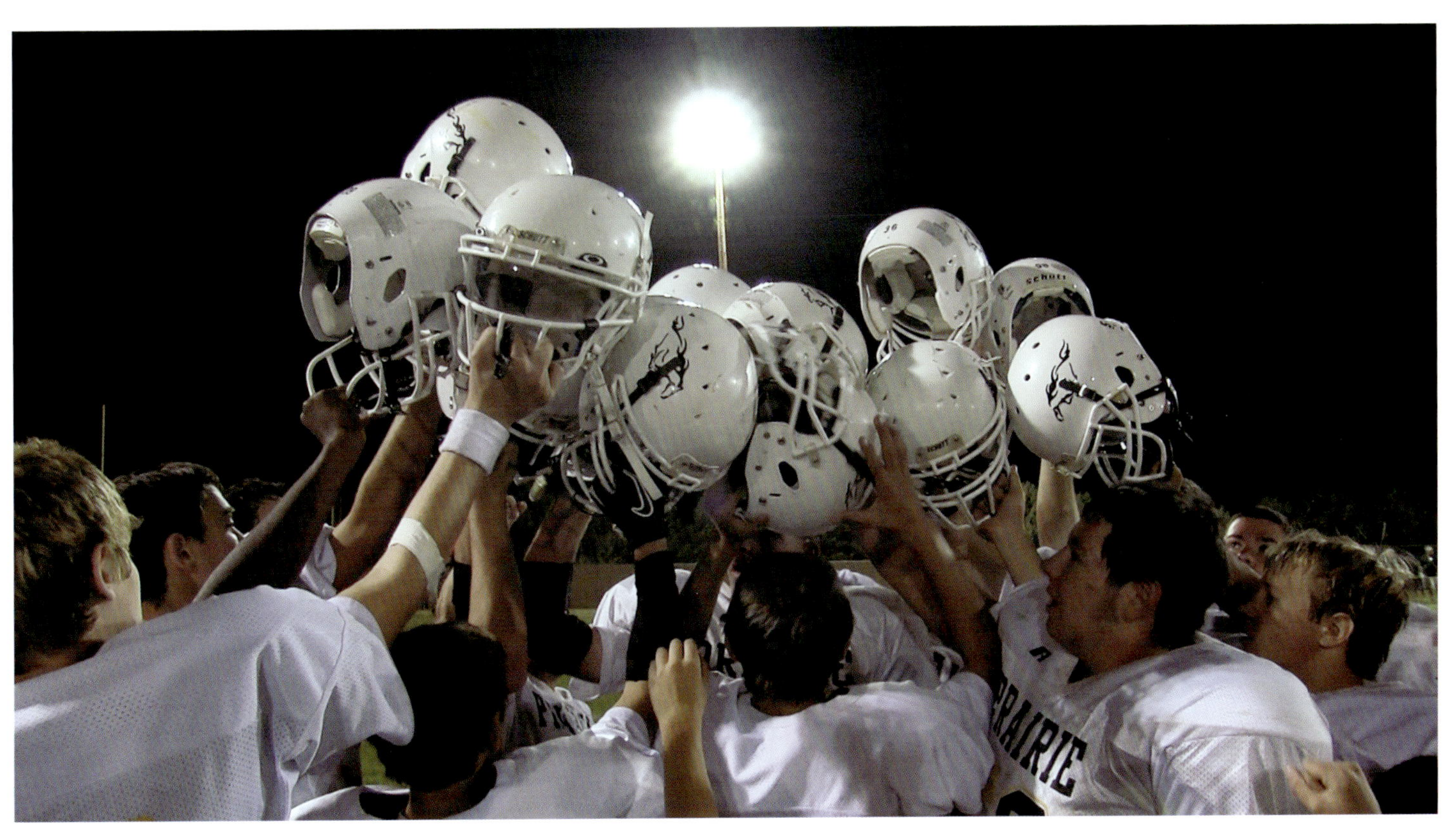

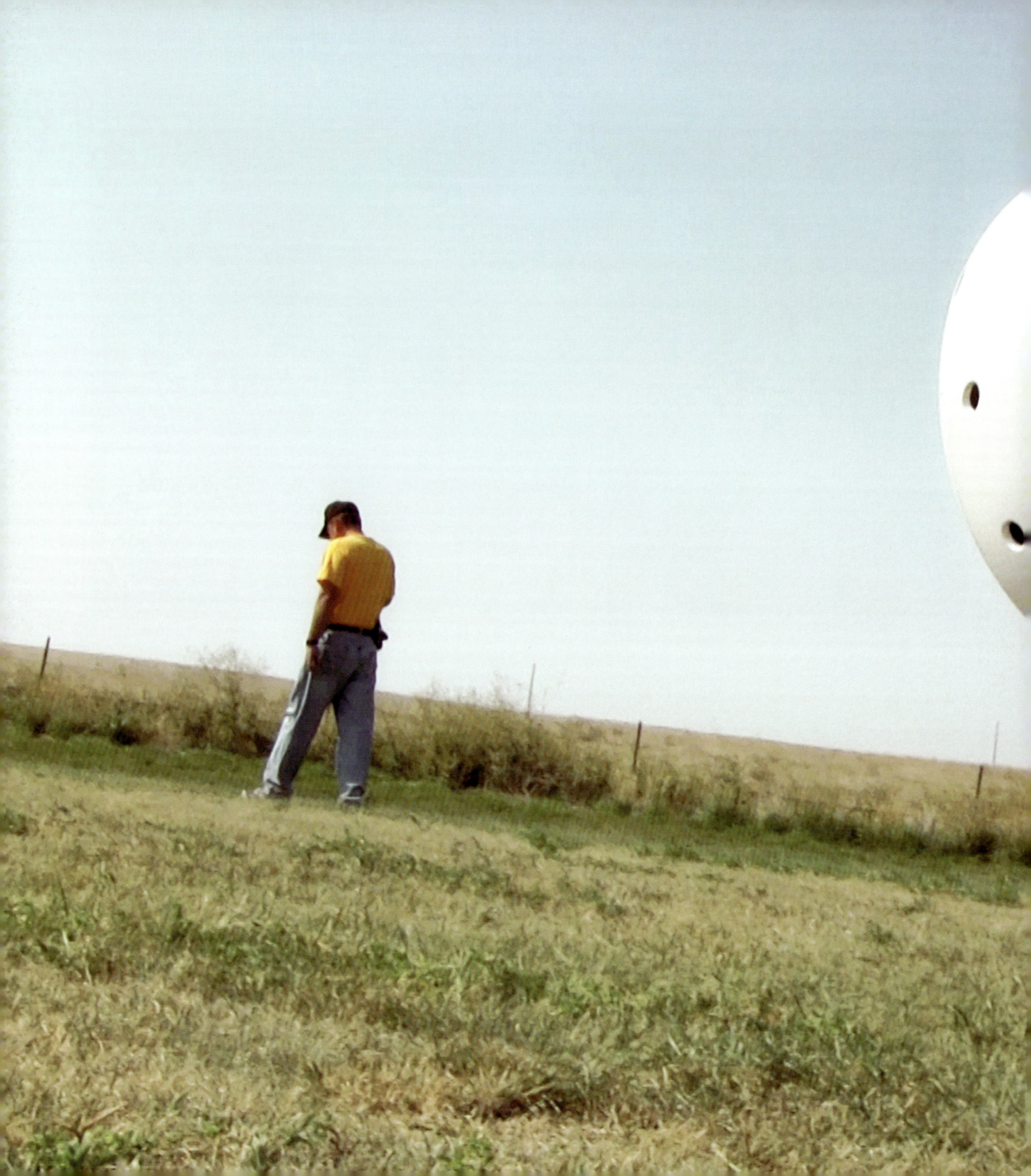

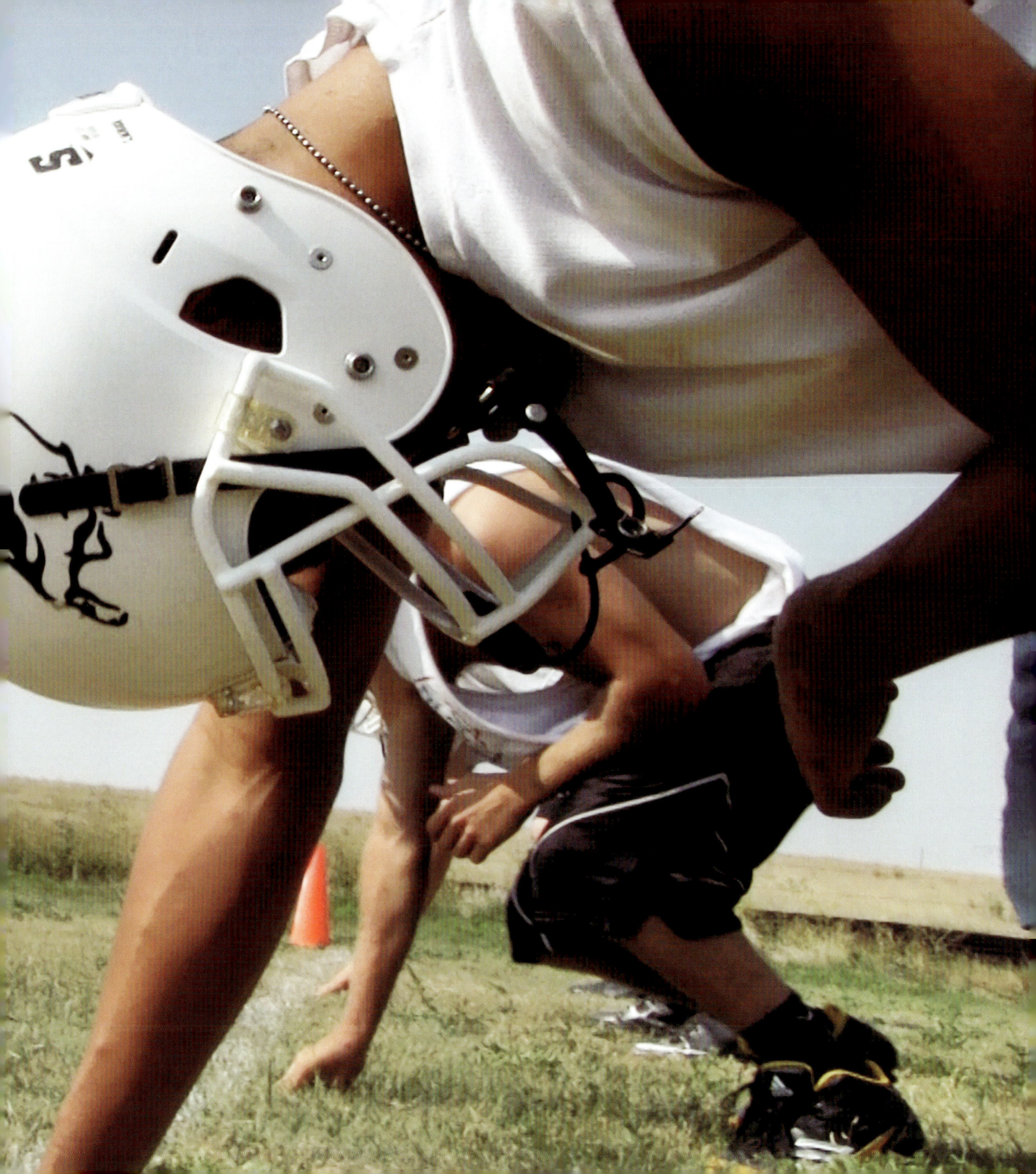

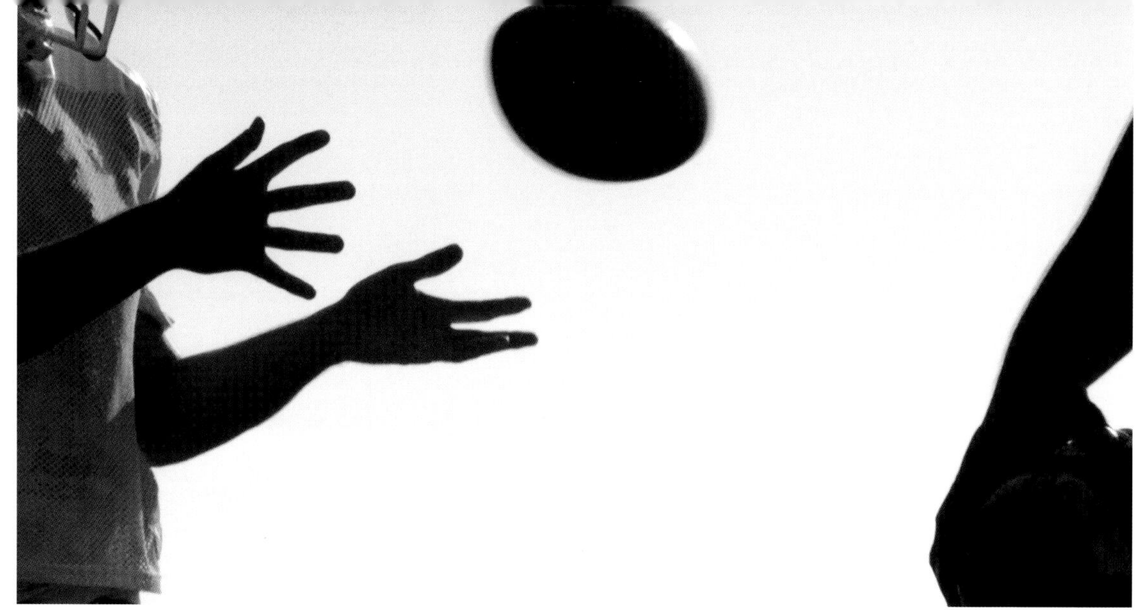

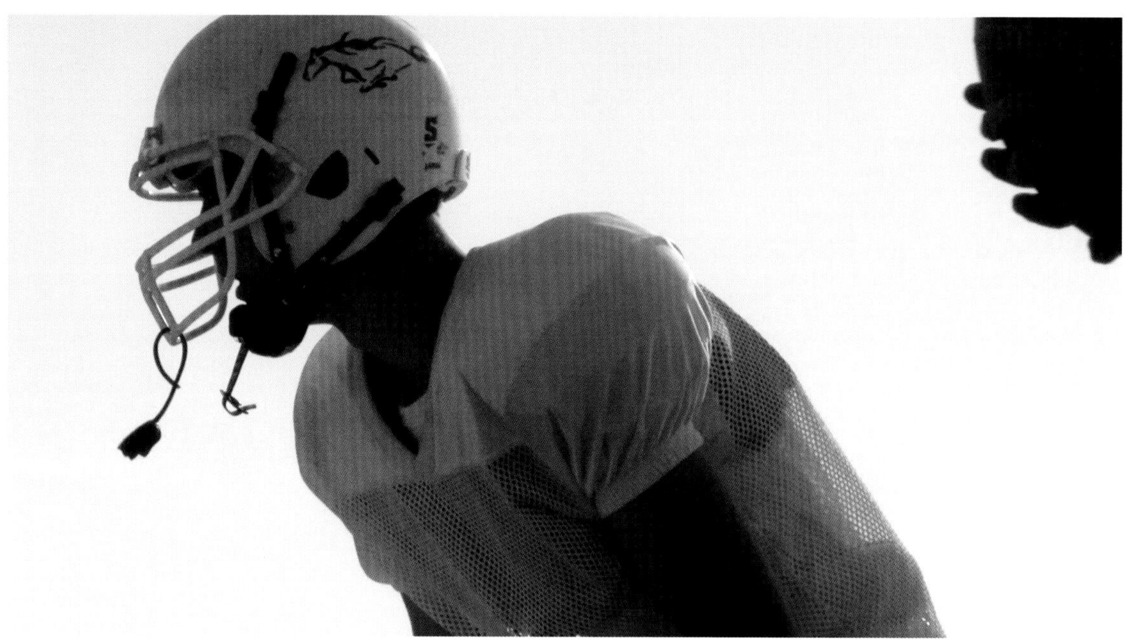

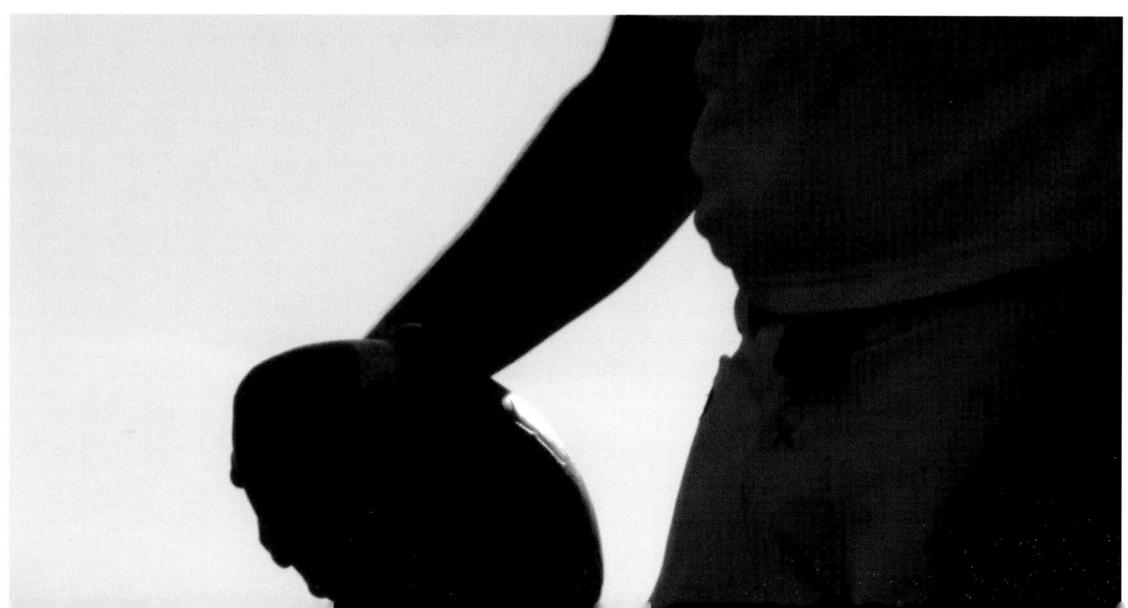

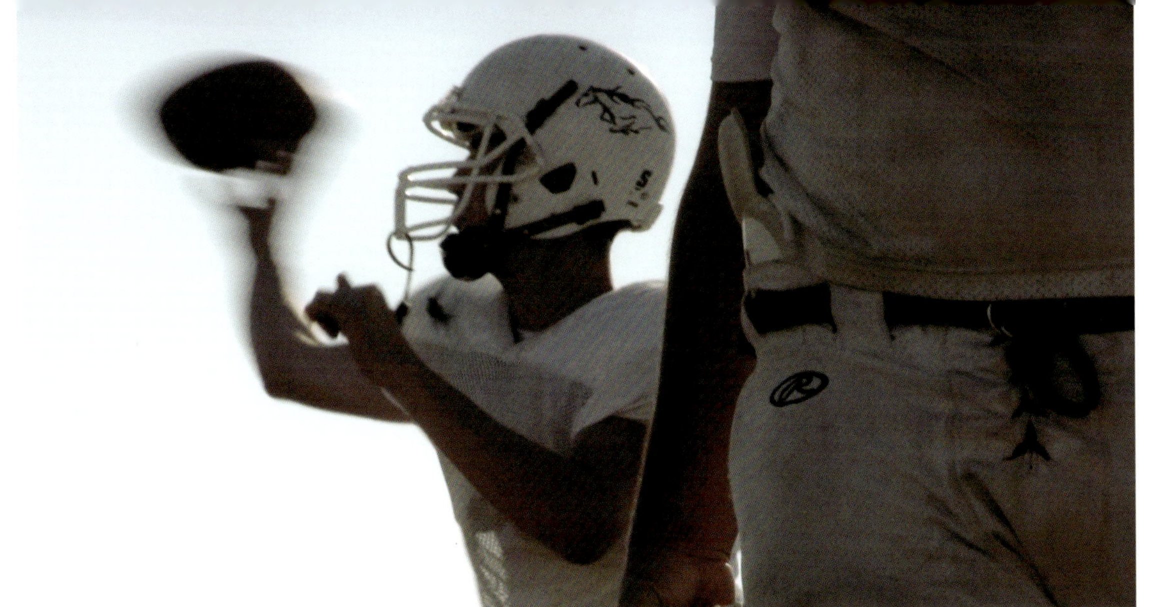

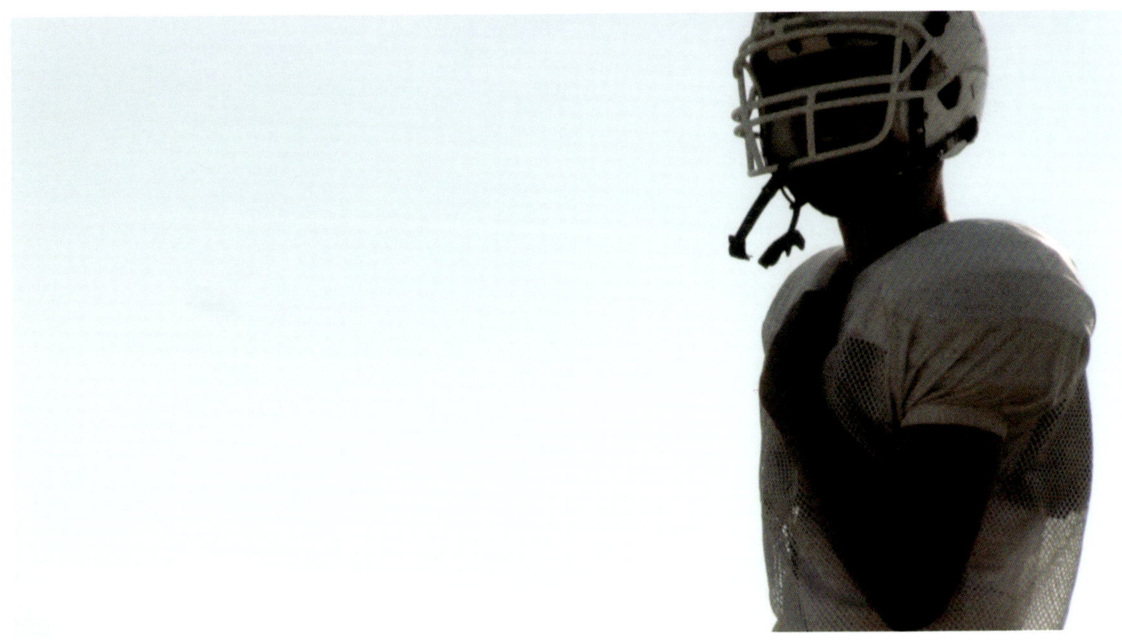

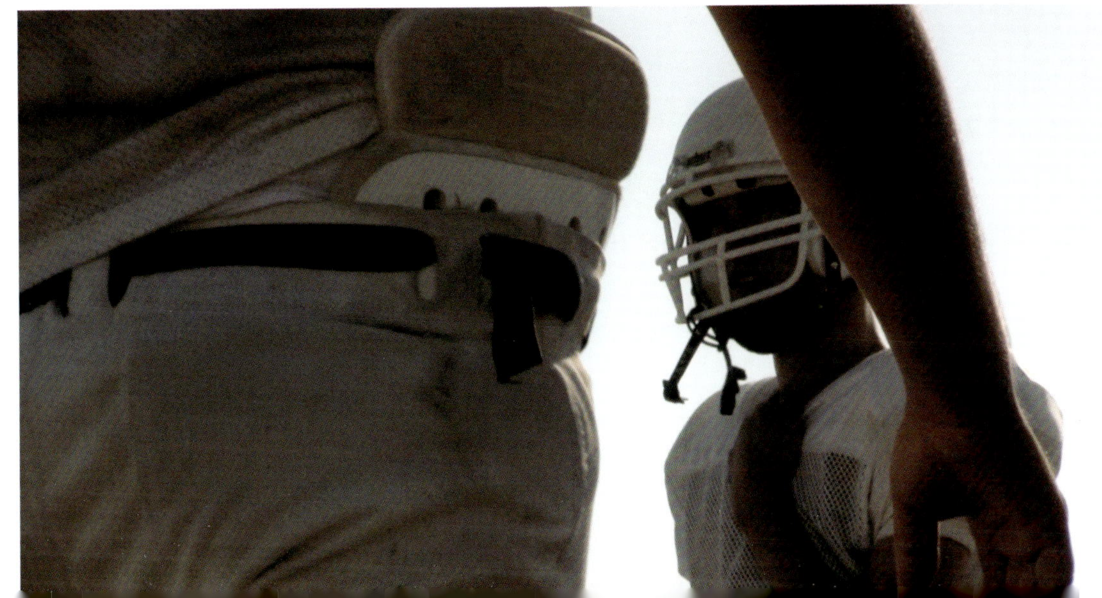

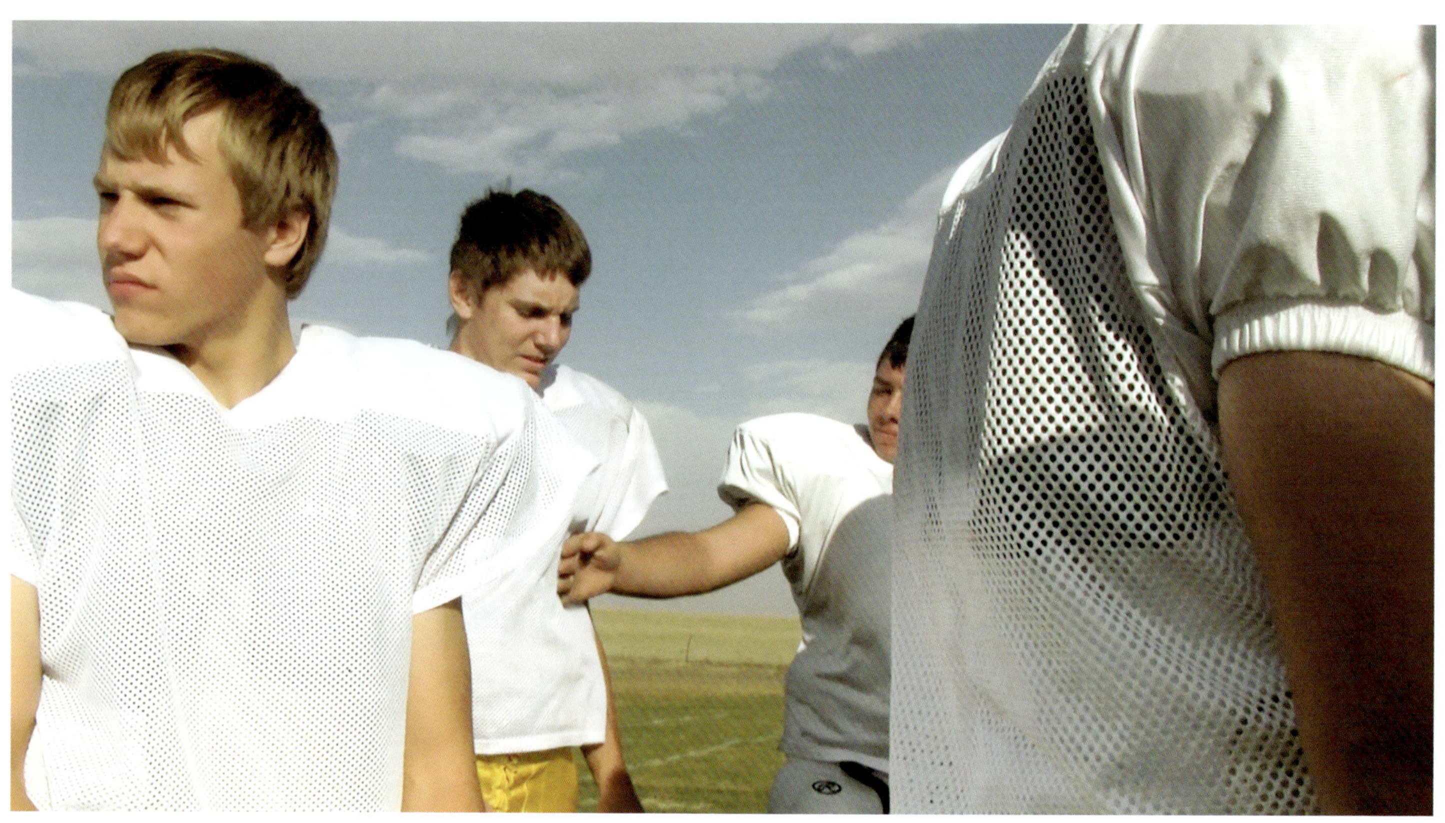

WELDON VALLEY WARRIORS

The next week the Mustangs faced Weldon Valley, the one school that didn't have lights for night games, so the event started at 3 p.m. After weeks of intense heat, the weather broke: the afternoon was gorgeous, 70 degrees with a few clouds. The Warriors football grounds sat just behind the school in the town of Weldona. Corn fields surrounded the other three sides, right up to the bleachers.

When the game began, Weldon scored first. Like the week before, the Mustangs quickly took stock of the situation and concentrated on the plays they had worked out in practice; the score was 35−7, Prairie, by half time. The starters played so well that subs were rotated in and took the score to 61−15 in the third quarter. By then the slaughter rule had kicked in, and the officials let the clock run. Prairie played the full roster, giving younger players like freshman Zachariah Hastings and sophomores Austin Littlefield and Eric Williams a chance to compete. Even the two big linemen, Bill Johnson and Trae White, made some pass receptions and ran with the ball. Prairie won handily, 61−29. Once again, Dustin Warboys was a major force for the Mustangs, with five touchdowns.

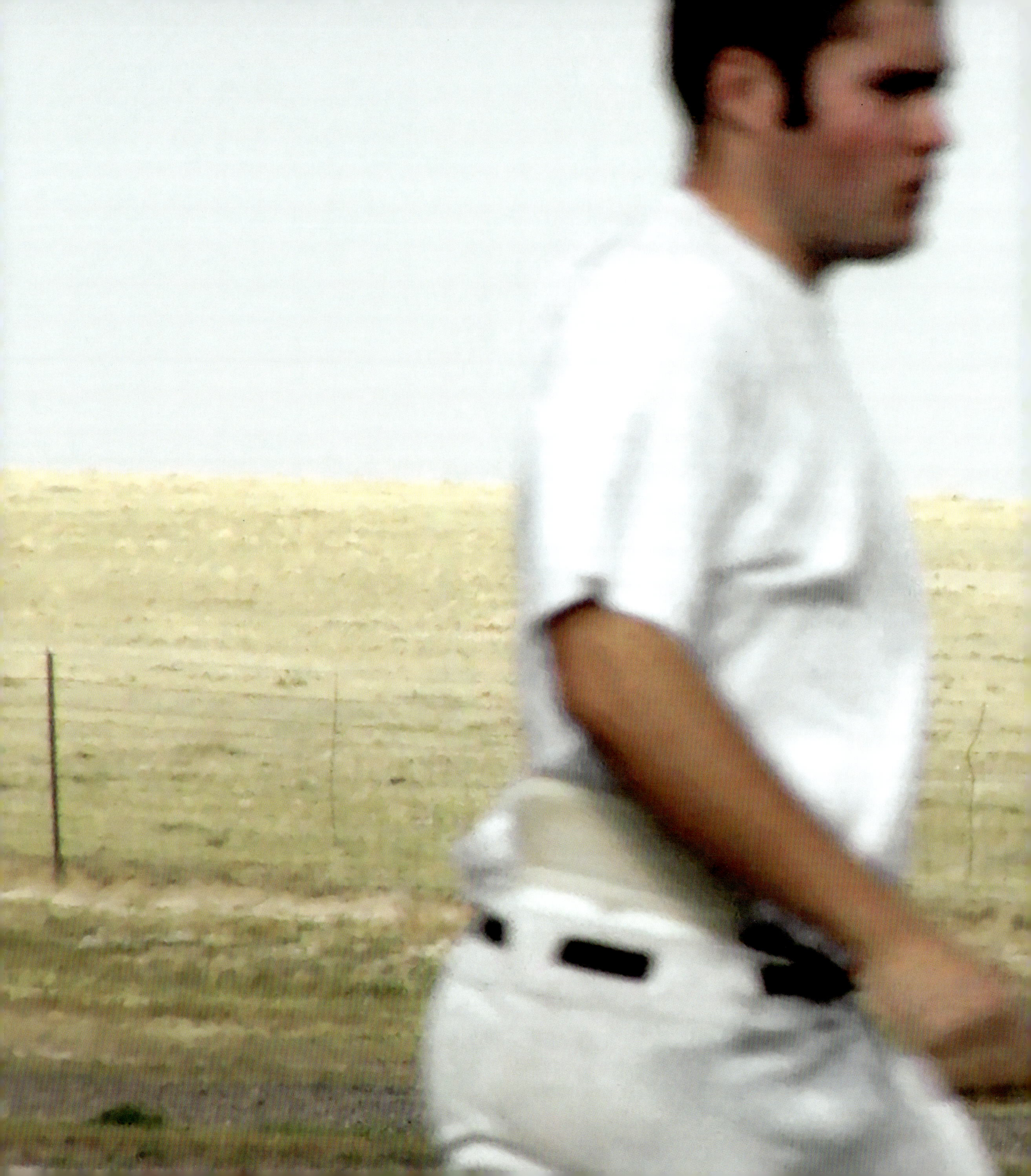

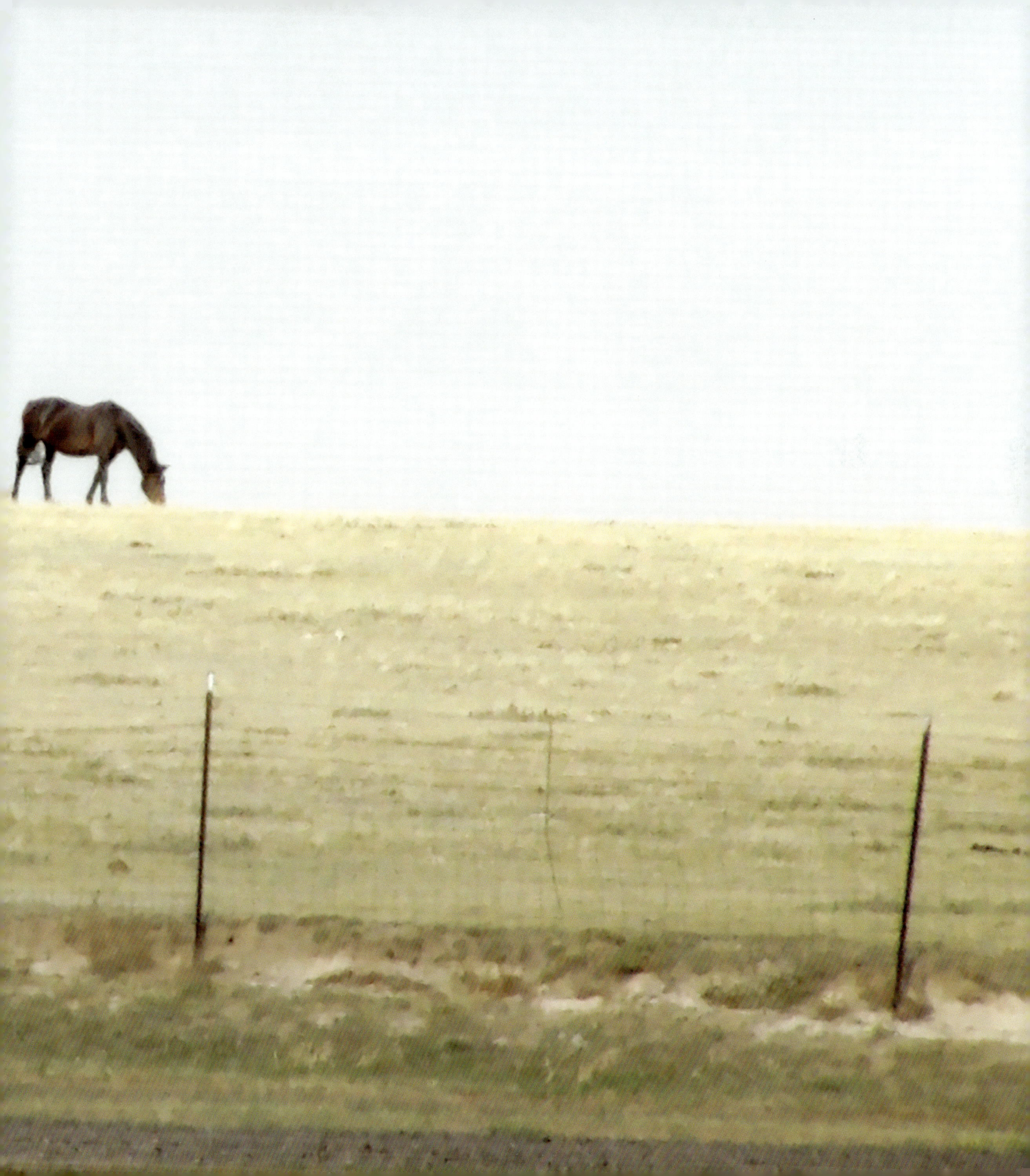

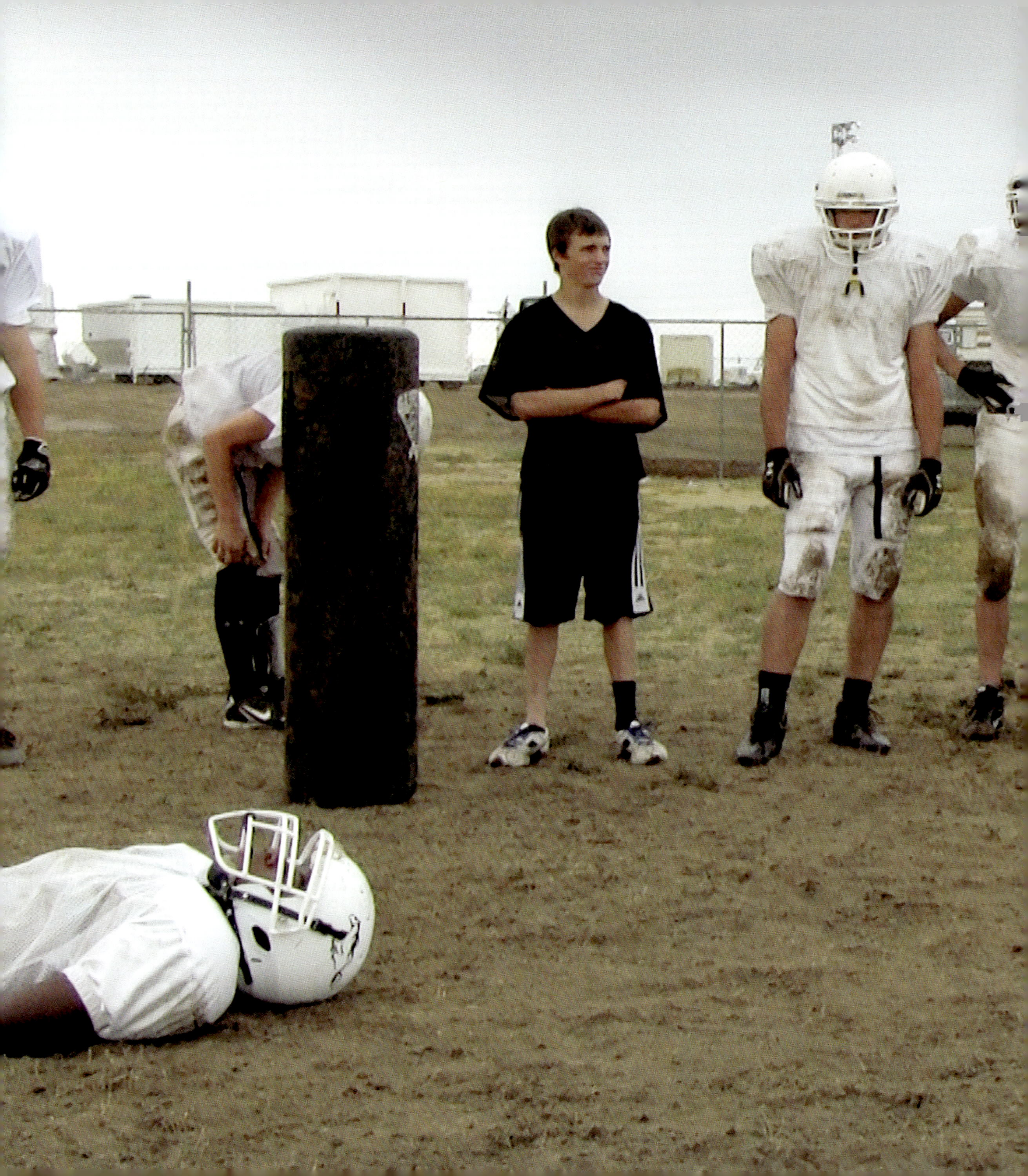

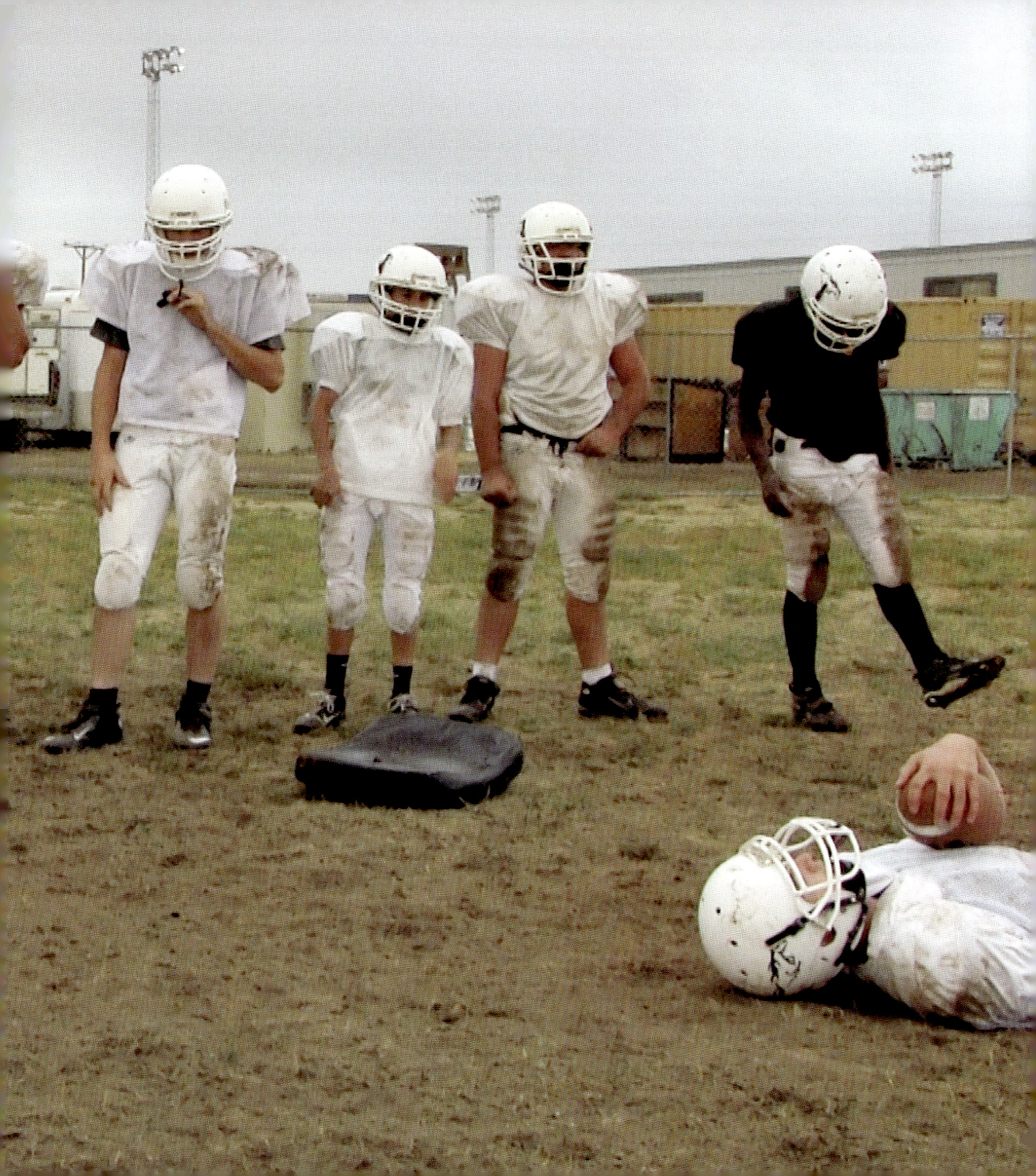

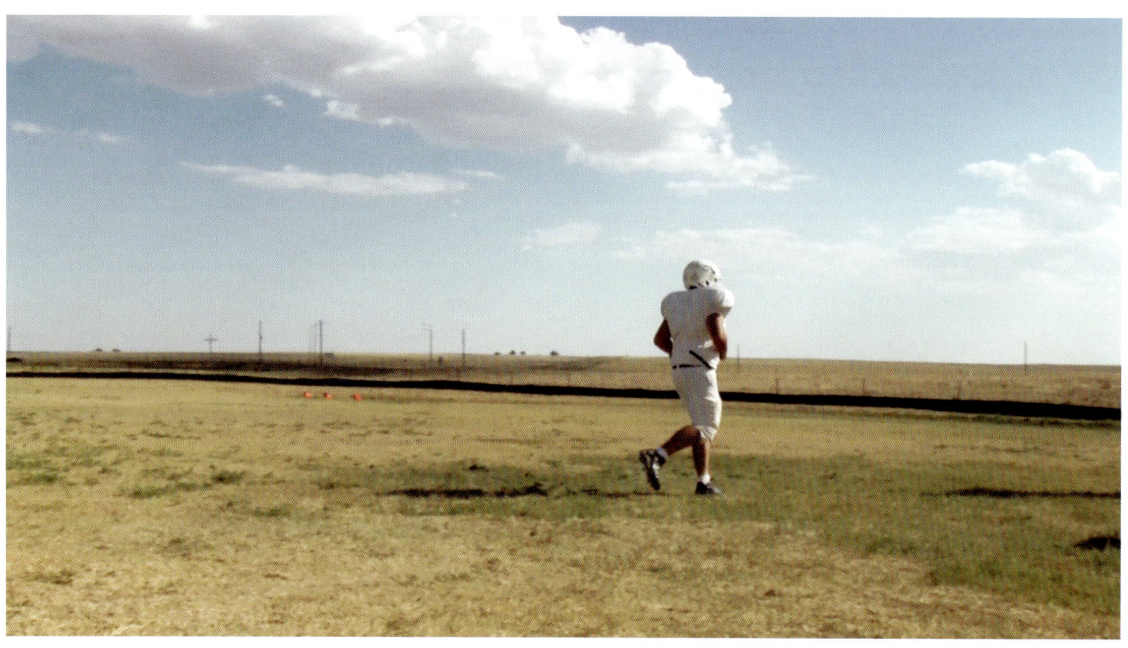

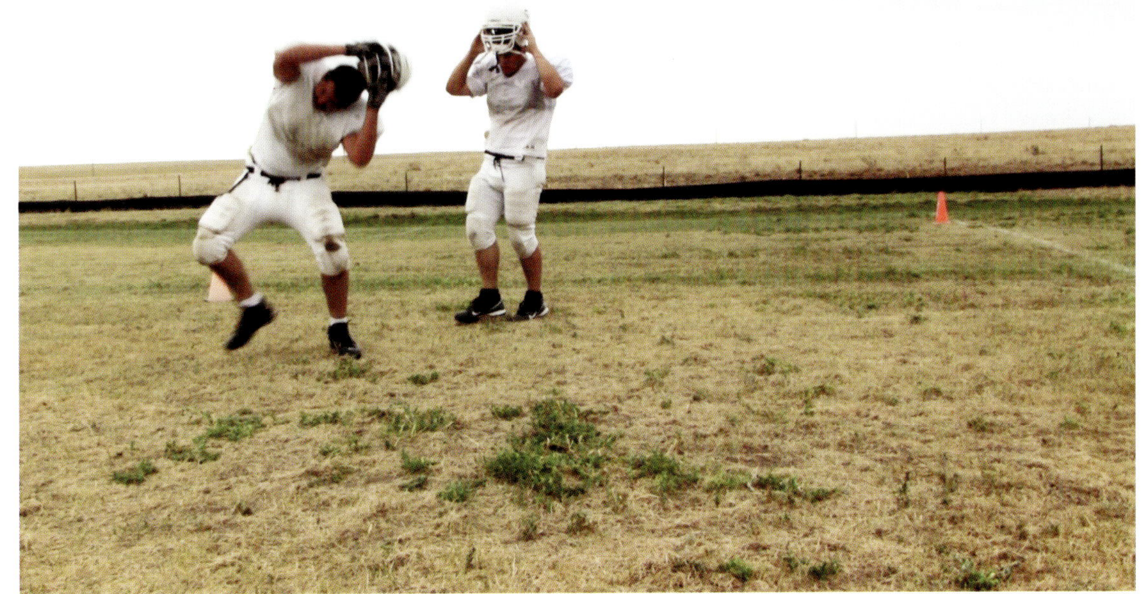

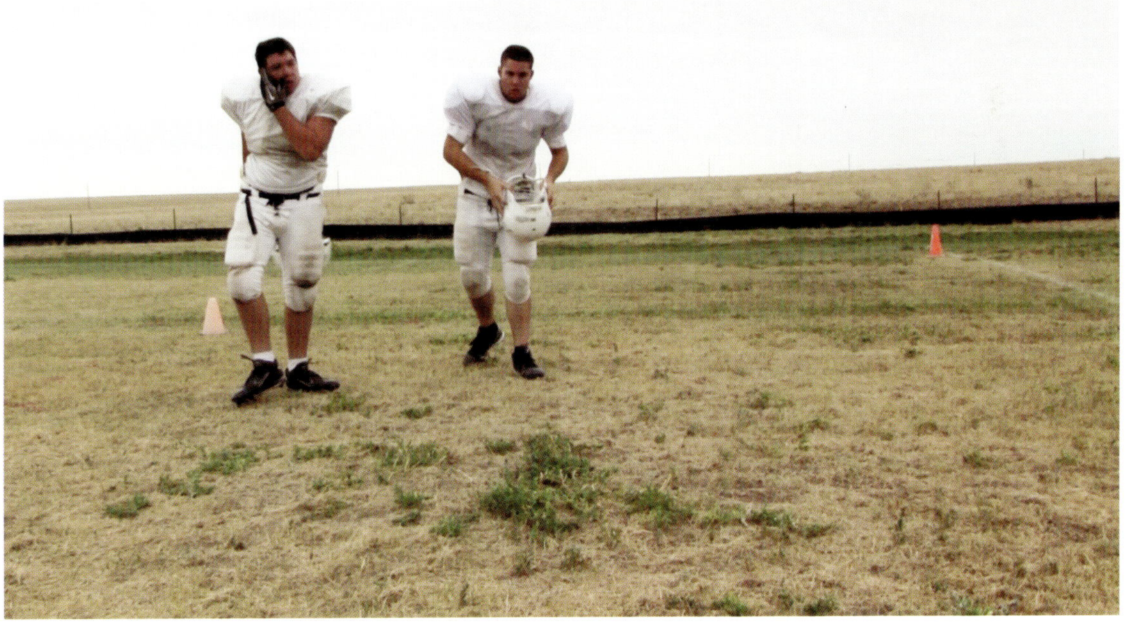

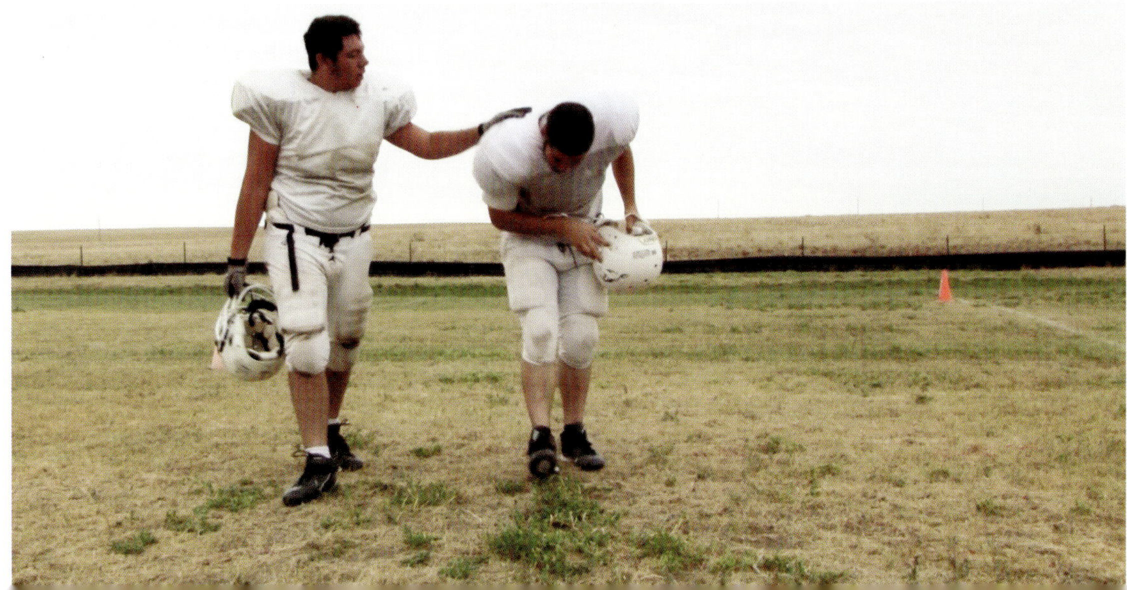

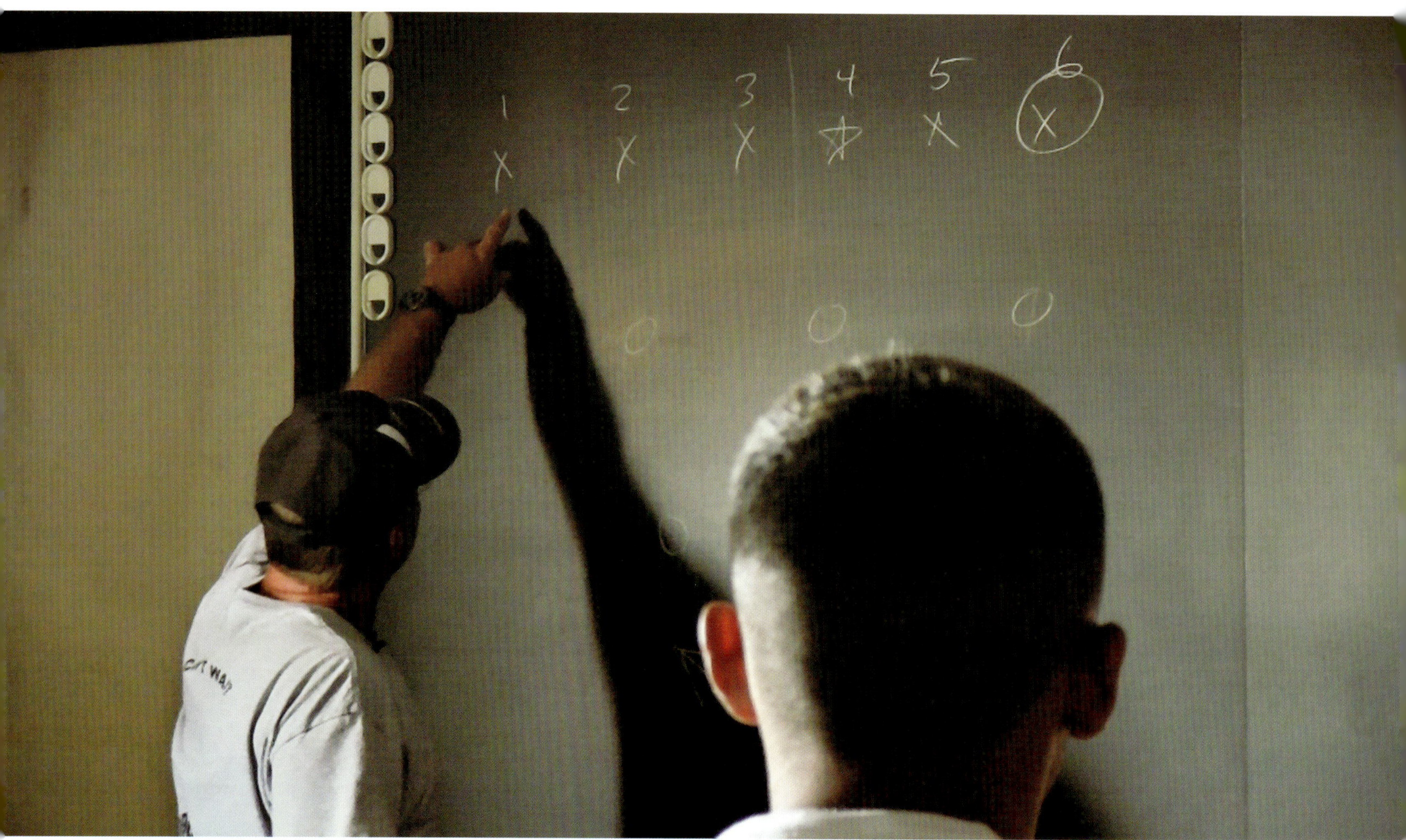

1 2 3 4 5 6
X X X X X X
O O O

OTIS BULLDOGS

Otis, south on Highway 34 just over two hours from Prairie School, was established as a camp
for railroad workers in the late 1800s. The town had about 475 people in the 2010 census.
Otis's historic school building and football field sit in the middle of town. Driving to the game,
I saw the Bulldogs' flaming red logo everywhere.

MaxPreps, the online stats keeper and general source of information on high-school
sports, favored the Bulldogs to win the six-man state championship that year, and the night
of the Prairie game was their homecoming. Otis had twenty-two players on the roster. When
they ran out on the field in their bright red uniforms and jogged around the perimeter, it
looked like they had fifty. Coach Carlson's squad of fifteen had worked all week to create
new plays that would use Otis' aggressiveness and size against them, to no avail. At halftime
Otis led 28–0. Prairie started the second half with an exciting charge, recovering their own
onside kickoff. Tyler Carmen managed a few good runs, but the Mustangs just couldn't block
the Bulldogs' defense and eventually the slaughter rule kicked in. With less than a minute
and the score at 46–0, Prairie had the ball. Dustin Warboys slipped through a hole in the line
and squeezed in Prairie's only touchdown of the night.

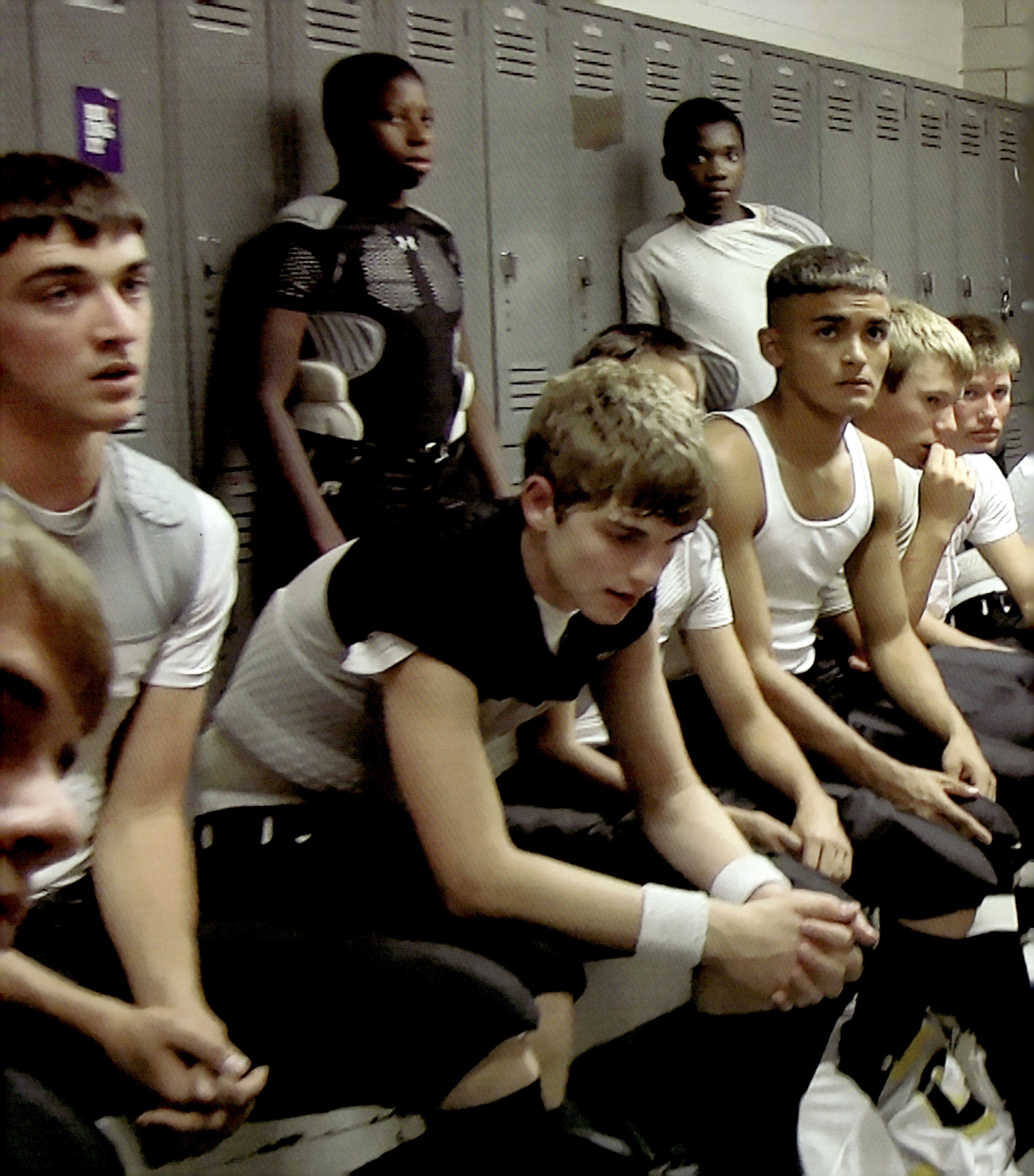

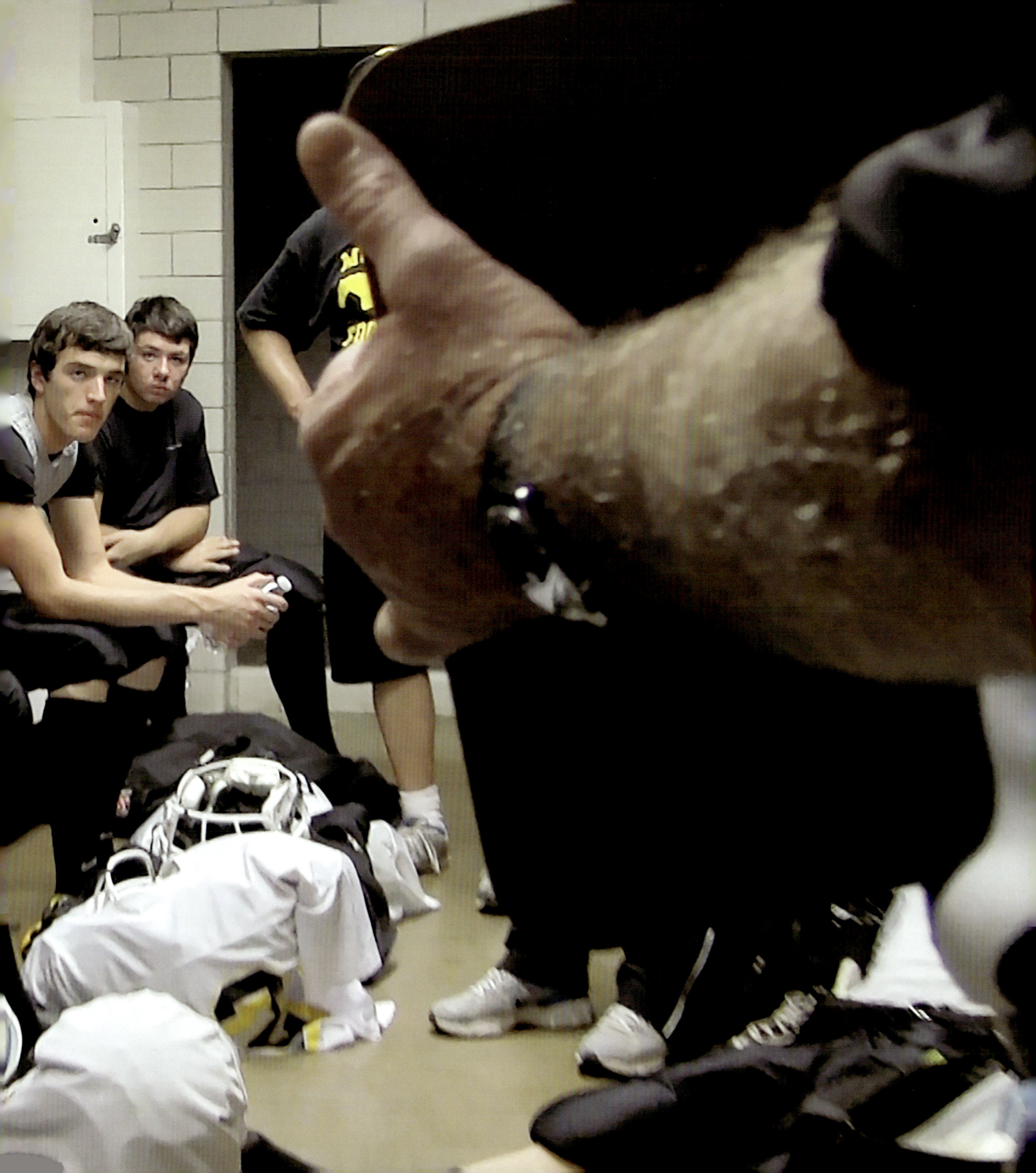

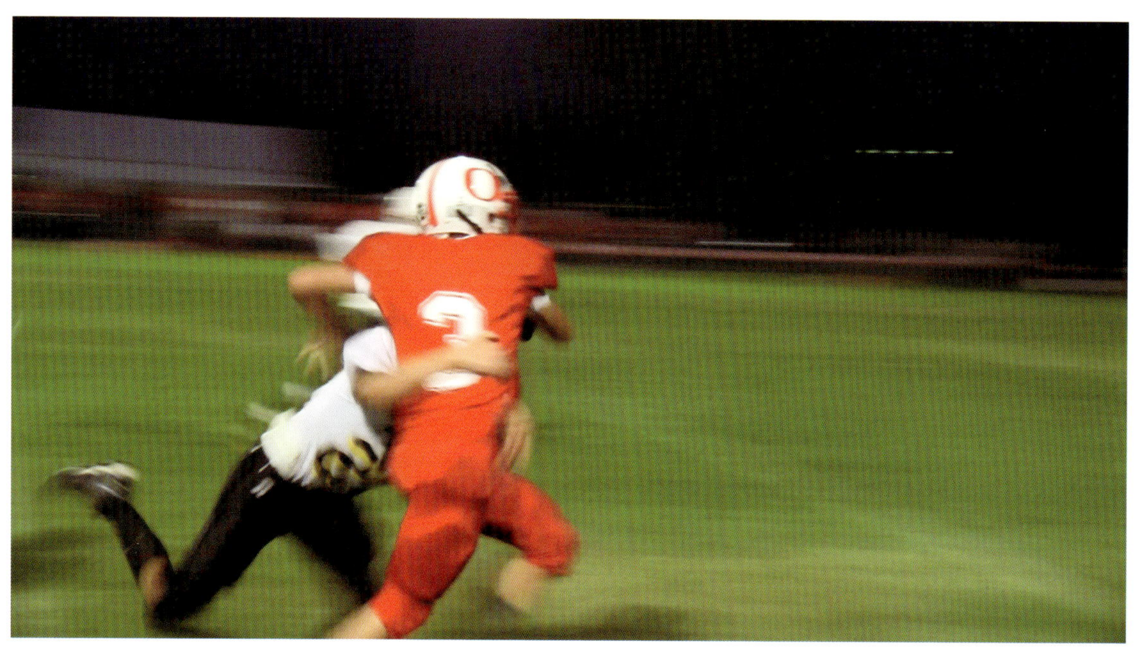

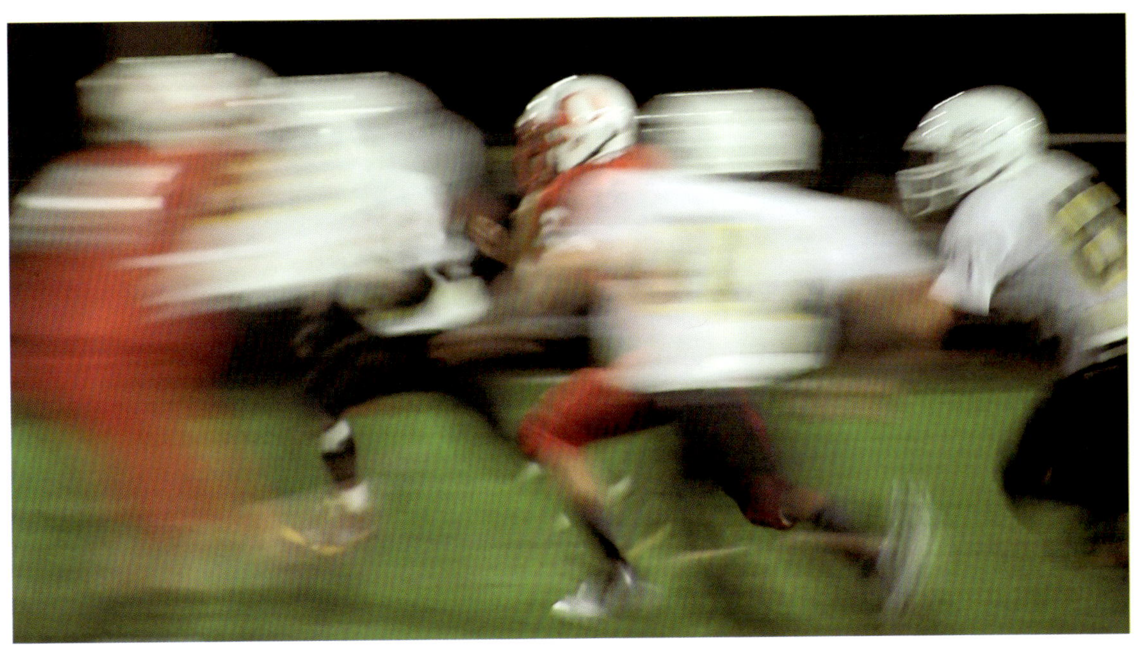

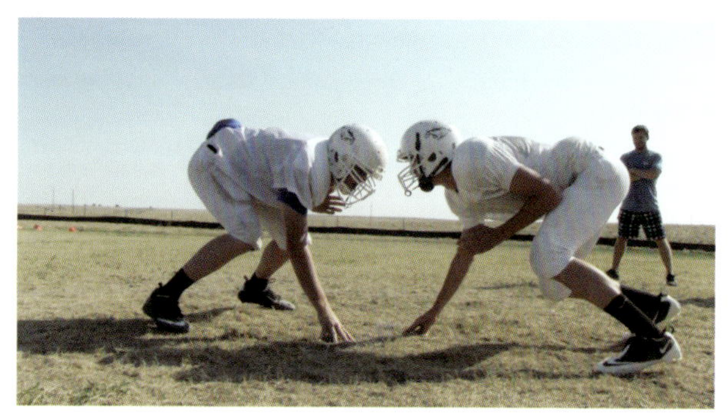
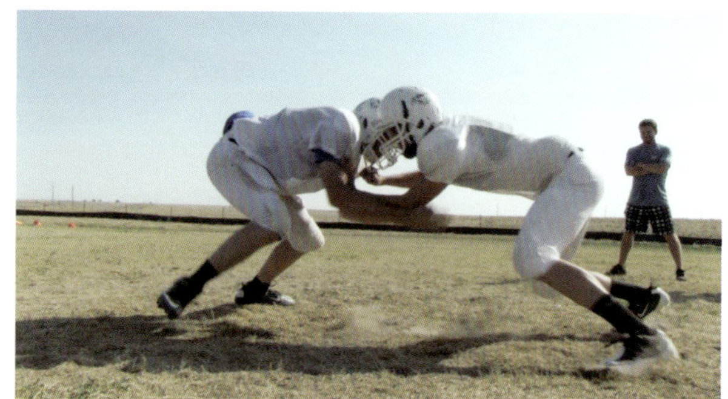
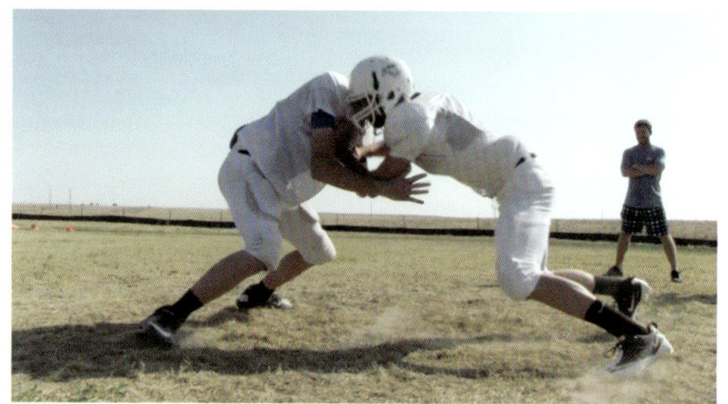
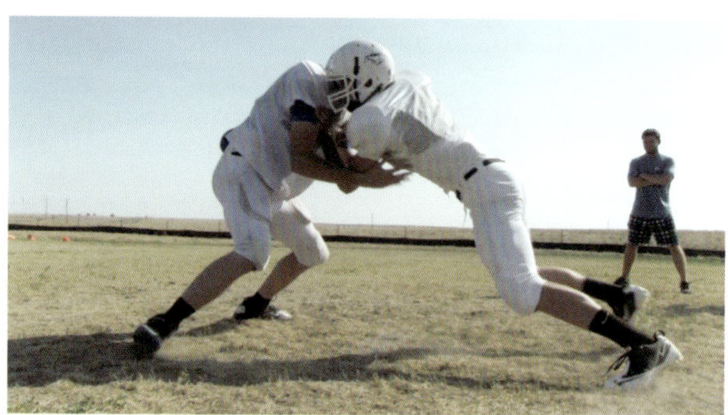
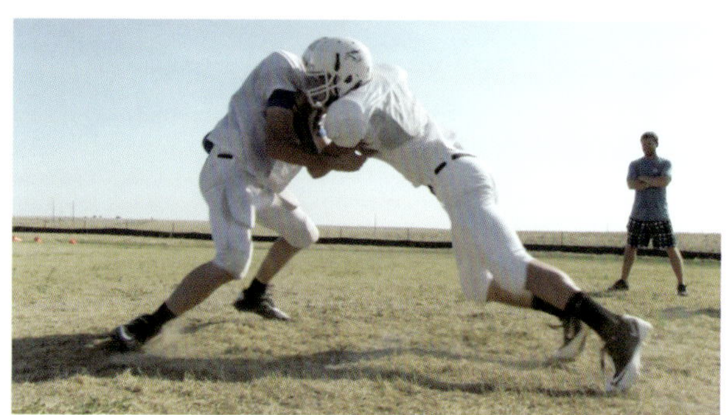
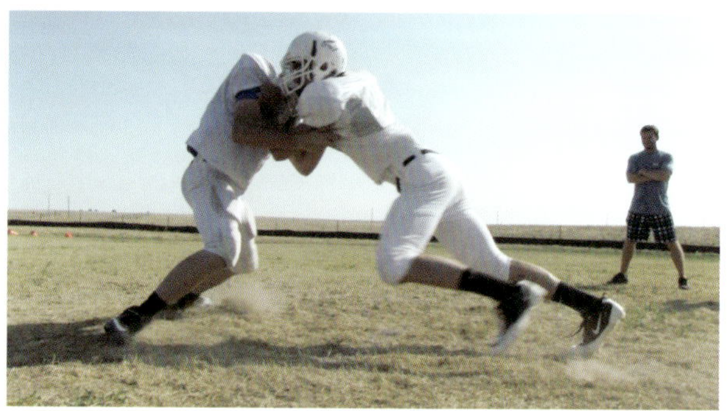
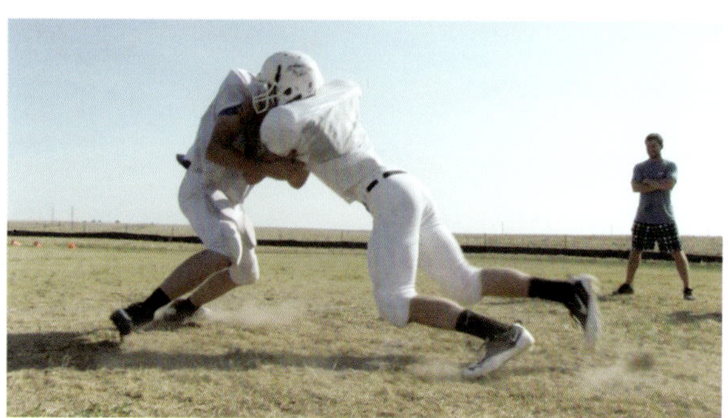
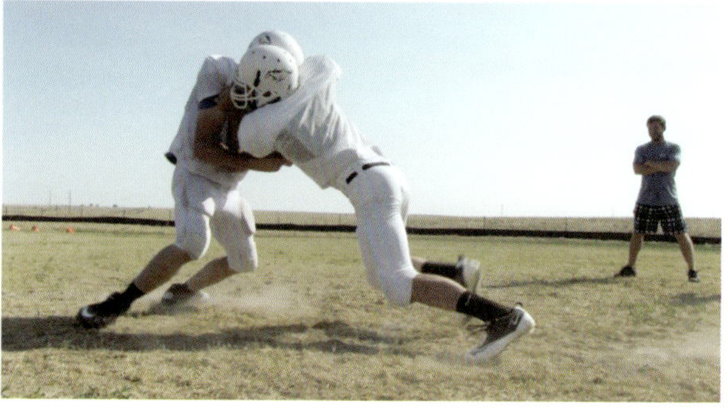

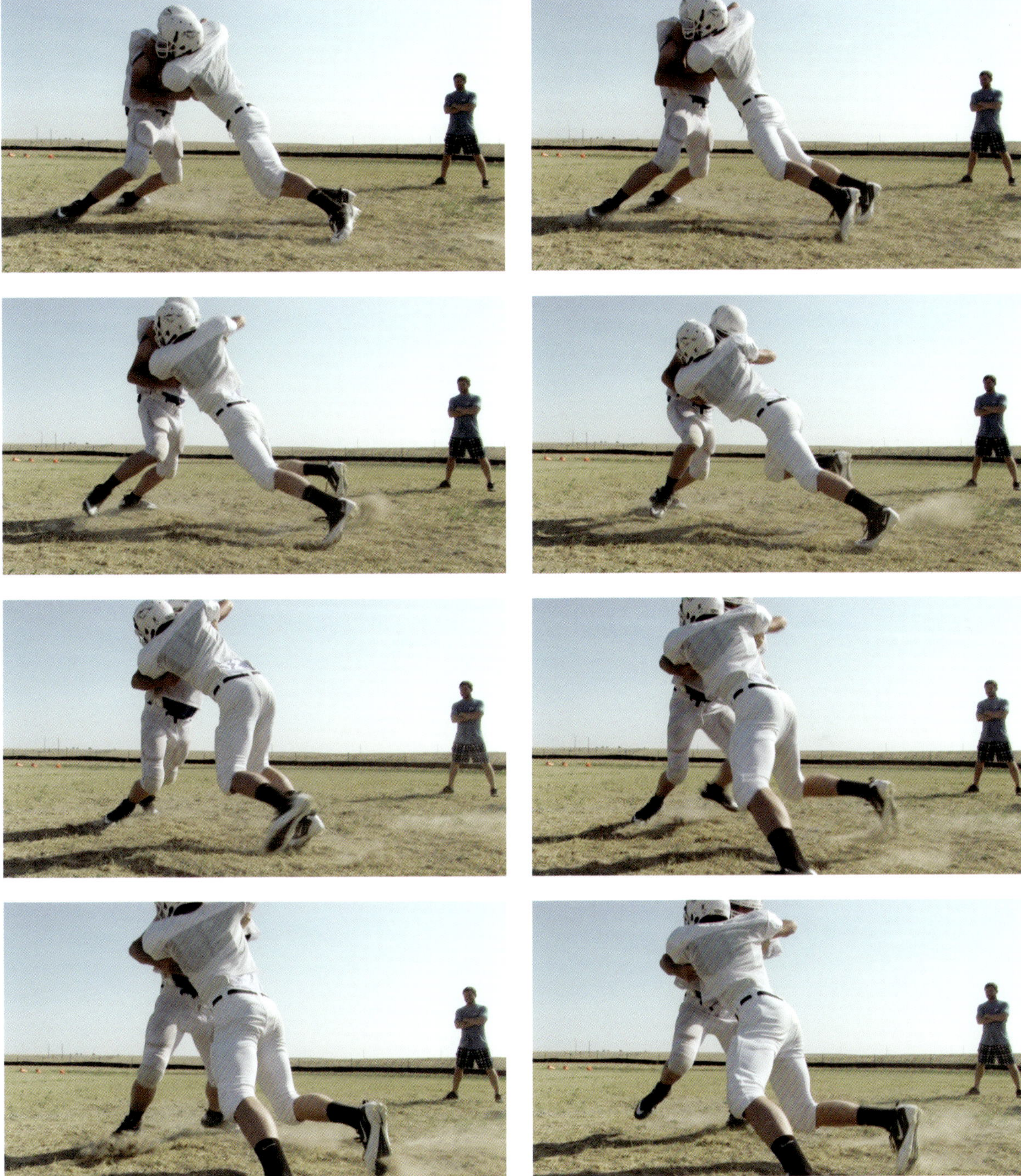

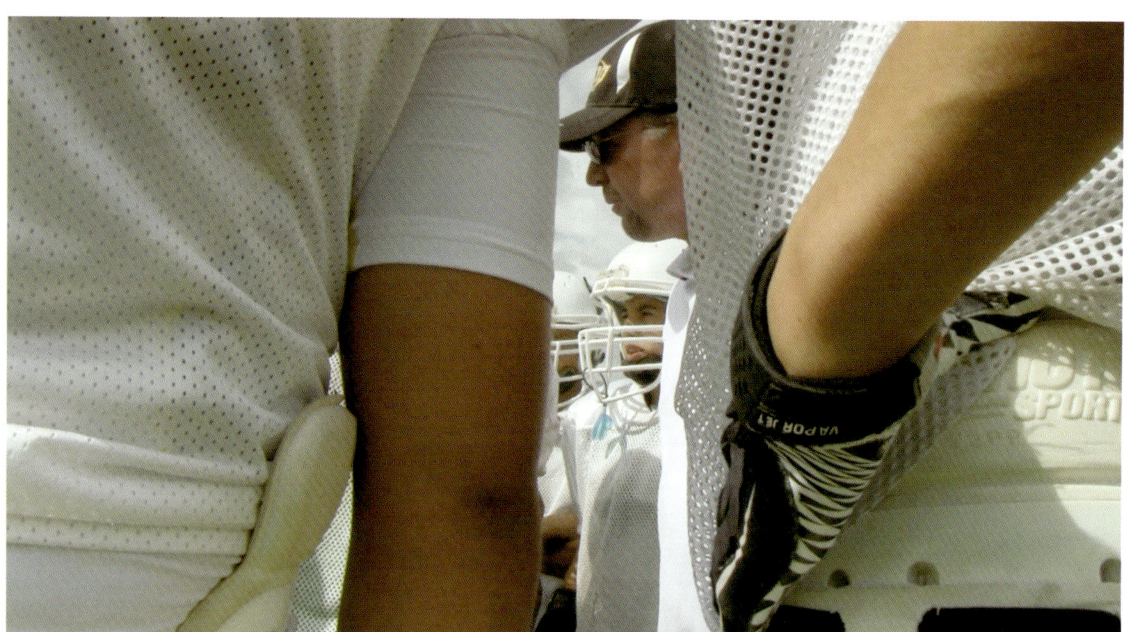

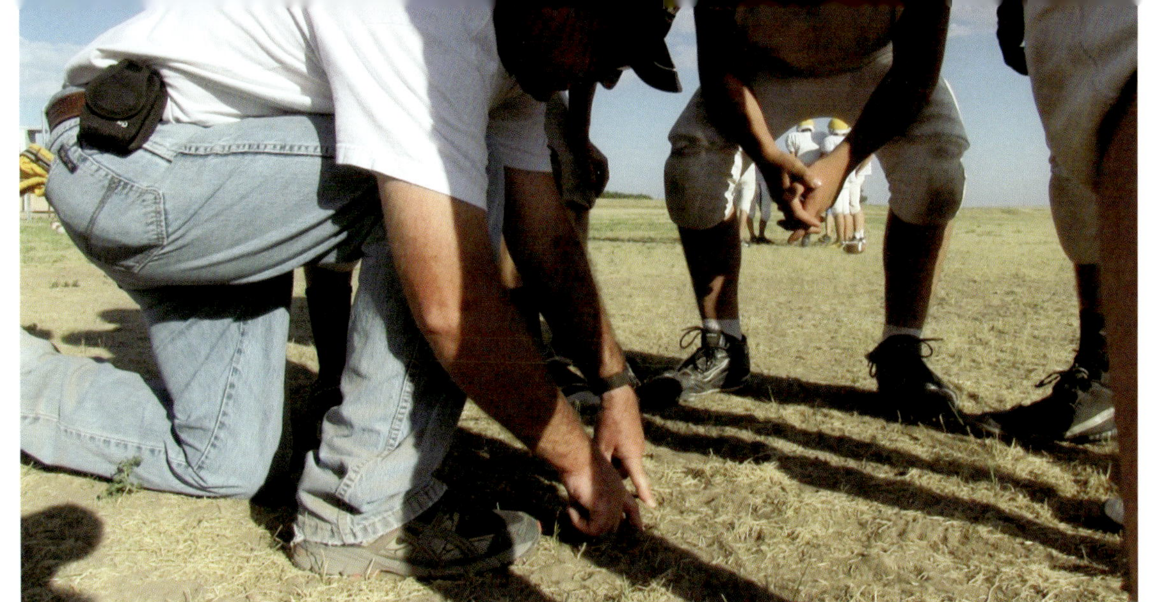

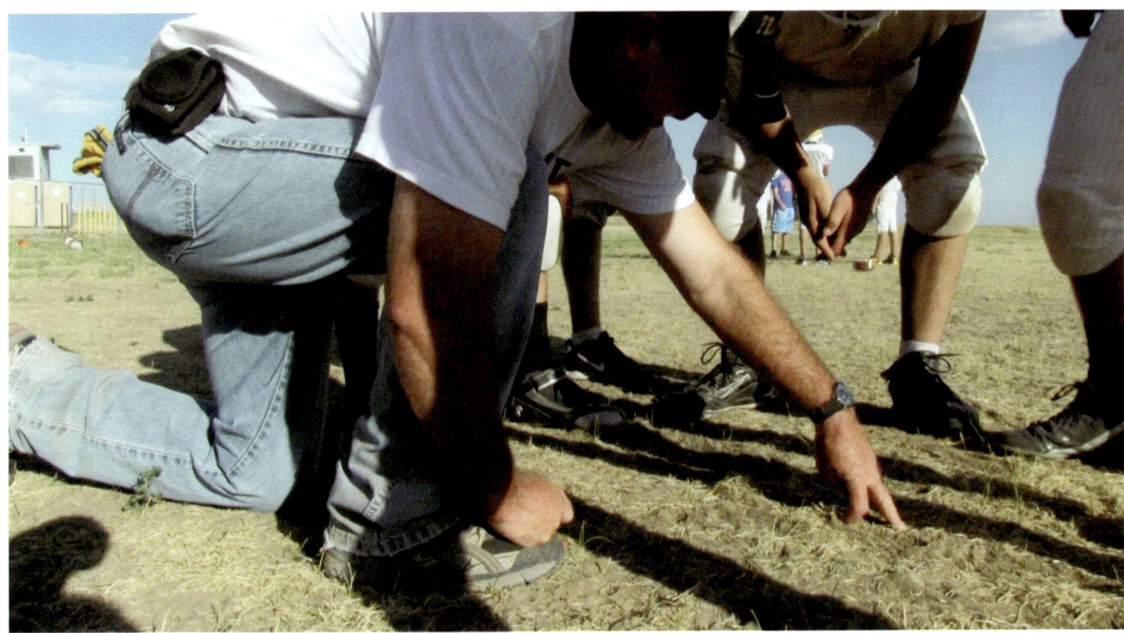

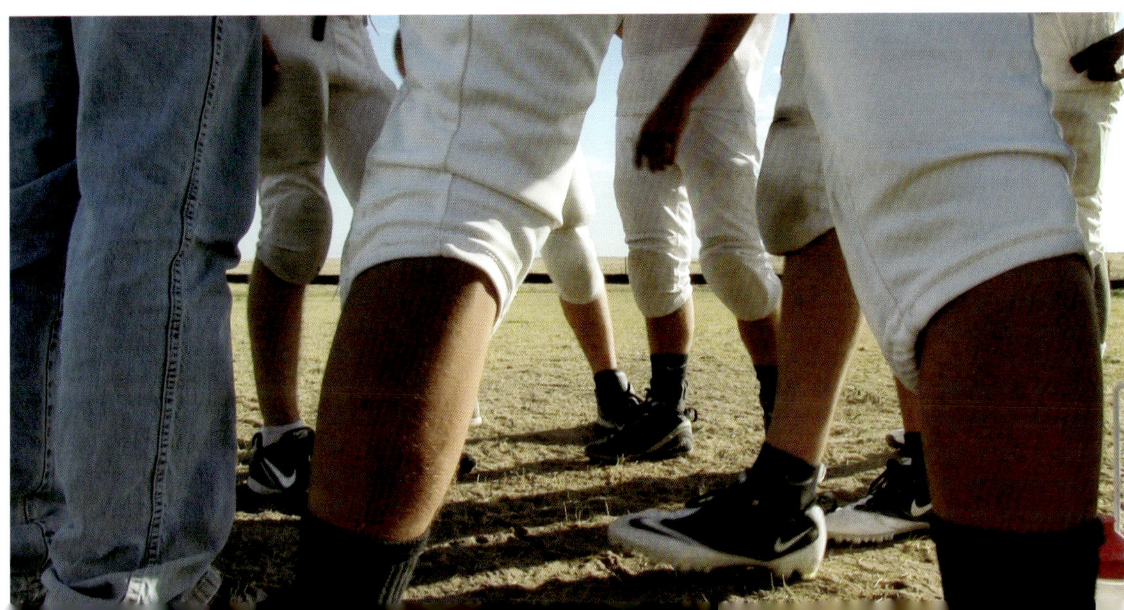

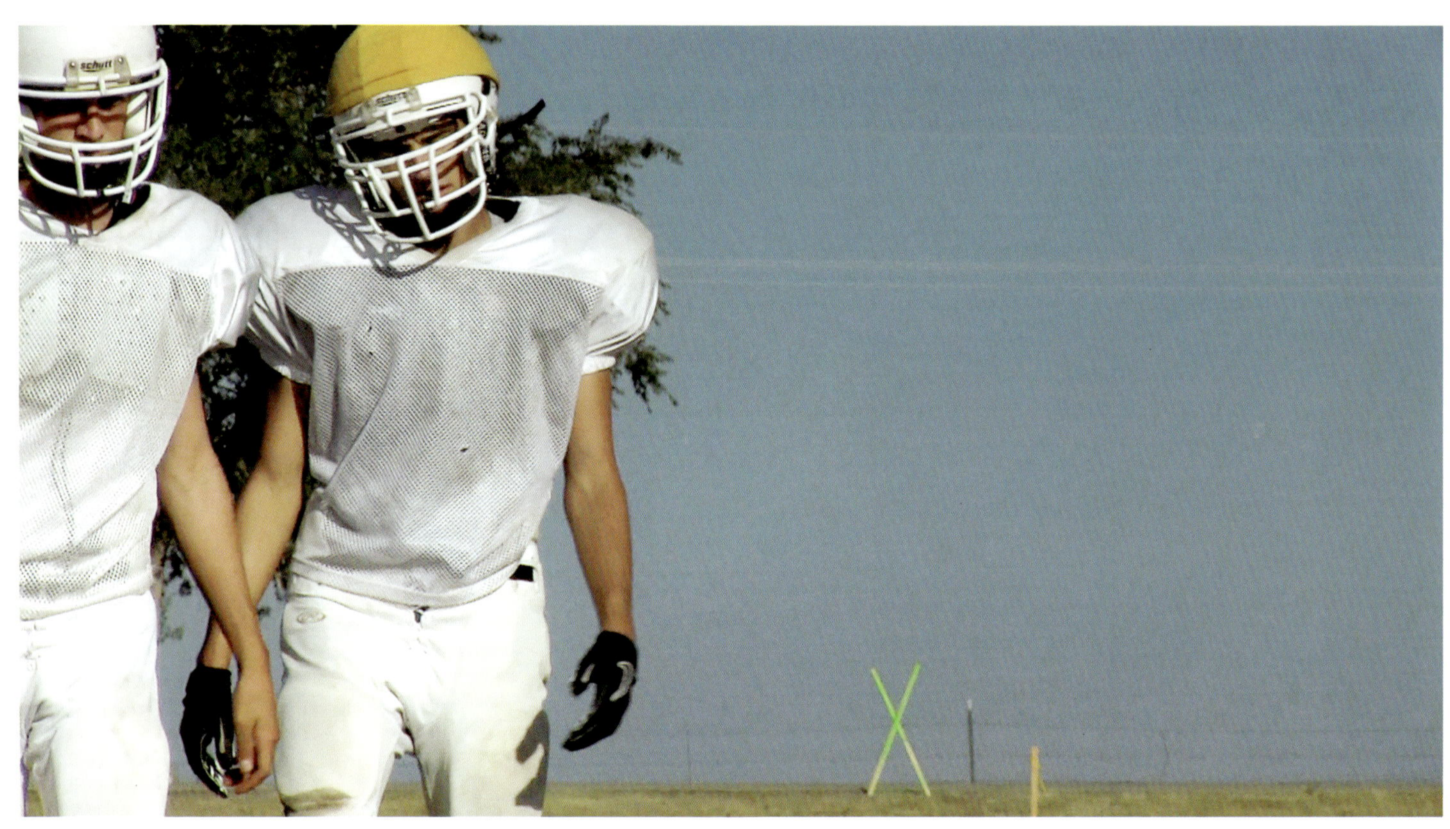

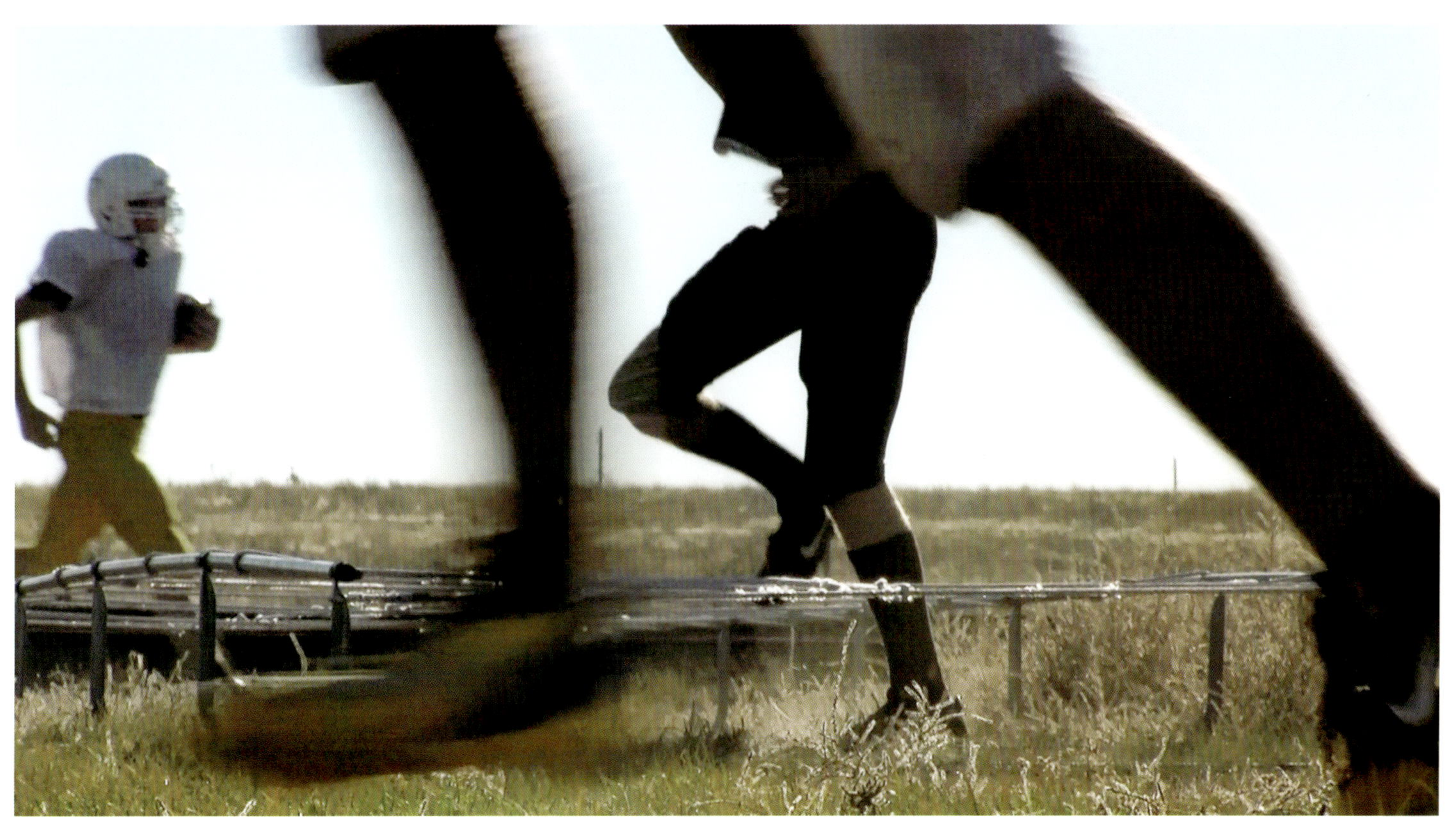

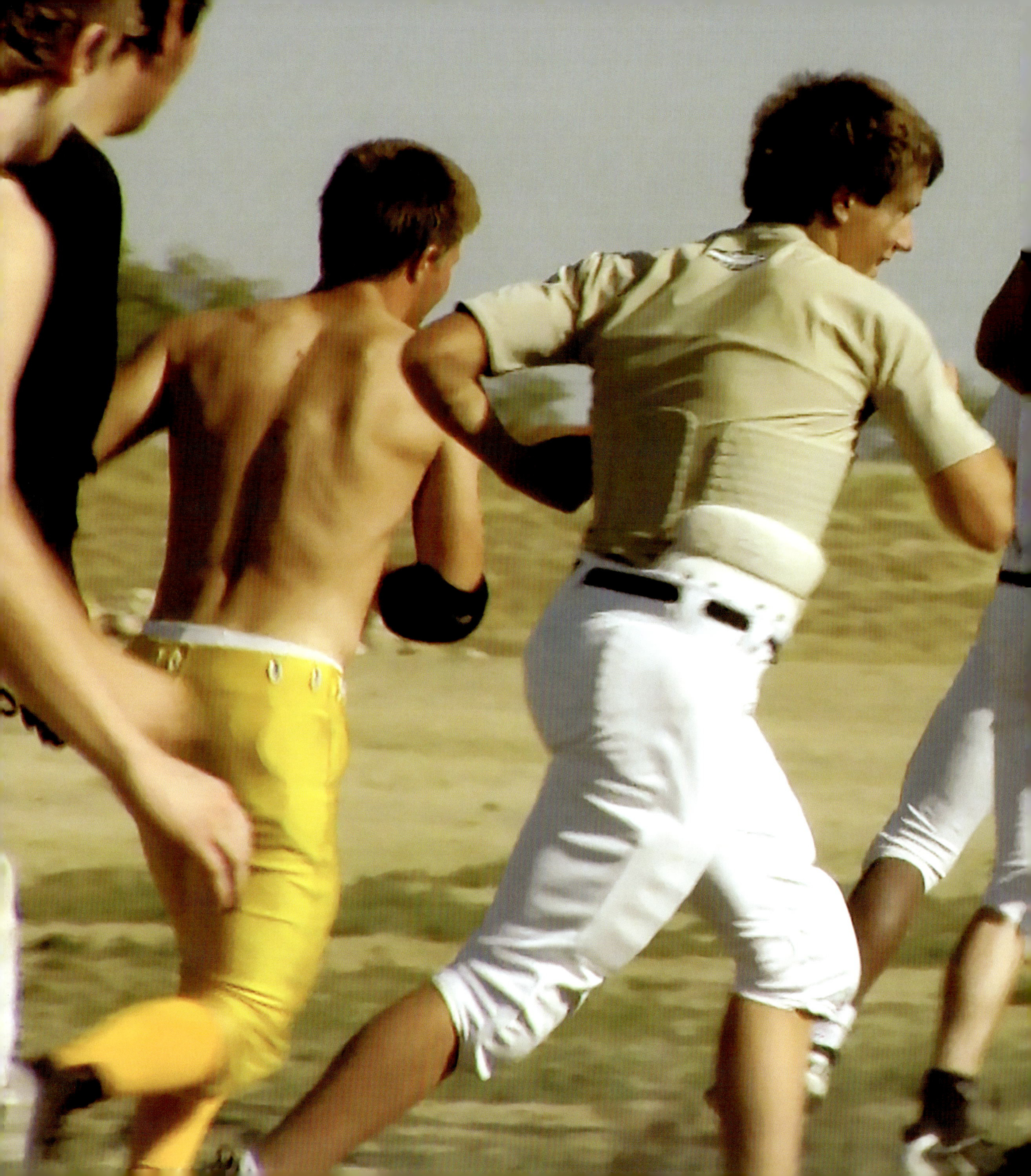

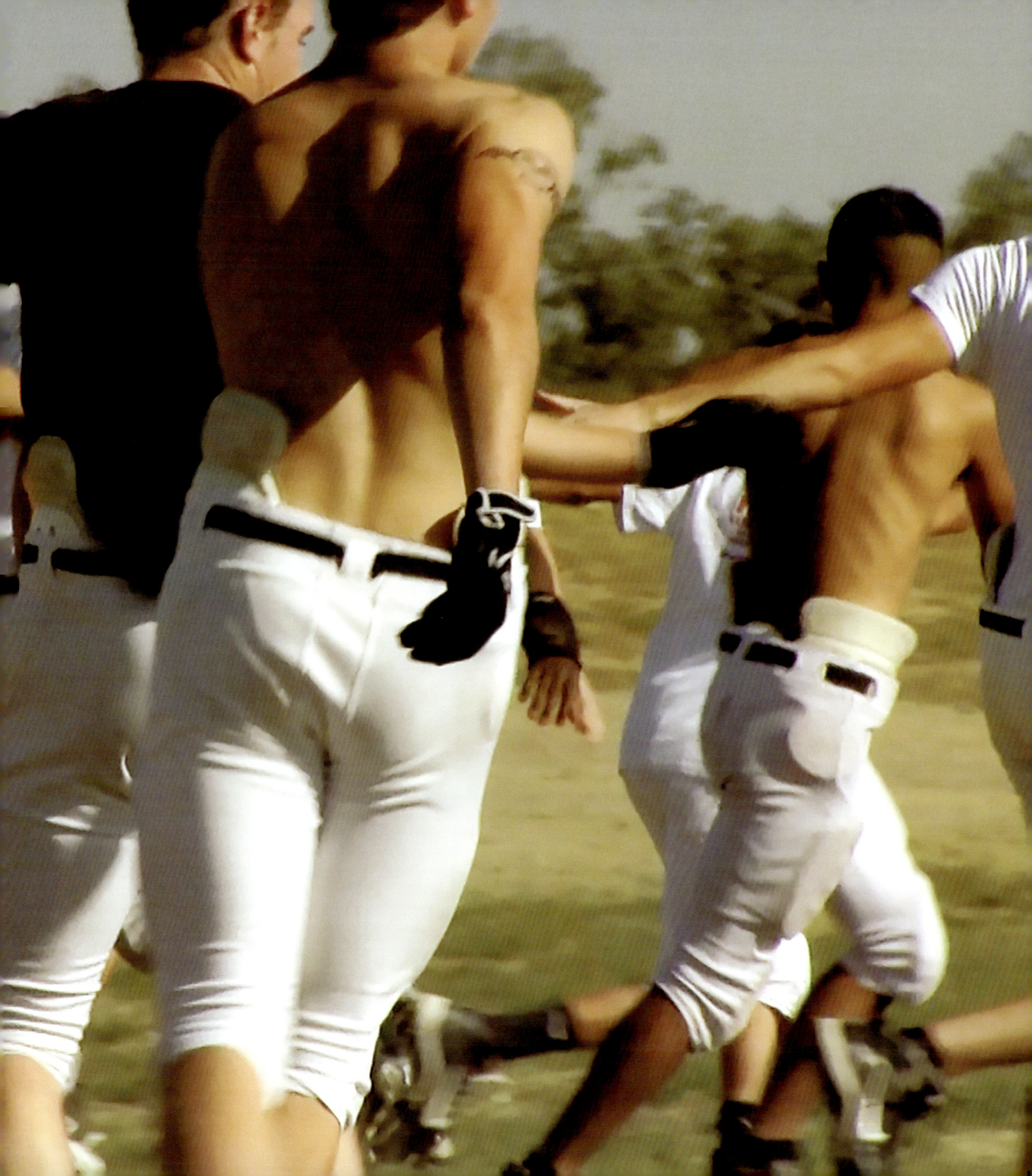

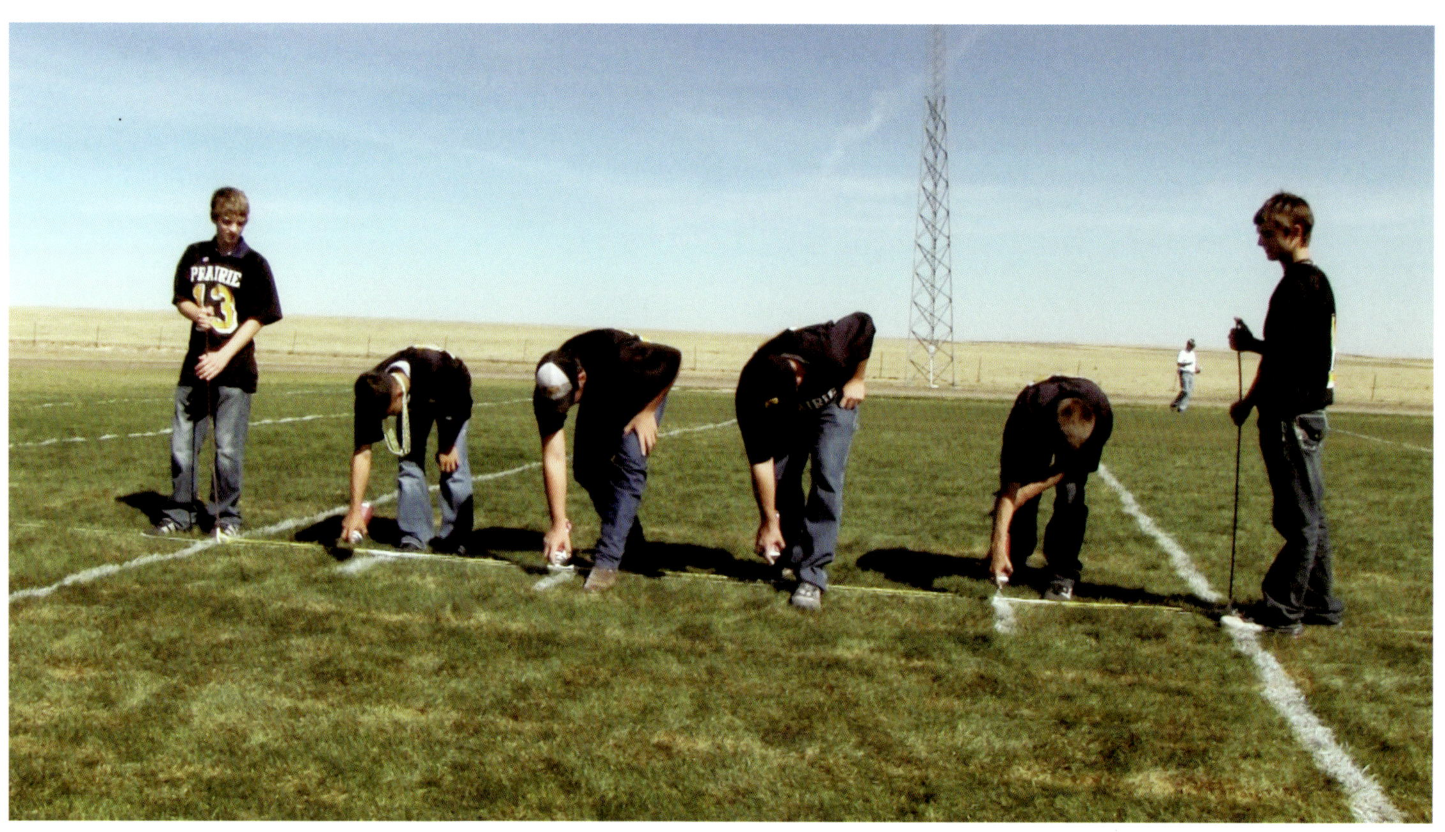

ARICKAREE INDIANS

The first home game for Prairie was homecoming, against the Arickaree Indians. On game day the temperatures hovered in the 70s. The new sod from August looked good, but the lack of soaking rain left it hard and uneven. The squad met right after school to paint the yard lines on the field, set out the markers, and raise the flags. Volunteers and school staff stocked the concession stand and set up the PA system. In the late afternoon, the Prairie girls' volleyball team won decisively against the Arickaree squad. Now it was up to the Prairie boys to rise above the last week's devastating loss.

The game got off to a swift start, and within minutes, Prairie scored. One of the dads (who would later DJ the dance) had made a recording of a herd of horses galloping and whinnying to be used as a post-touchdown salute for the Mustangs. Each time the team scored, he played the clip at full volume through the PA system, sending the sound of a stampede echoing out across the landscape. The first time they heard the soundtrack, a nearby herd of a dozen skittish mares and a lone donkey, often seen grazing in the distance, came running excitedly up to the edge of the football field. Stamping their feet and calling out, they looked everywhere for the provocateurs, before slipping back into the darkness beyond the lights.

Arickaree and Prairie had identical records at 2-1-0. Both teams had only lost to the tough Otis squad. But by halftime the Prairie players had racked up some points and pulled ahead 38–13. Then the homecoming festivities began.

Six football players ushered the queen's court out onto the field. Freshman Zach Hastings, sophomore Austin Littlefield, and junior Seth Gapter each escorted a member of the queen's court from his respective class, while seniors Dustin Warboys, Brady Stump, and Bill Johnson accompanied two seniors—and potential queens—each. Few were surprised when volleyball star Savanah Hastings and football star Dustin Warboys were crowned homecoming queen and king. They took their place, under the waxing moon, on an Ikea leatherette couch perched on a wide flatbed trailer as the crowd cheered. Then a "dually" truck pulled the trailer around the field, out beyond the scoreboard, back past the visitors and the ghost horses, and then off toward the parking lot behind the gym, completing the ceremony.

In the second half, the coaches felt confident and tried out a range of new run-and-pass plays. Offensive ends Michael Kaiser and Brady Stump traded off grabbing passes and racking up yards. By the start of the fourth quarter it was 44–13. A spectacular score-saving tackle at the one-yard line by the Mustang's Seth Gapter held Arickaree for a second-half shutout. Inspired, Coach Carlson sent in a full lineup of backups. Both sophomores Ian Fauconier and Austin Littlefield scored their first touchdowns of the season, and the game ended with a Prairie win, 63–13.

On Saturday, students and teachers decorated the lunchroom with the theme "A Night in Las Vegas" for the homecoming dance. Students arrived after dark and stood awkwardly around in knots until the music got going. Then the football and volleyball teams performed a perfectly choreographed line dance to V.I.C.'s song "Wooble," and everyone joined in the fun.

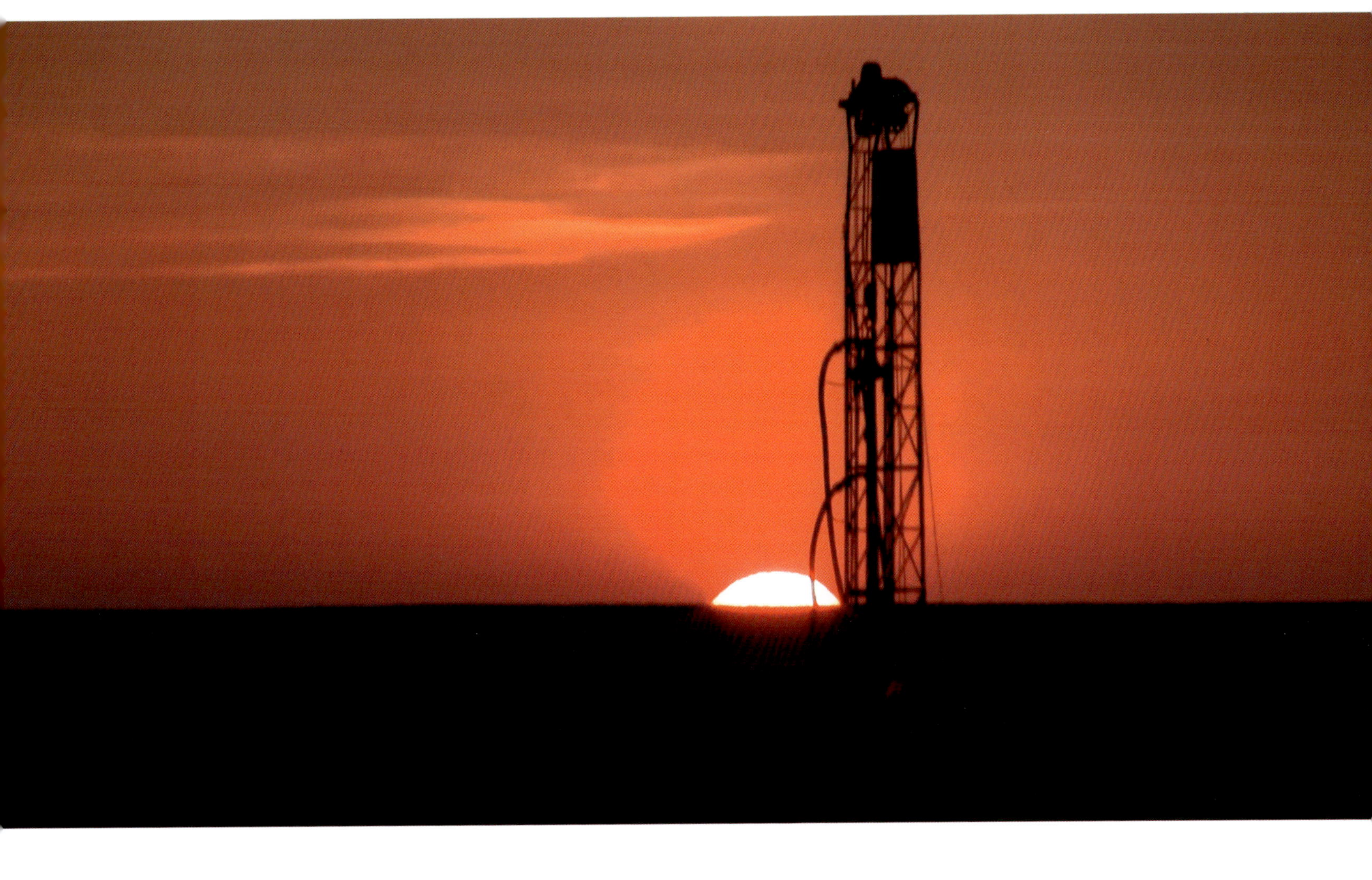

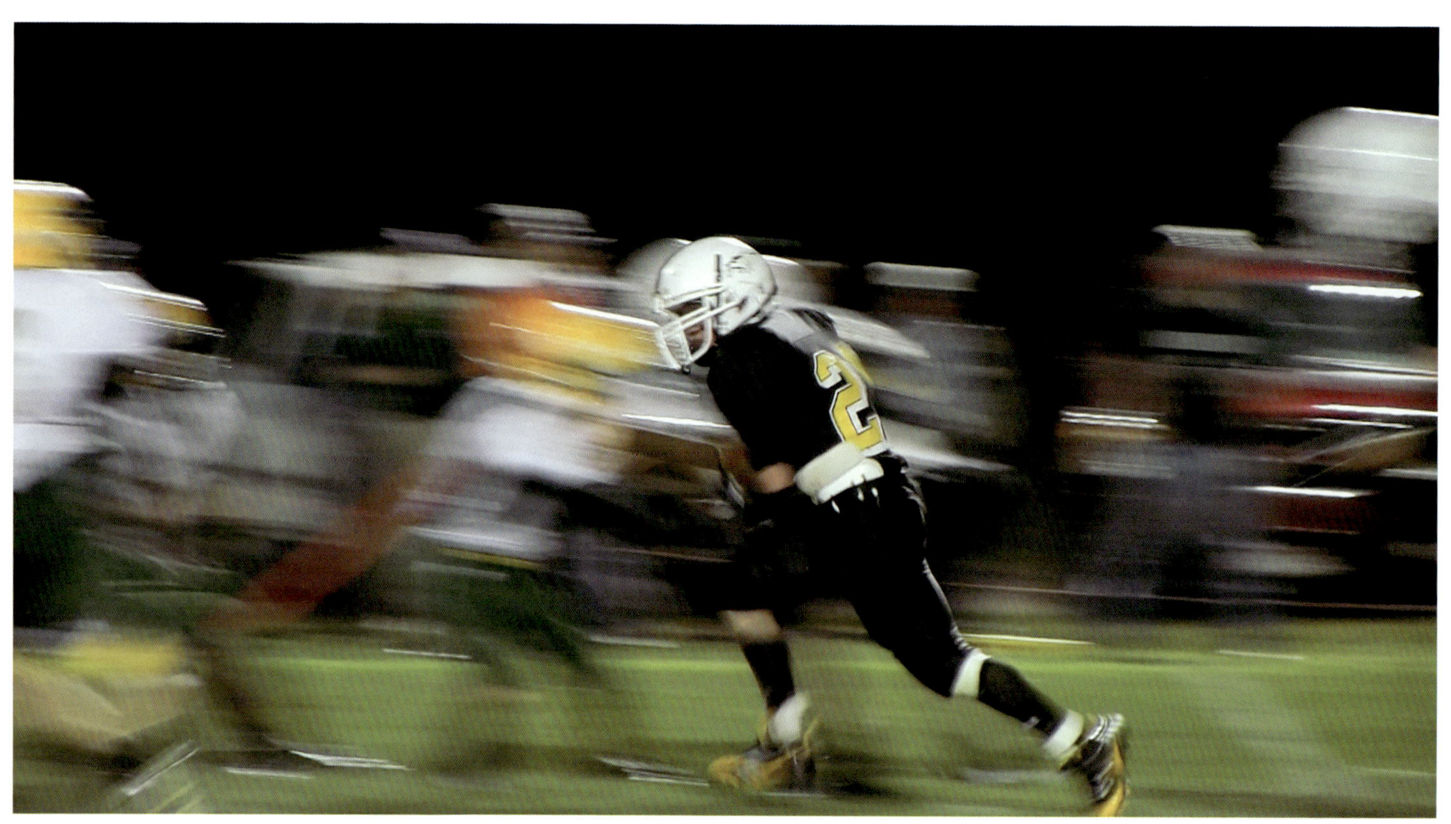

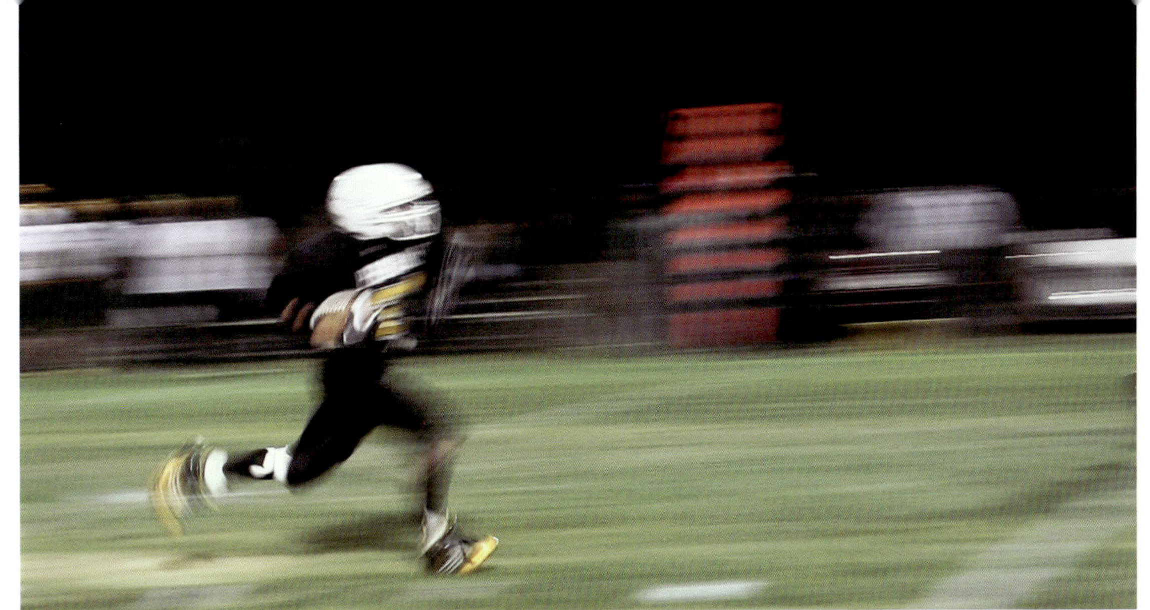

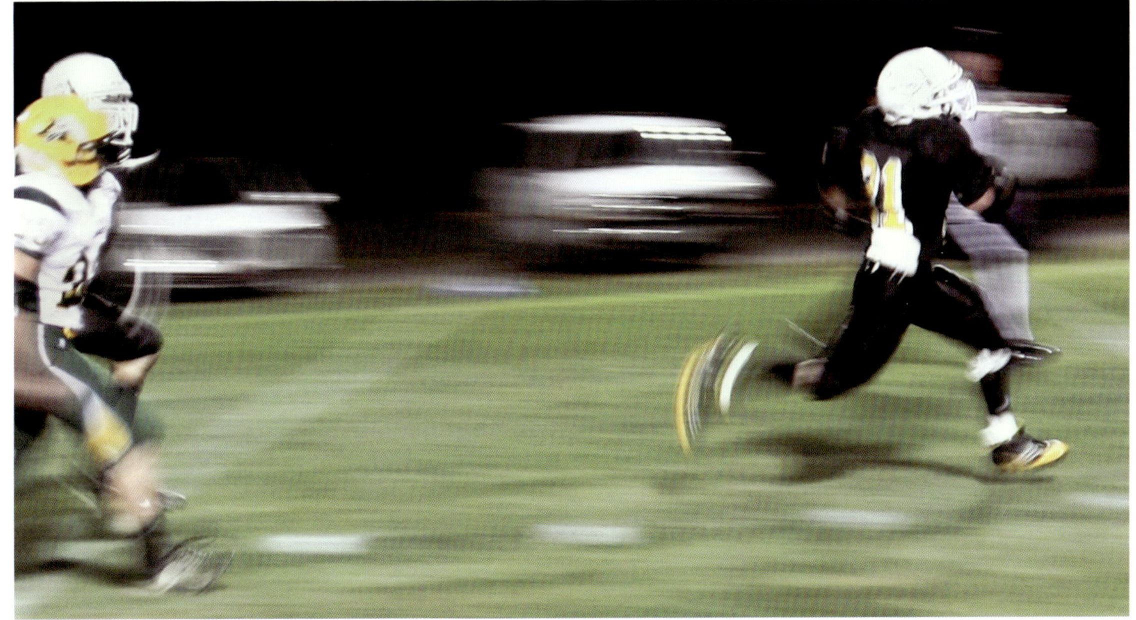

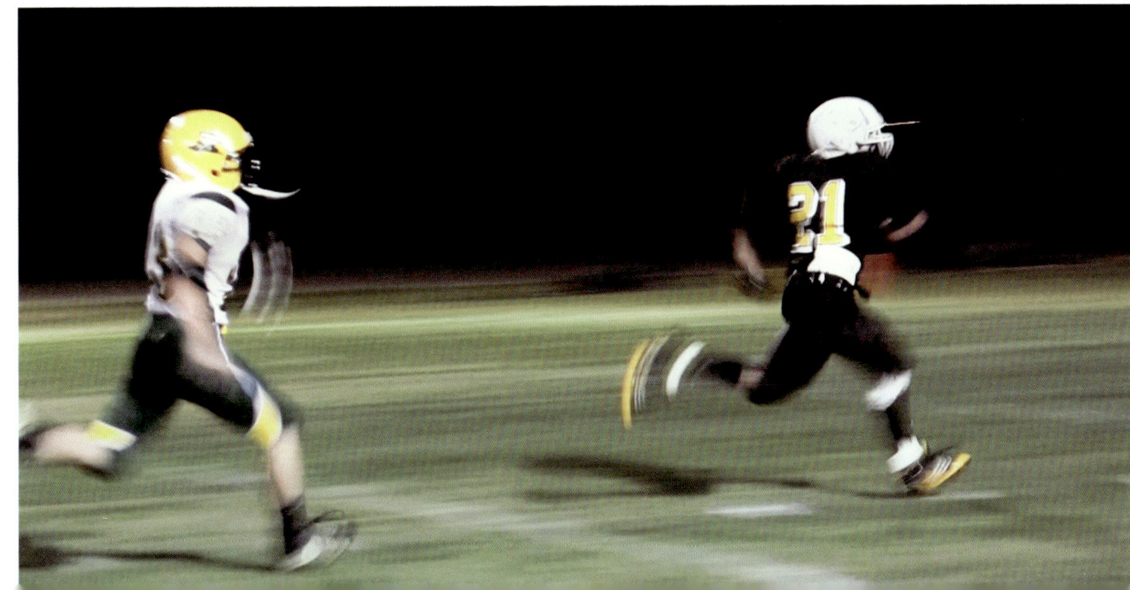

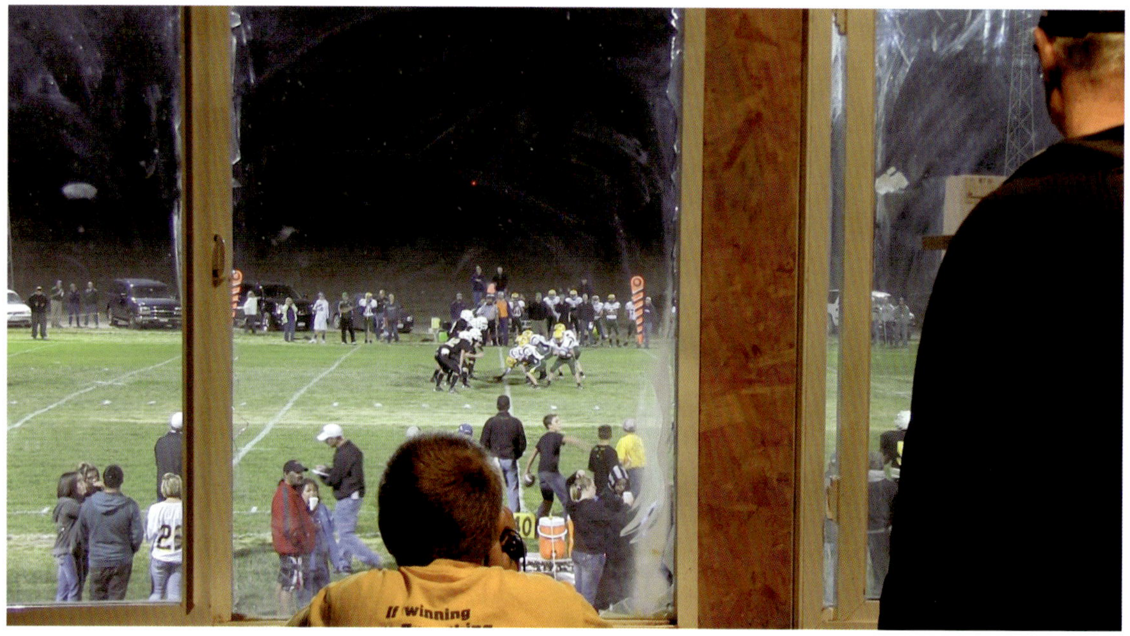
If winning

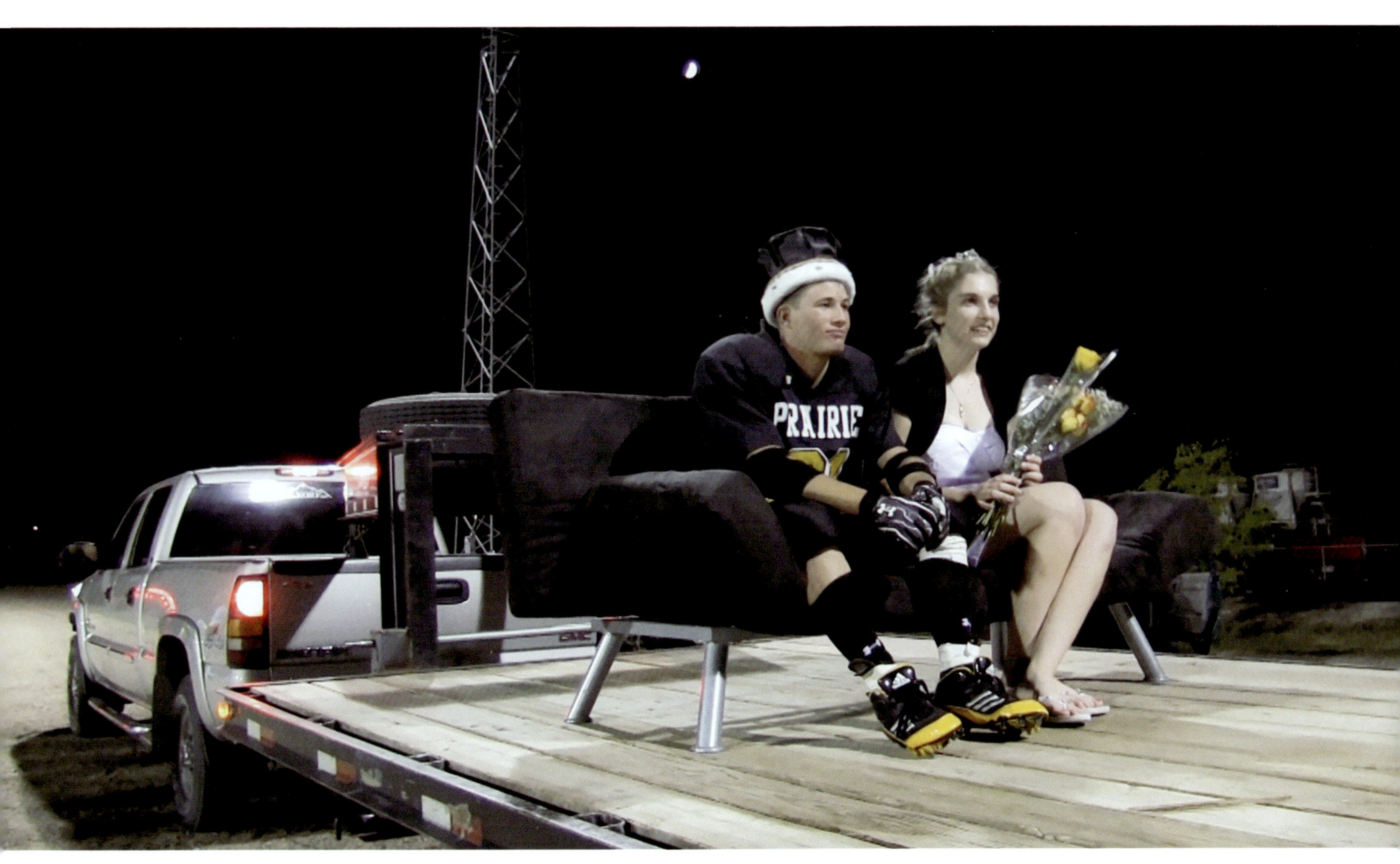
PRAIRIE

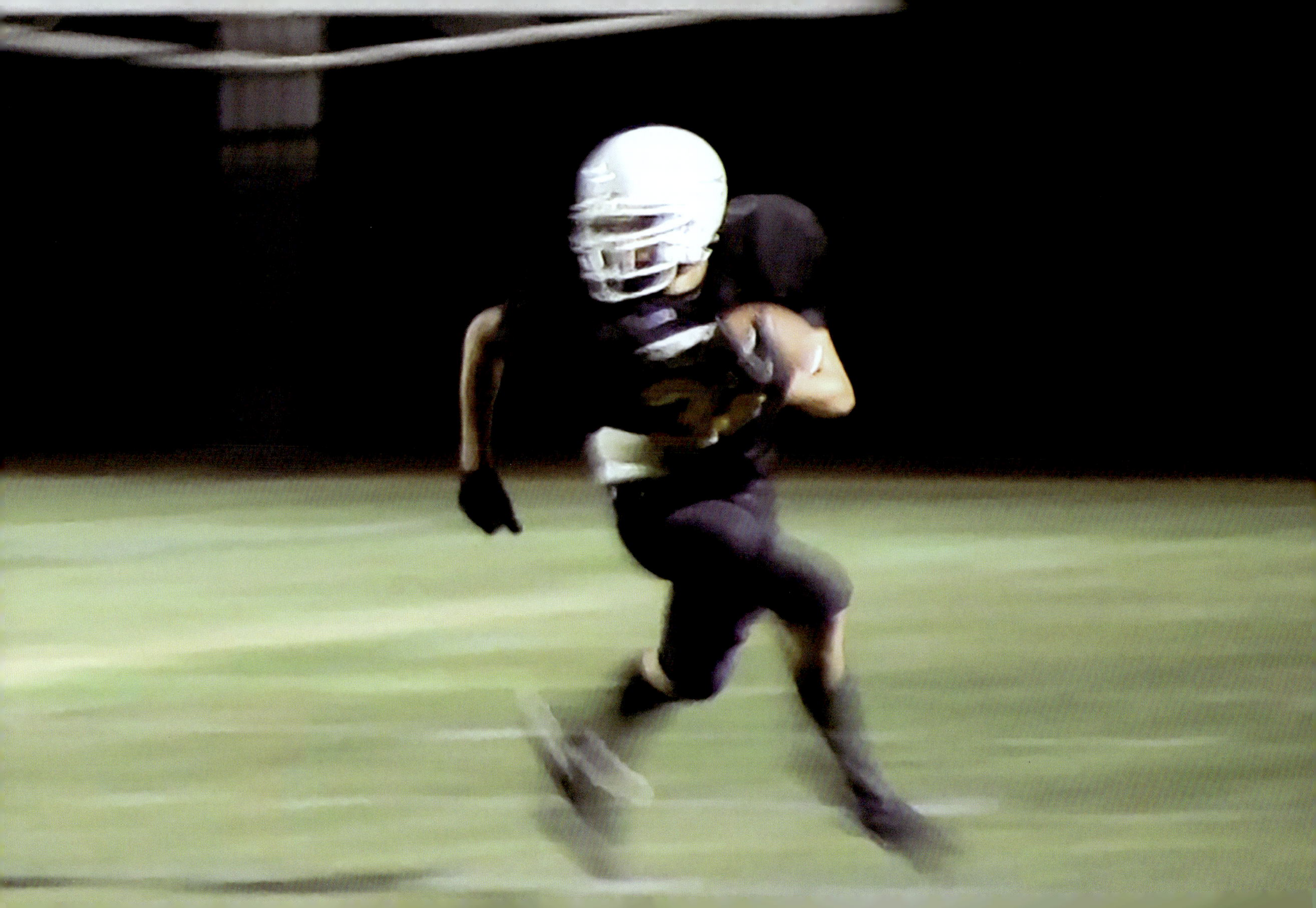

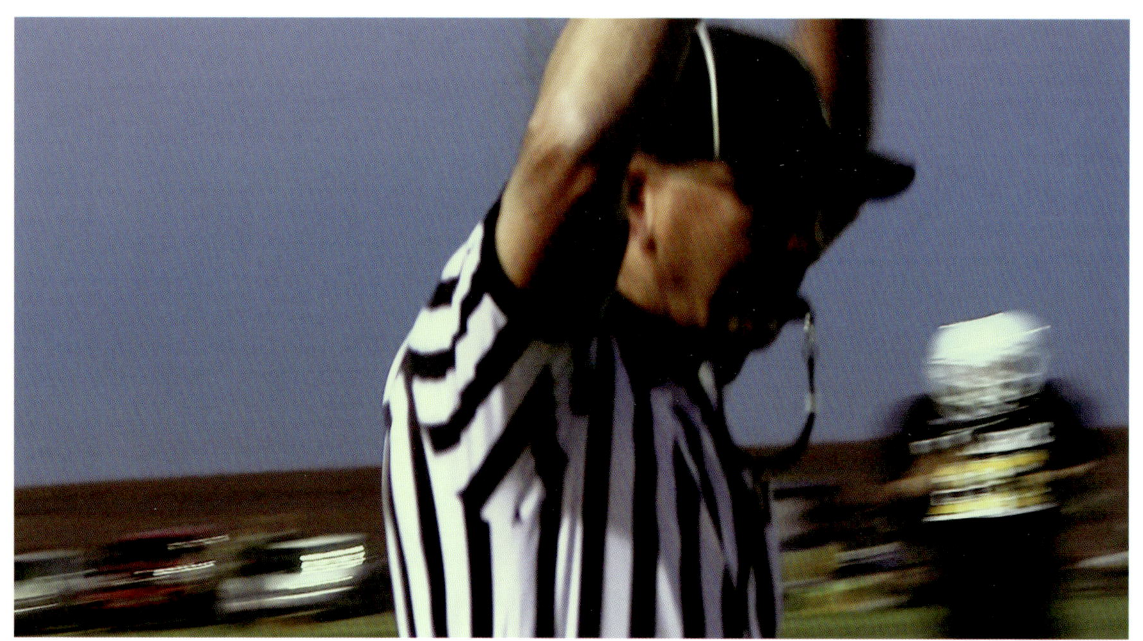

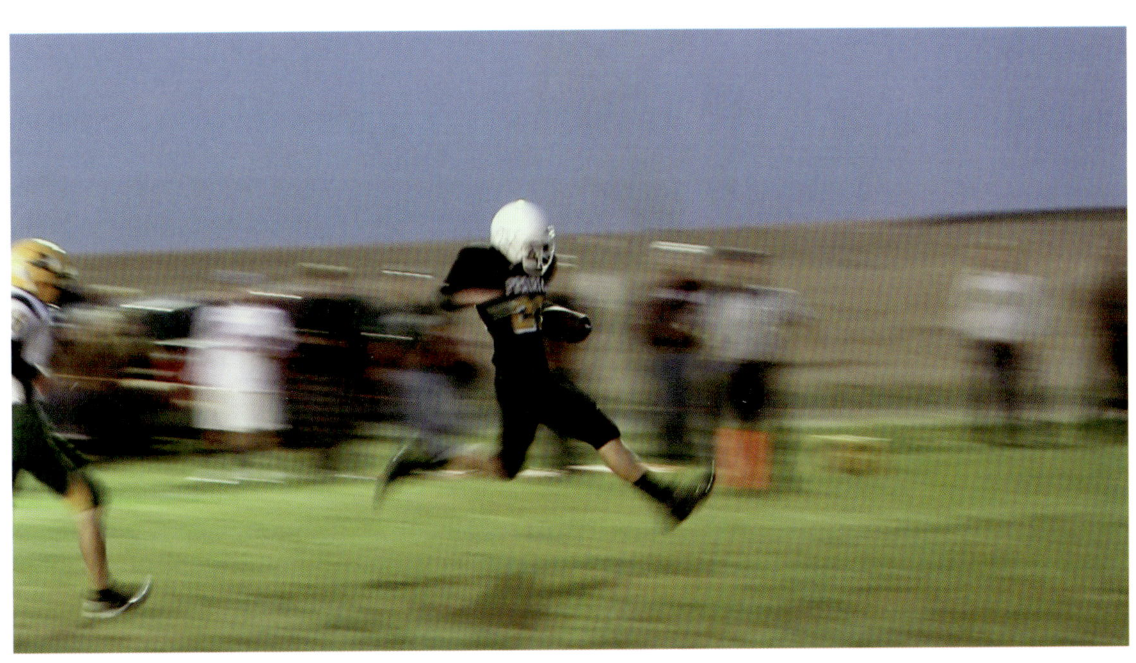

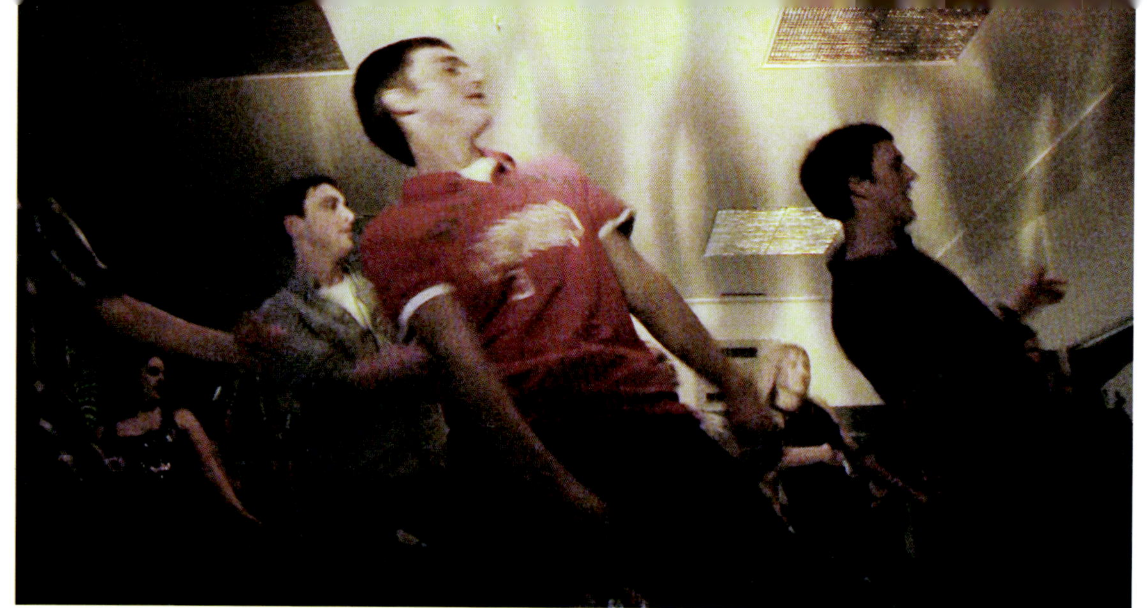

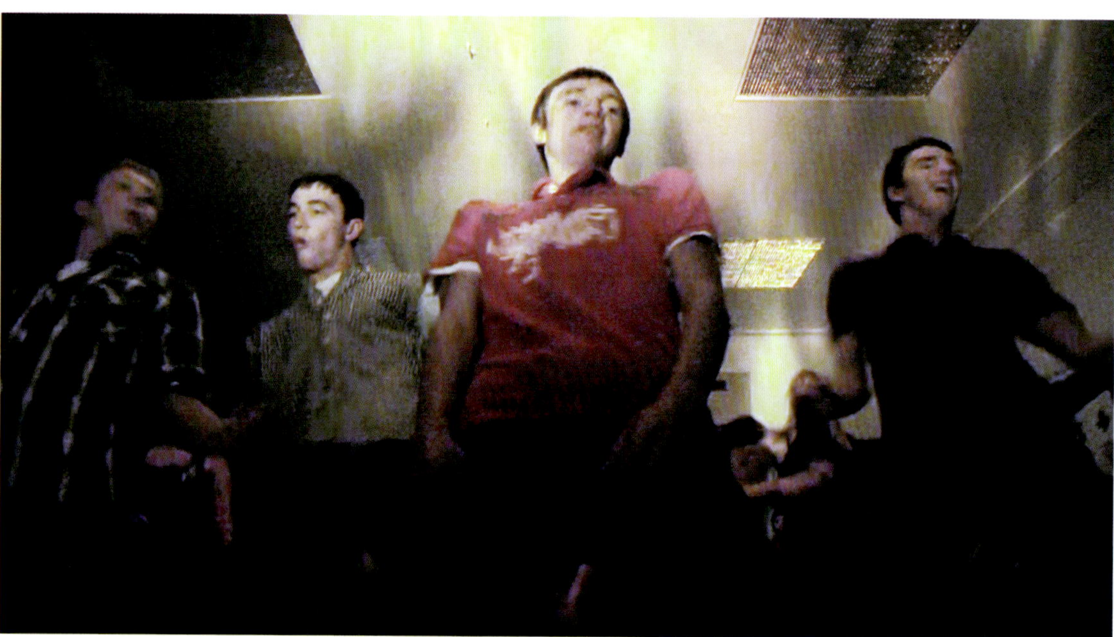

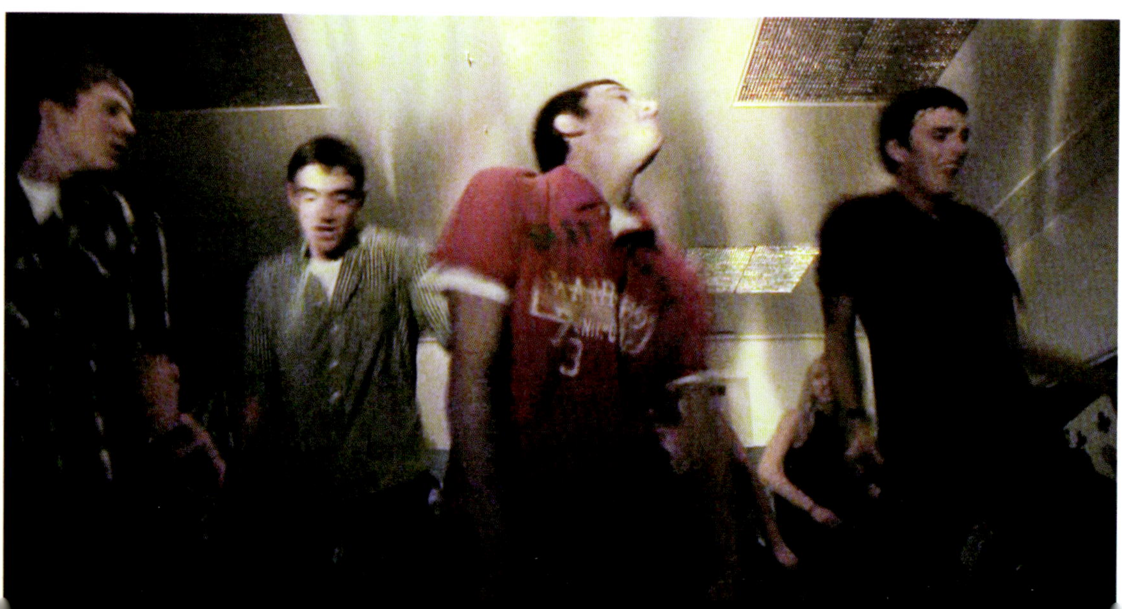

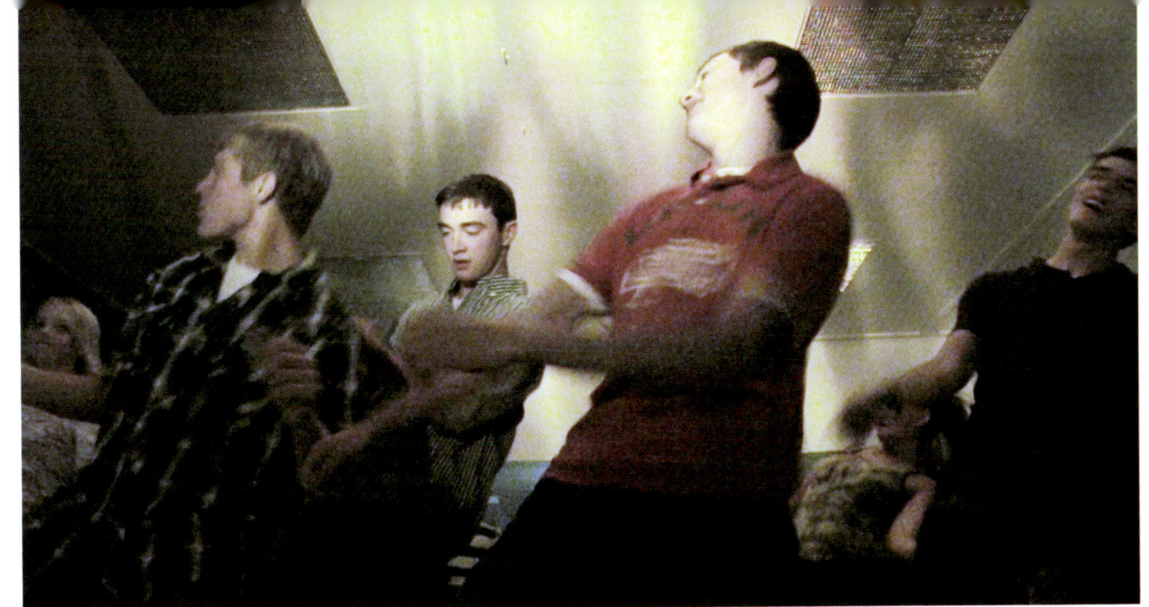

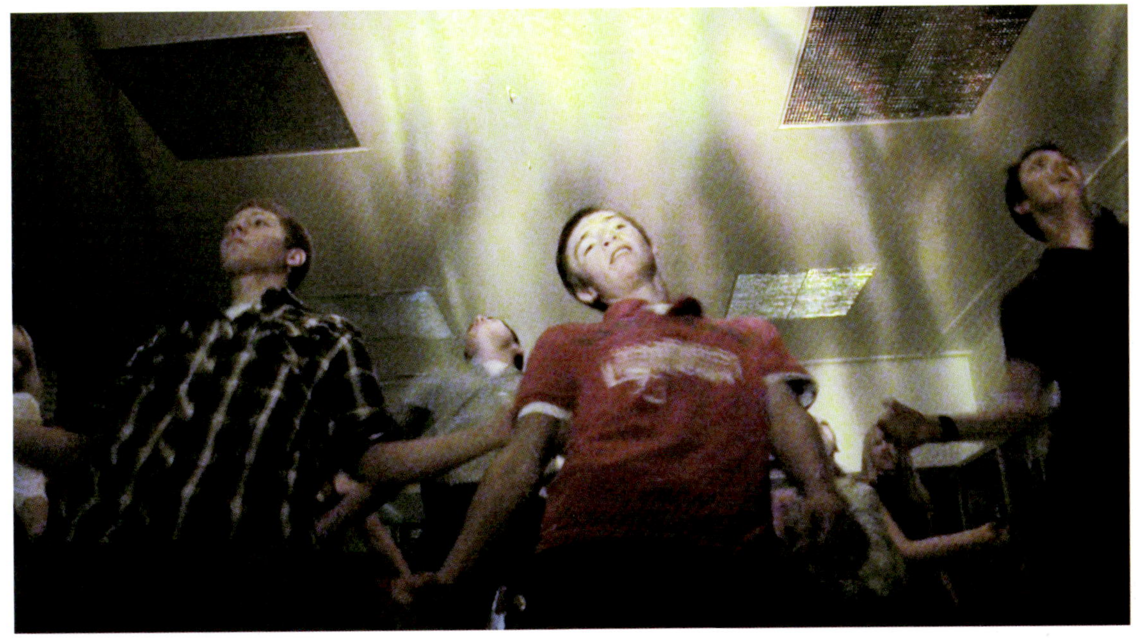

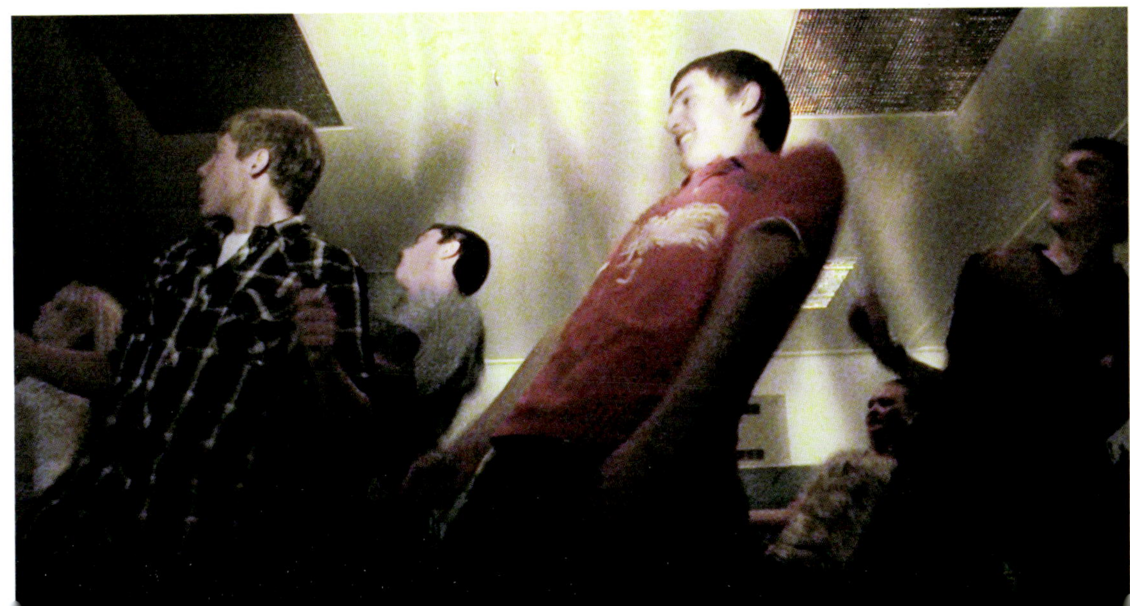

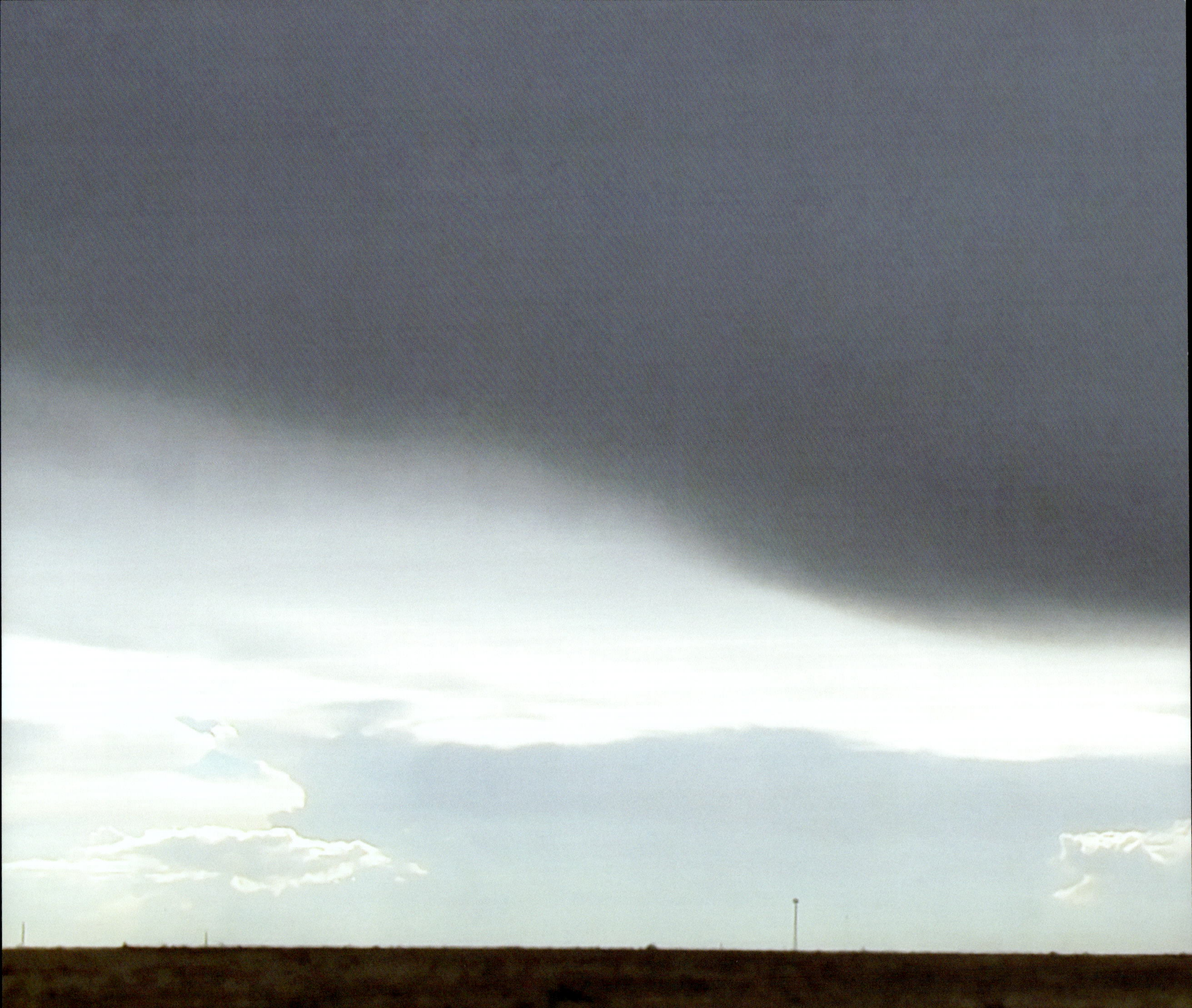

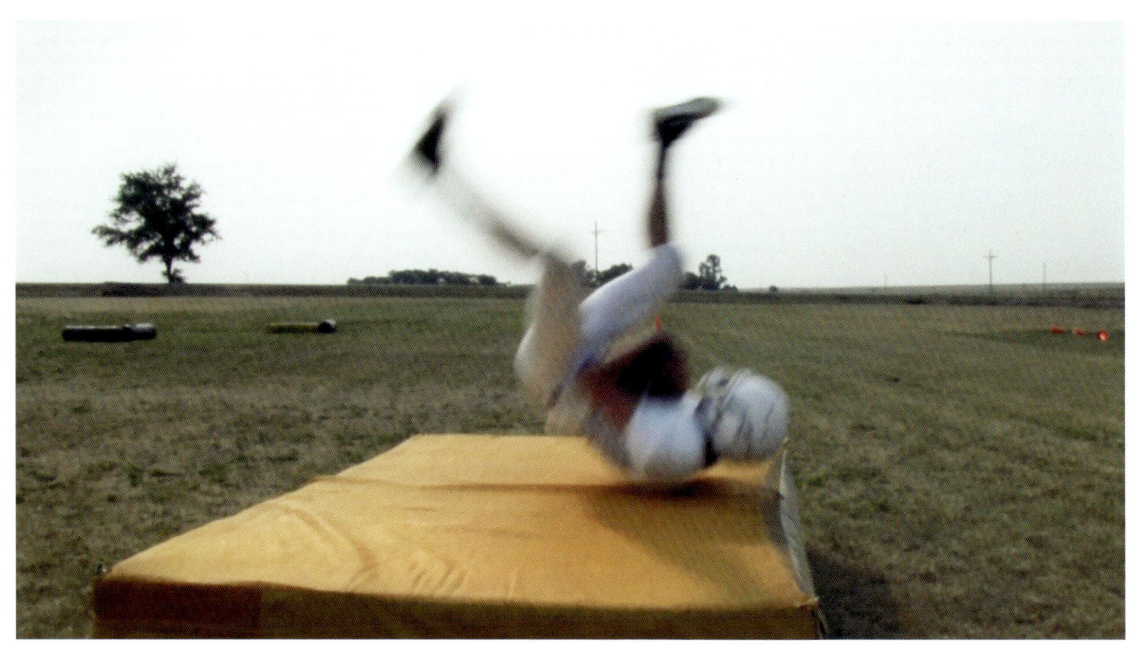

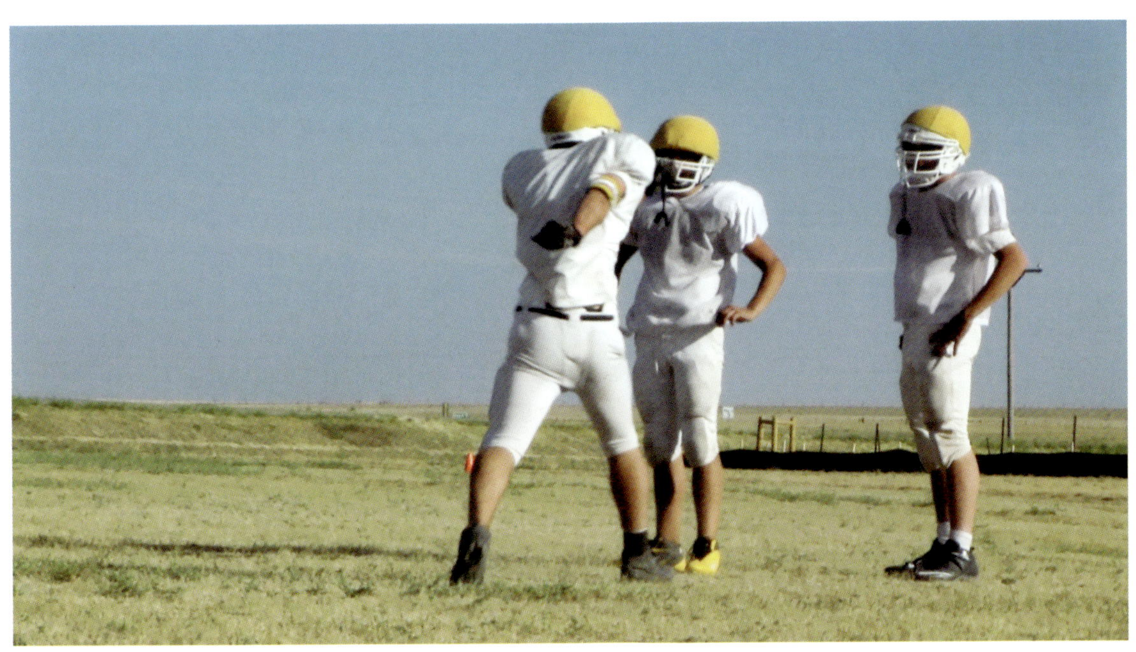

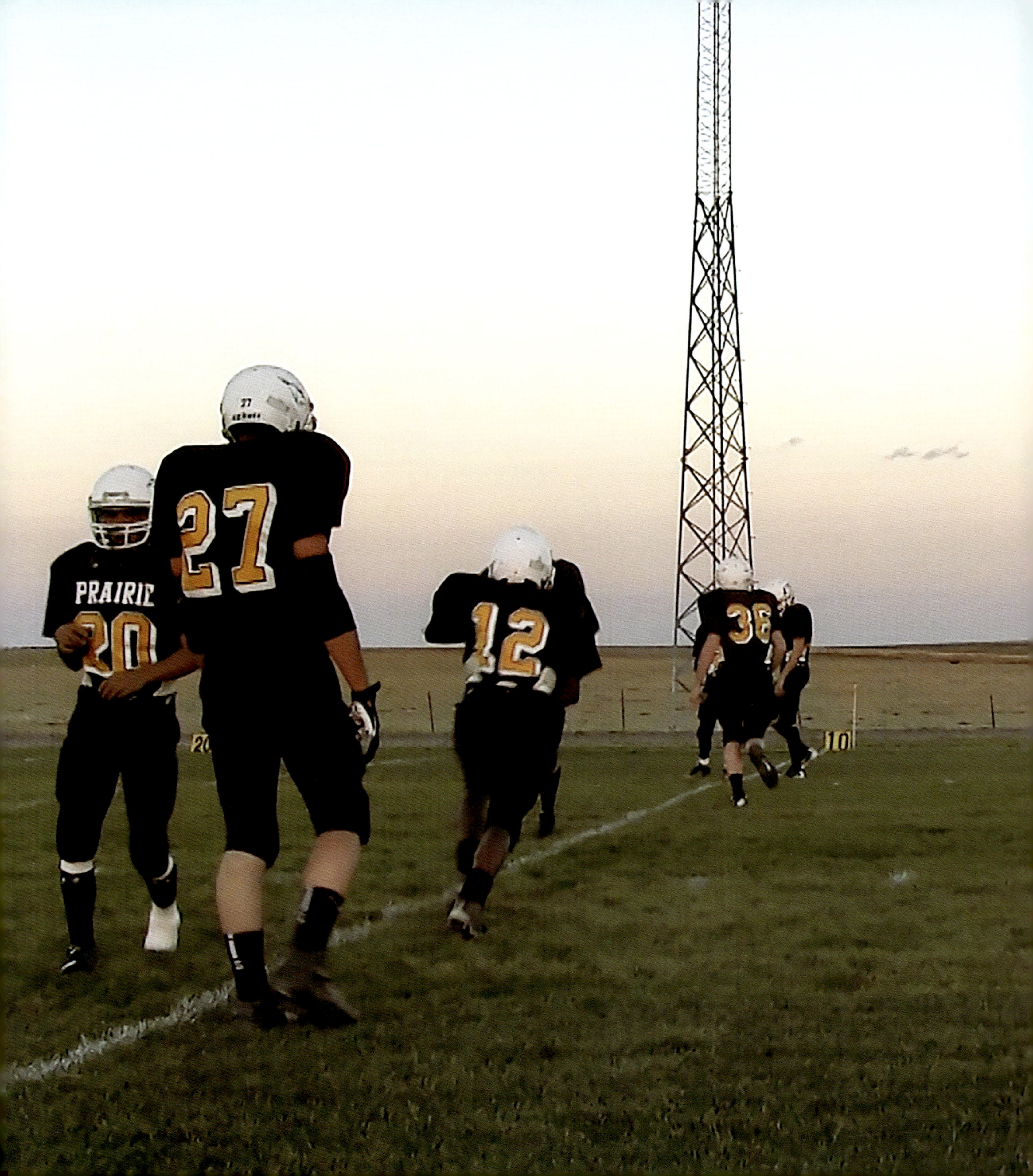

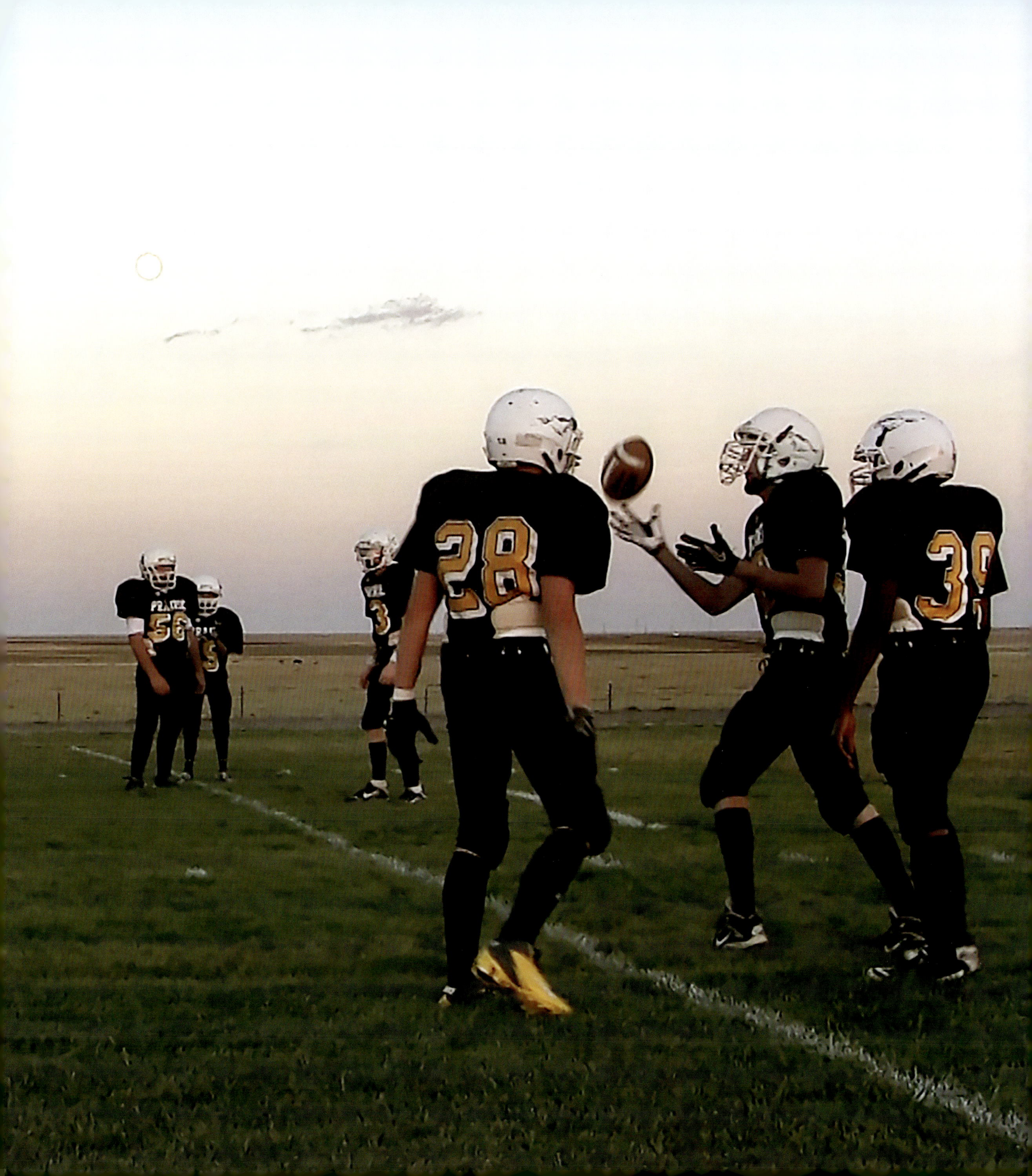

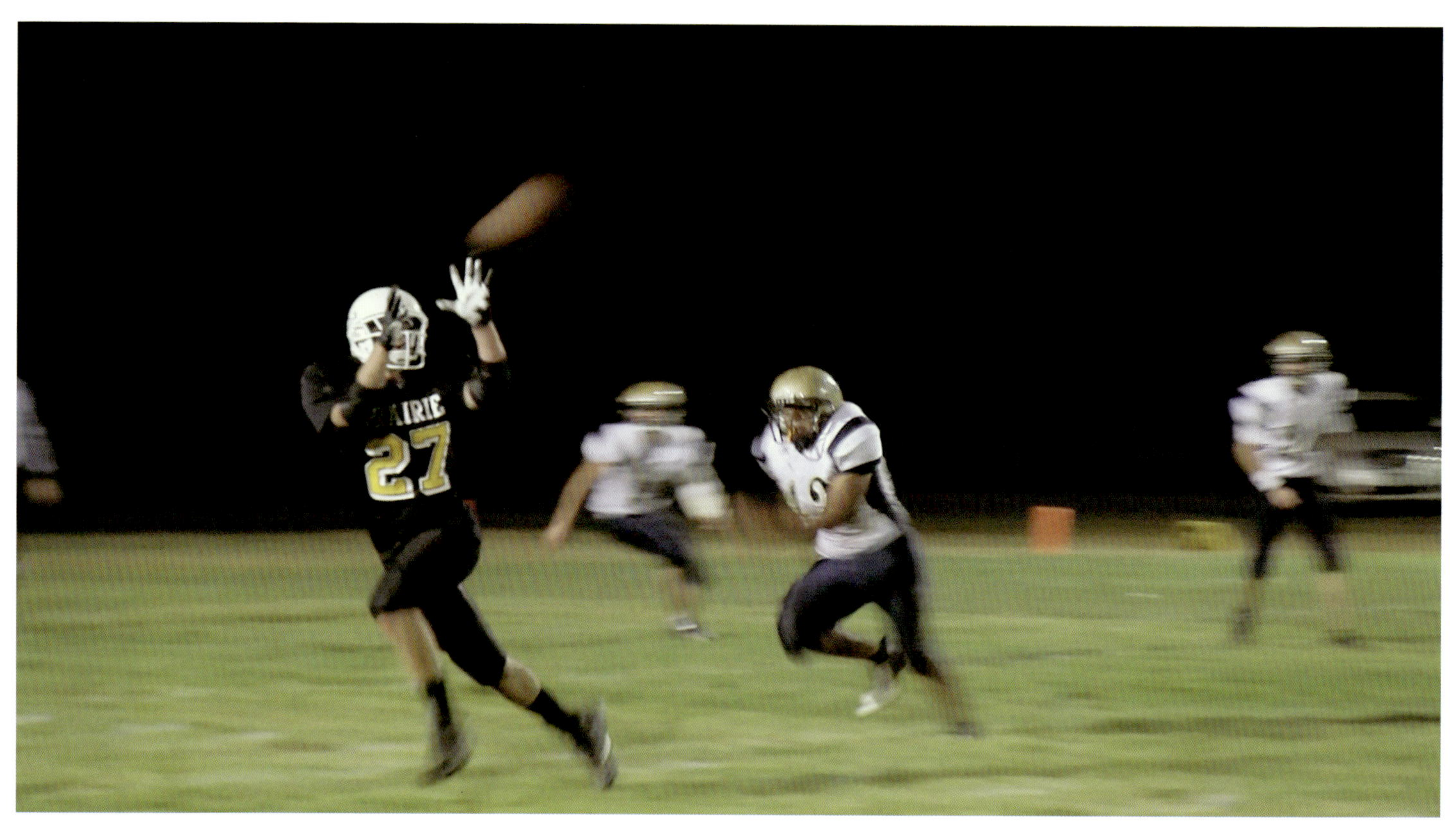

NORTH PARK WILDCATS

Clear skies, a full moon, and a temperature in the 50s made for a perfect football night in New Raymer, and the fans, staying warm in their pickups, were clearly excited about the game. The North Park Wildcats had traveled four hours from Walden, Colorado, a quiet town located in a sparsely populated, high-altitude basin along the Wyoming border. It's not uncommon to find a herd of elk grazing on their football field.

The Wildcats had come to Prairie School with a 3-1-0 record, fresh off a win against Weldon Valley. It had been a rainy week, and the re-sodded field had turned from the hard and dry ankle-twisting slabs of the previous week into a soggy mess of loose turf. Prairie kicked off first, and the ball soared almost to the end zone. The Wildcats shocked the Mustangs by scooping it up and running it all the way back for a touchdown in the opening seconds, silencing the crowd. After Coach Carlson settled the team down a bit, Godinez fielded North Park's kick and made a long return that changed direction a half-dozen times before being brought down midfield. A few plays later, the Mustangs scored, and then it was all Prairie. The game ended with a score of 53–12. As the Mustang players shook hands with the Wildcat players, the announcer asked everyone to please help repair the torn-up field. The North Park team and parents joined together with the Prairie folks to replace divots and smooth out rippled sod.

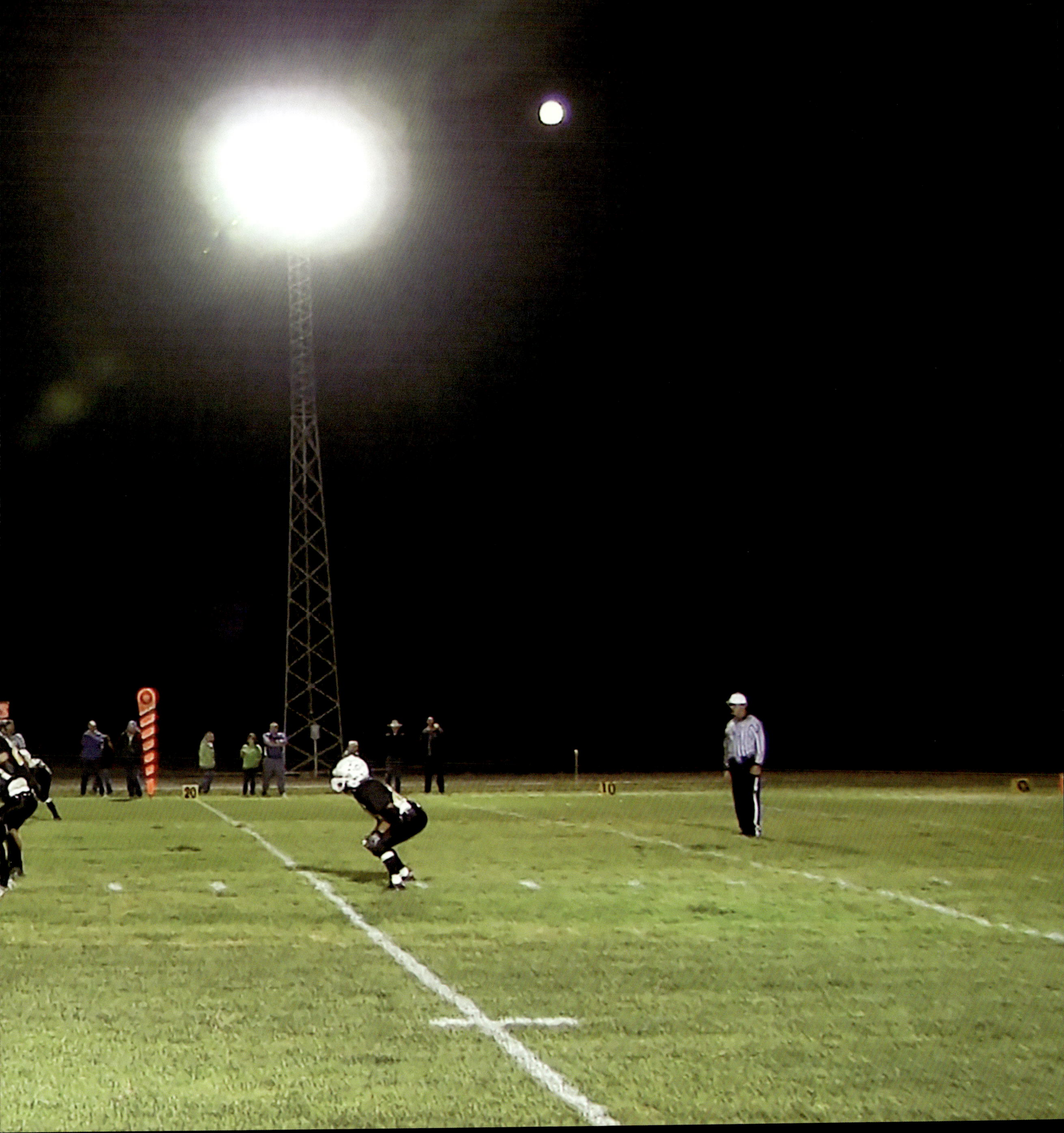

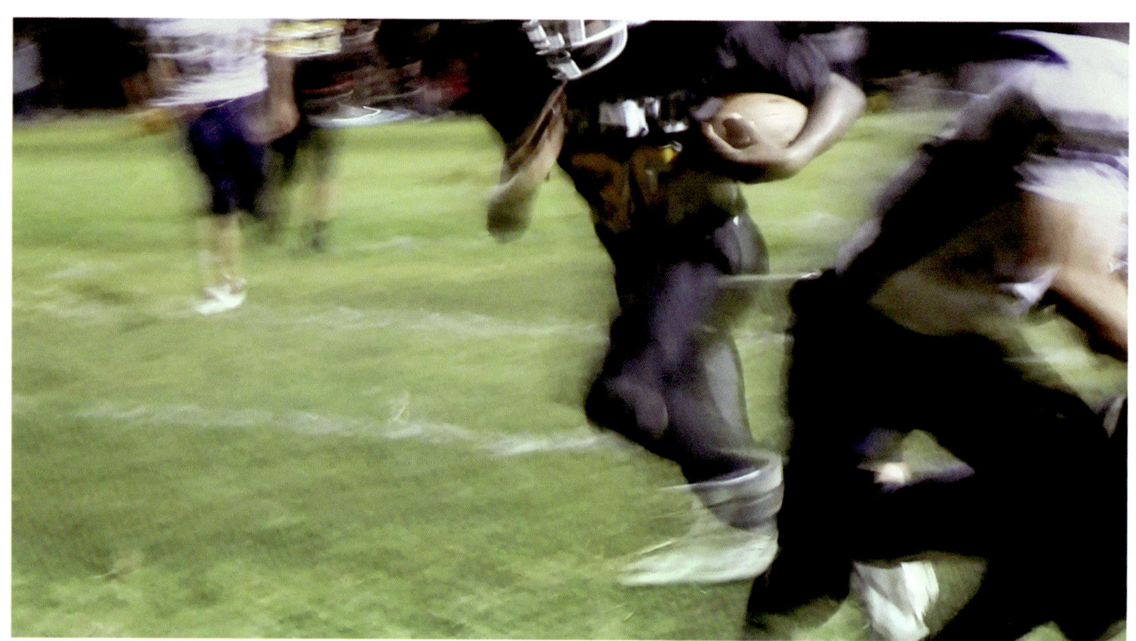

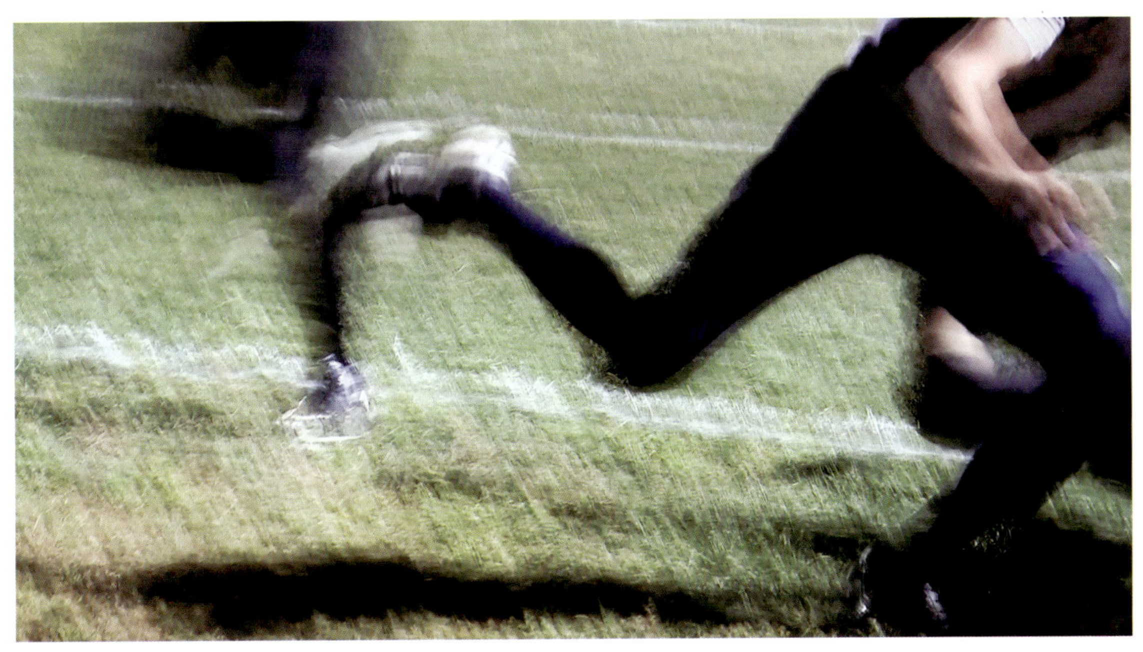

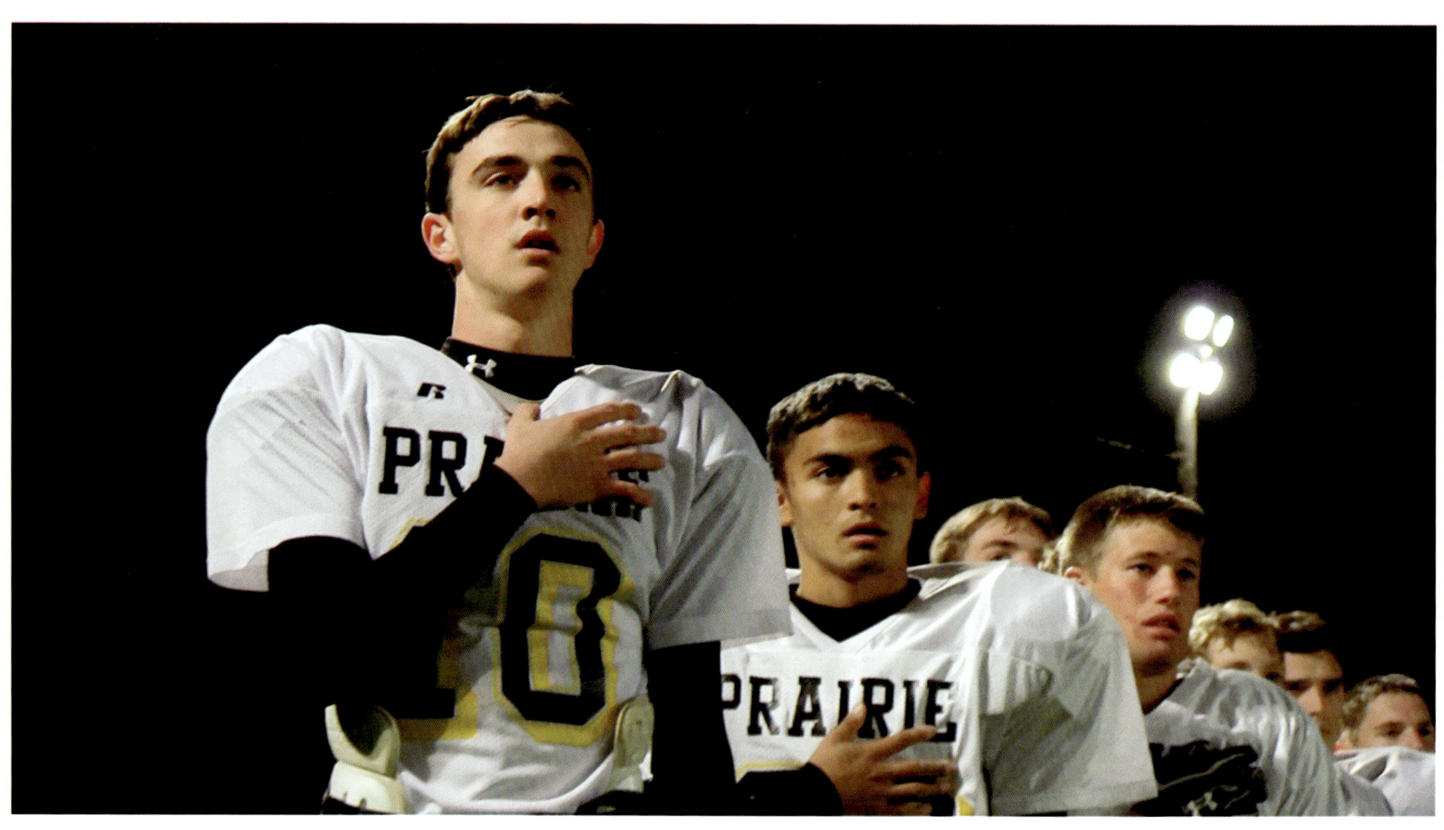

PAWNEE COYOTES

The next week's game against the Pawnee Coyotes was billed as the Colorado marquee game of the week by MaxPreps. The number two and number three leading rushers in Colorado six man were pitted against each other and both teams had strong defensive squads. The school was in Grover, a town of about 150 people, located in the center of the Pawnee National Grasslands. Willa Cather's description of "a little group of dwellings at the end of everything, with the desert running out on every side to the sky line" fits Grover perfectly. On game day it was cold, and the forecast indicated snow by late afternoon.

At kickoff, the temperature was 35 degrees and dropping. The first quarter ended a nippy 0–0. Warboys was struggling to get out of the backfield. It seemed too cold to try and block anyone, and the Coyote defenders were all over the Mustang runners. Prairie's defense was holding its own until midway into the second quarter, when the Coyotes completed a quick pass that should have only been a short gain but ended up a touchdown. Warboys ran the ball the next four plays in a row, trying to get the Mustangs on the scoreboard before the half, but the drive failed.

Prairie needed to come out after halftime ready to play, but key players were feeling sick, and the cold had everybody down. The Mustangs kicked off, and the Coyotes ran it straight back for a touchdown. Prairie didn't score until halfway through the fourth quarter and then tried an onside kick, but the Coyotes fell on the ball quickly, giving them great field position. A few minutes later they scored again, making it 28–8, sealing the defeat for Prairie.

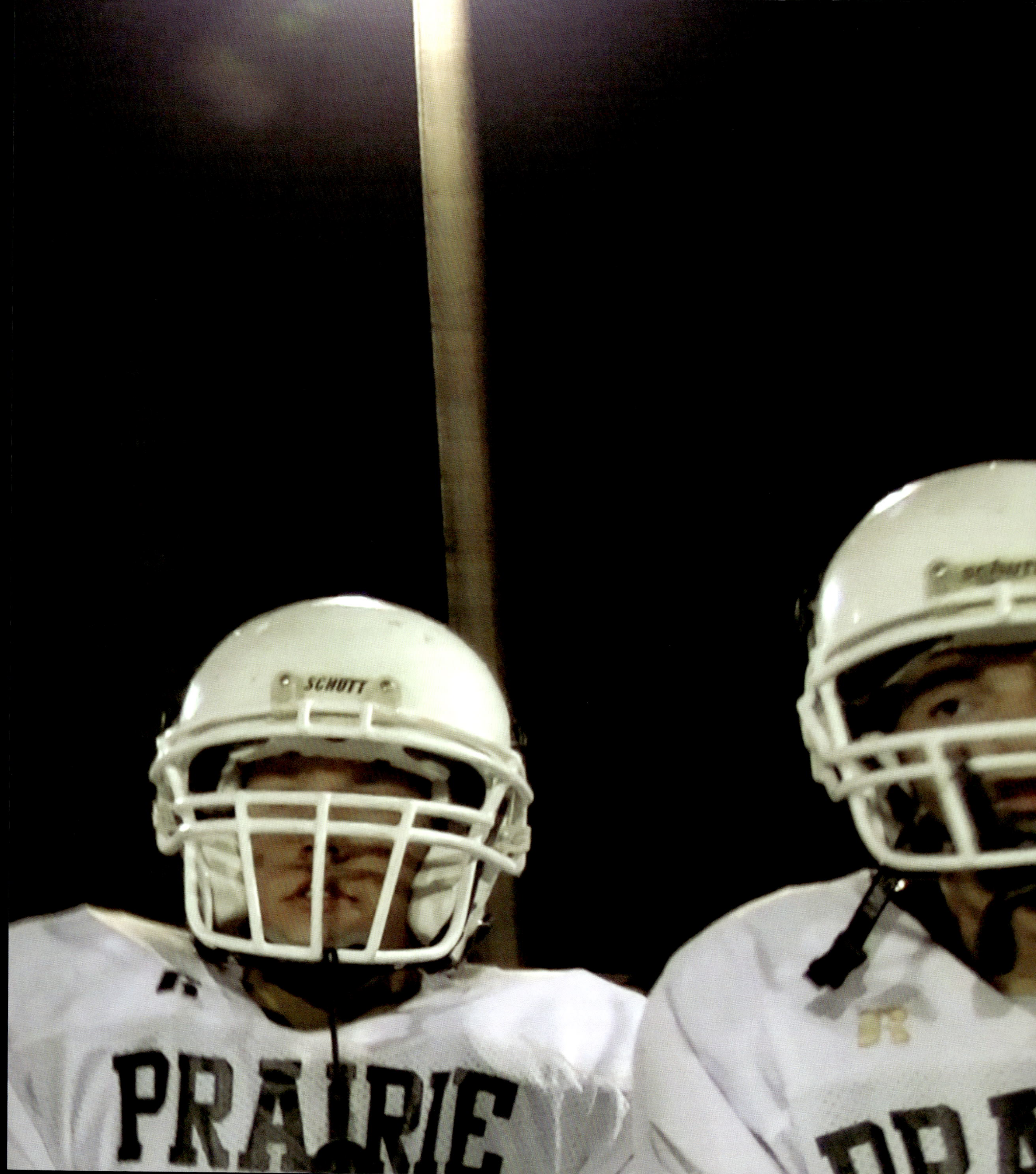
SCHUTT
PRAIRIE

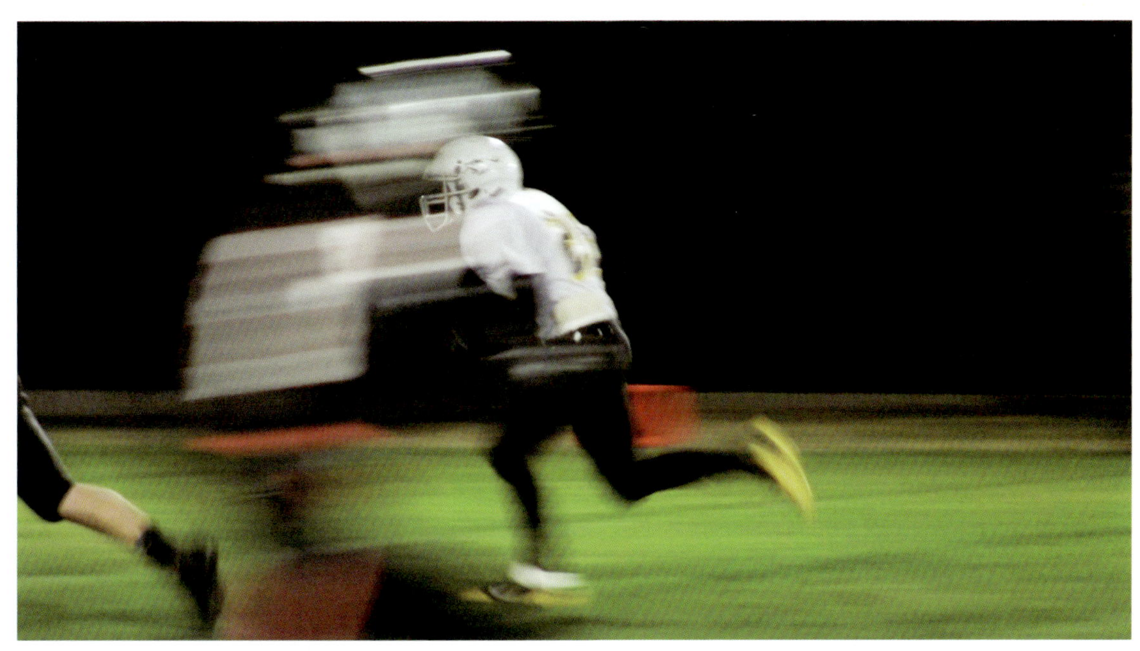

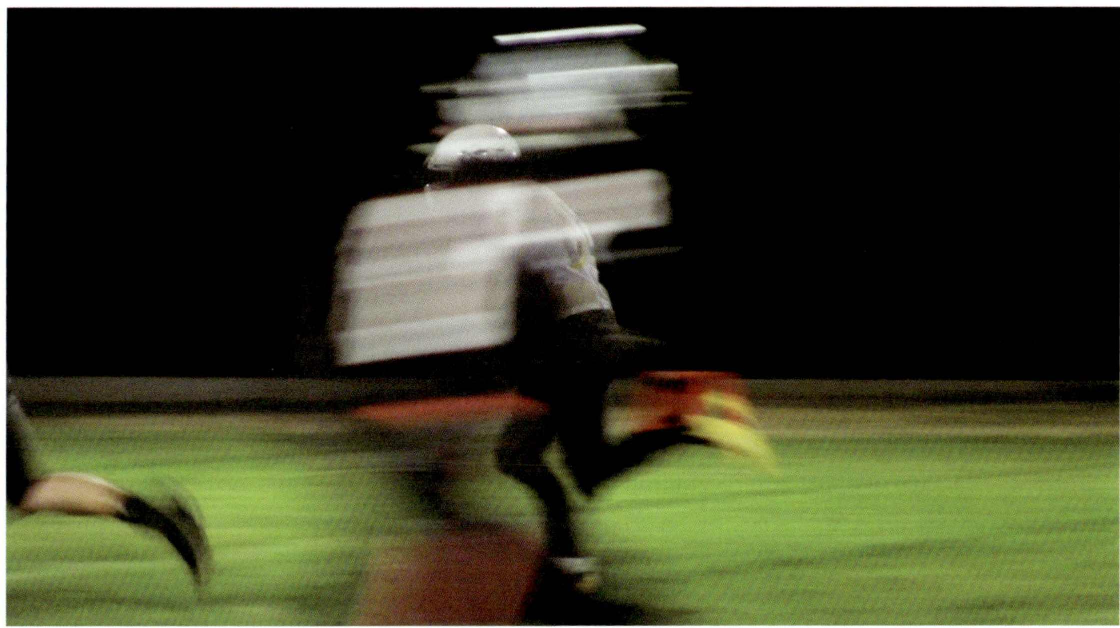

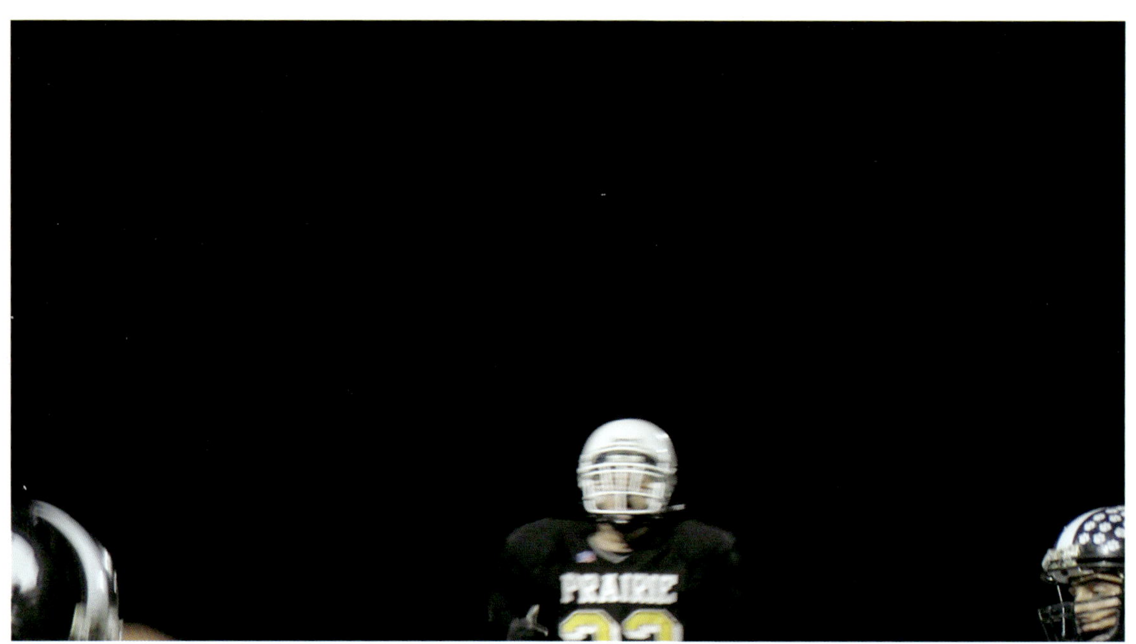

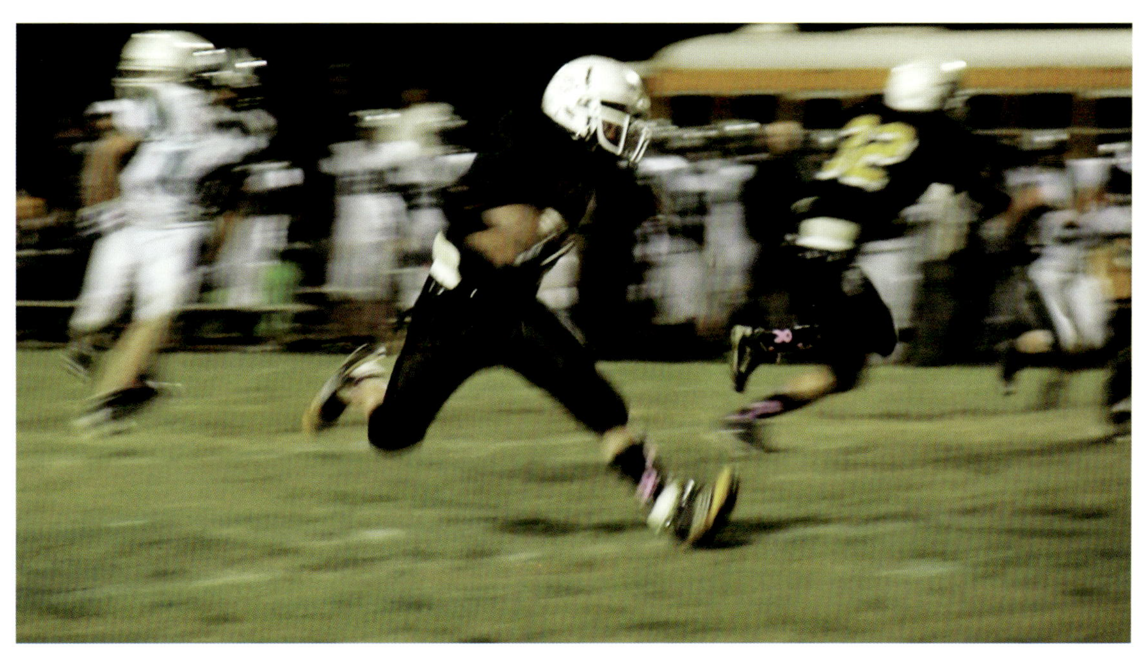

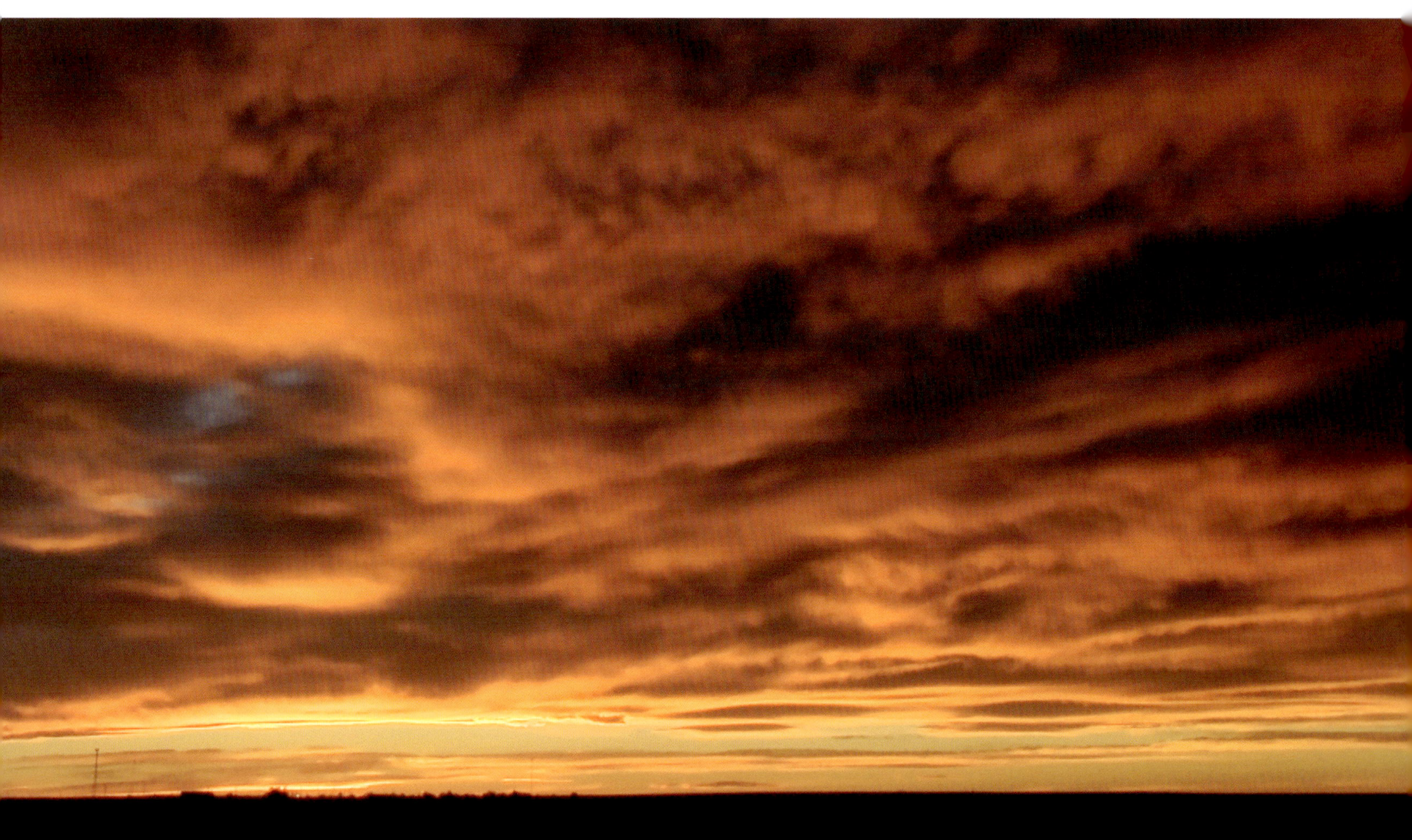

FLEMING WILDCATS

The hard loss to Pawnee brought a renewed intensity to the following week of practice. The formidable Fleming Wildcats were undefeated and ranked number one in Colorado six man and number twenty-sixth nationally. They also had the leading rusher in the state, Trevor Chintala, who always managed to stay 50 to 100 yards ahead of Warboys each week in the stats. But the game was at home and the weather was perfect. The New Raymer chapter of the Future Farmers of America was hosting Cancer Awareness Night with *Got Pink* t-shirts and ribbons, special socks for the Prairie football team, and a family walkathon around the field under the lights after the game. Like many schools, Prairie also held Parent Appreciation Night for the football team, on the last home game of the year. The Mustangs won the toss and elected to receive.

Prairie couldn't get anything going on the first three plays and had to punt the ball away. On the next play from scrimmage, Fleming ran it in for a touchdown. By the end of the first quarter, Fleming ran up the score 40−0. The Mustangs dug in, trying to stay in the game. Carmen and Warboys in particular made some spirited runs into the Wildcats' big defensive line. Great defensive efforts by Gapter and Funk kept the Wildcats out of the end zone in the second quarter. Finally, Ross Stump connected on a 35-yard pass to his brother Brady, who dragged a few defenders 10 more yards. The next play saw Warboys power over two defenders, break a few tackles, and slide into the end zone. Another Prairie touchdown followed soon after, and the Mustangs went to the locker room optimistic, at 40−16.

When the second half began, Fleming put up a quick score, but the Mustangs were not ready to let this game go. Quarterback Stump connected again with his brother Brady for a long gain, and Warboys scored again a few plays later. Prairie's onside kick was successful

"

and the Mustangs quickly took it in for another touchdown to make it 48−24. Prairie gambled and tried another onside kickoff. Tyler Carmen fell on the loose ball as it bounced between the Wildcats players, recovering it for Prairie as the crowd erupted and the truck horns honked. They drove down to the eight-yard line, but on fourth down came up short of another touchdown. The final score was 72−38, Fleming.

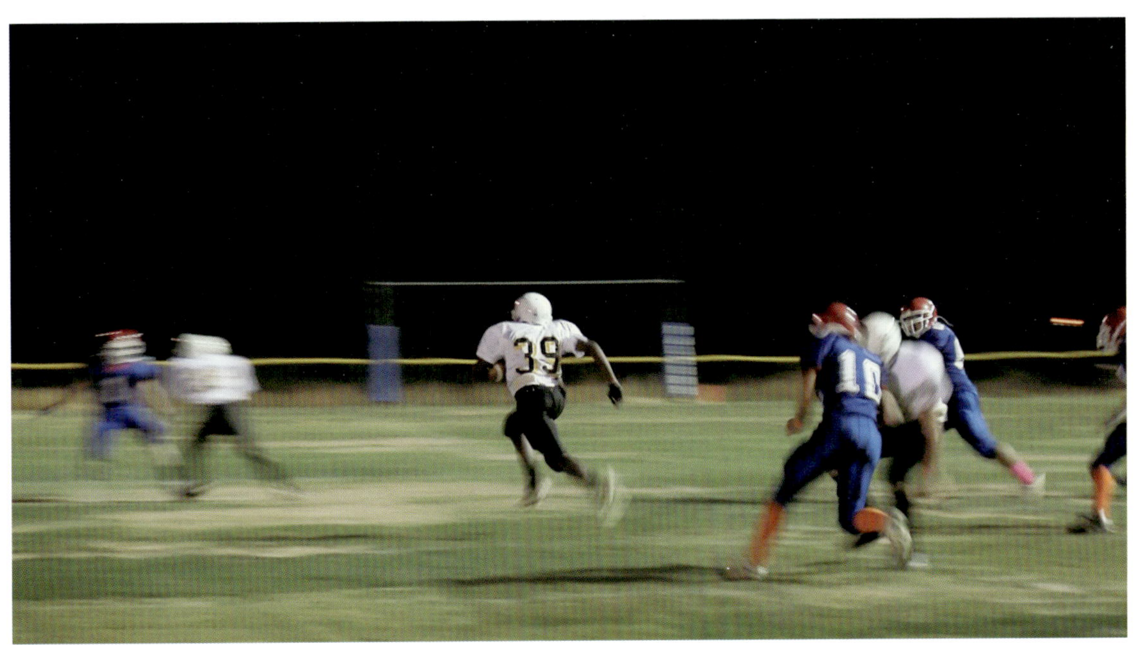

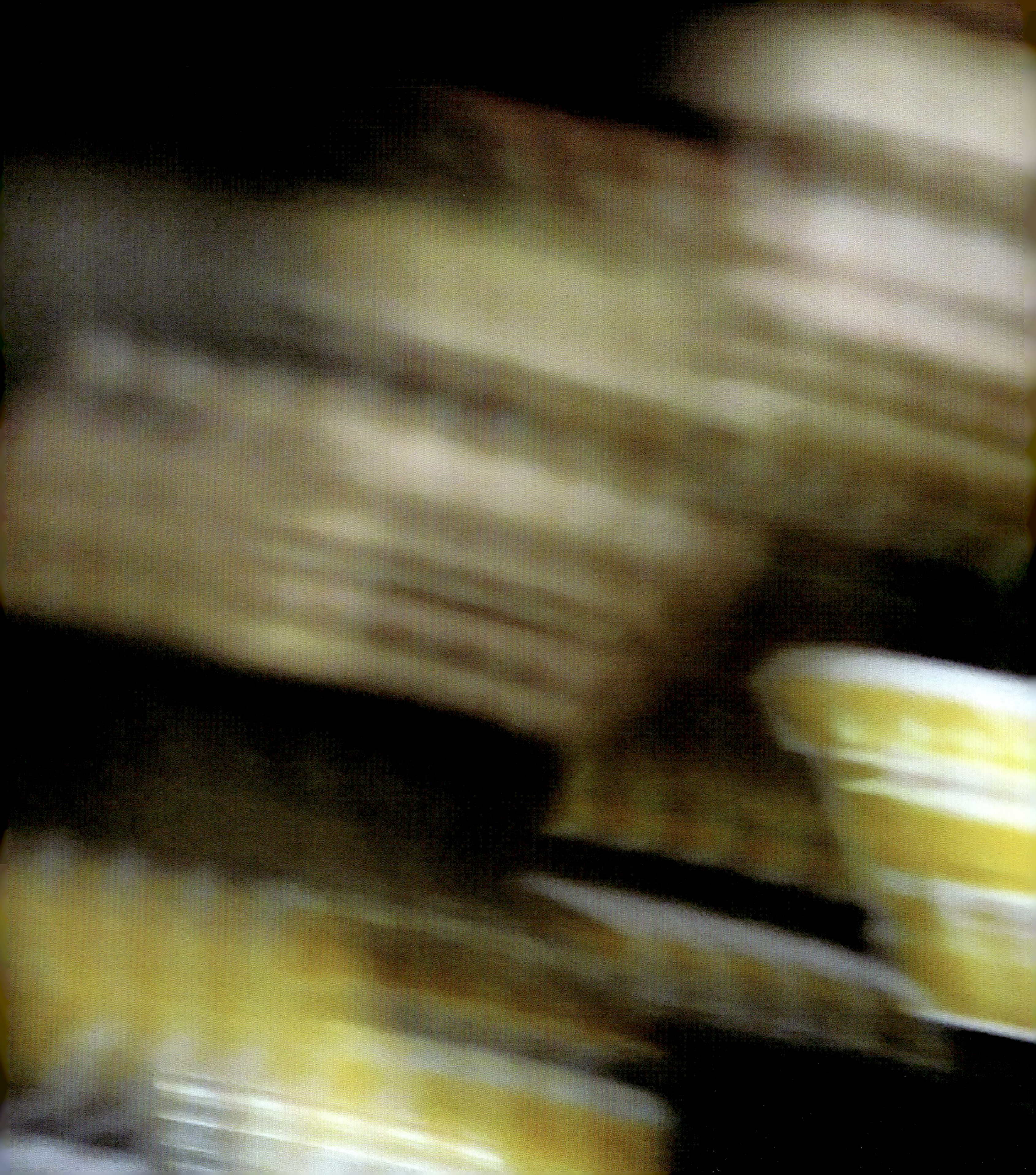

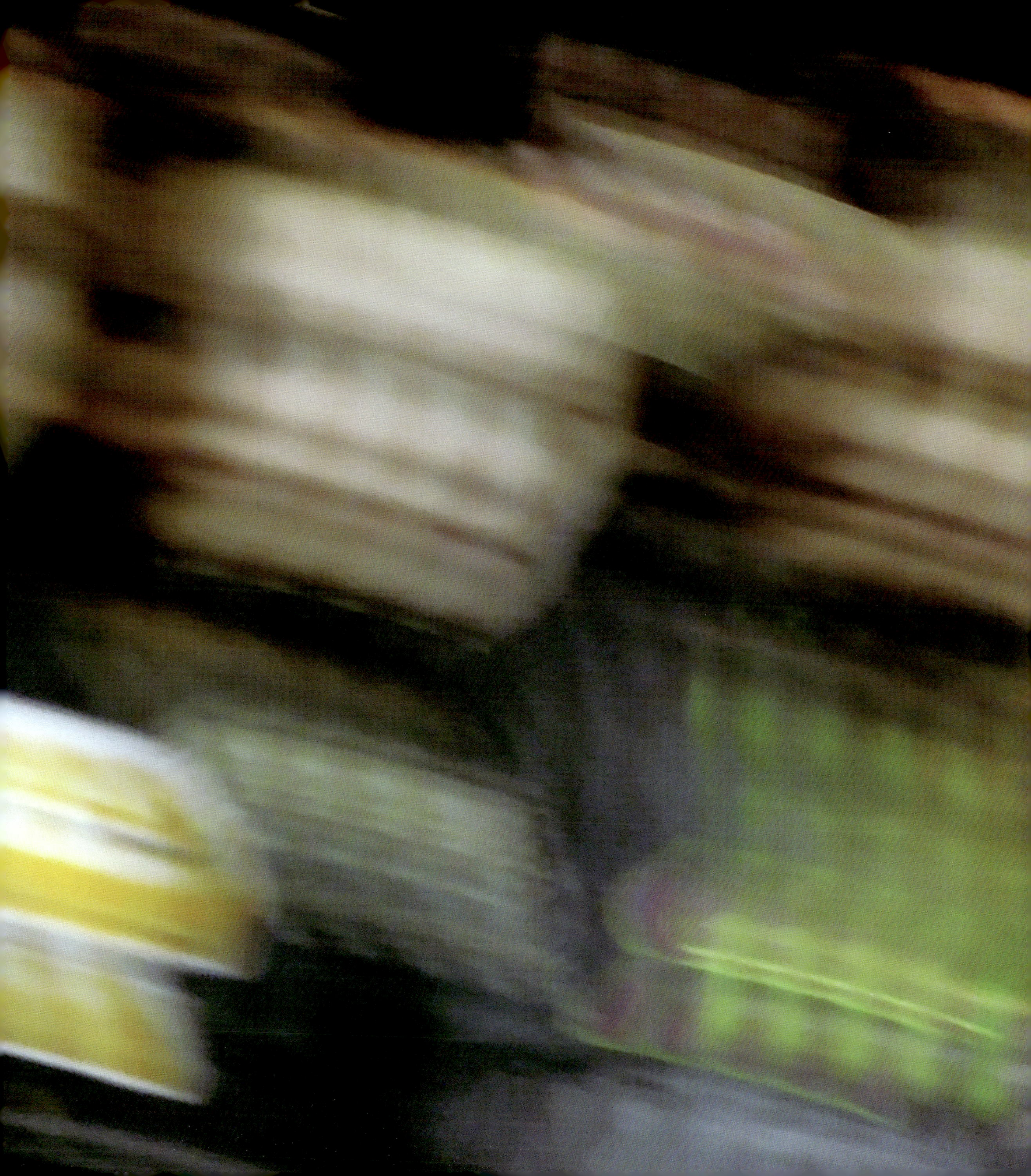

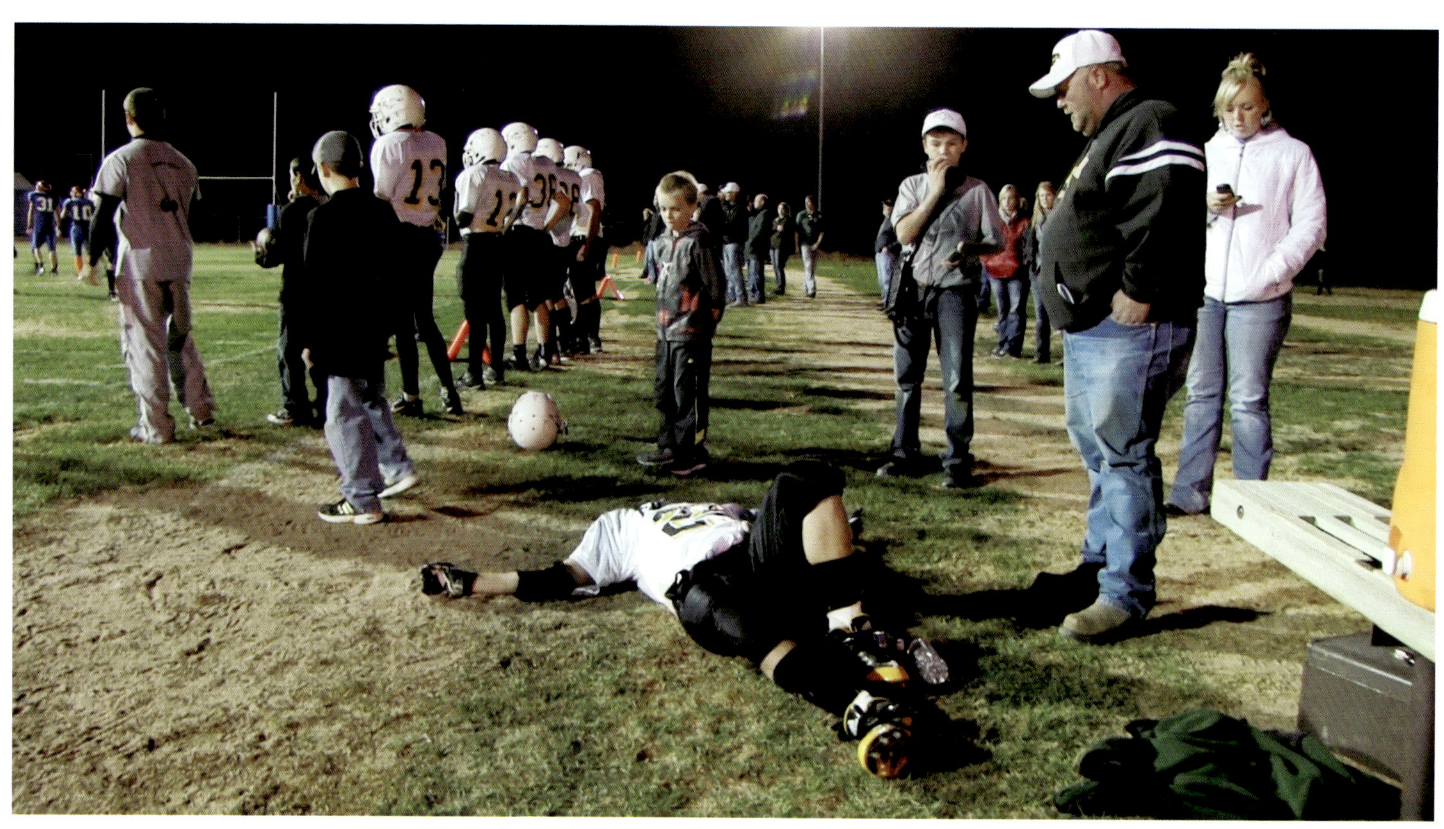

BRIGGSDALE FALCONS

For the last game of the regular season Prairie, at 4-3-0, faced off against Briggsdale, at 5-2-0. Located only forty miles apart along Highway 14, these two schools had a longstanding rivalry, and the players knew each other well though local chapters of Future Farmers and rodeo competitions. With each week that passed, the pregame sunsets grew more impressive. From the Briggsdale field, the sky lit up with dramatic streaks of orange and red clouds.

The Mustangs scored on the first set of downs on a 40-yard run by Warboys. The Falcons came right back with a long pass play on their first possession, making it 8–8 only five minutes into the game. On the next Prairie possession, after a half-dozen plays working the ball down the field, Ross Stump pitched the ball to Warboys on a sweep play. He tucked the ball under his arm and launched into the line, only to be smothered by the Falcon defense. Warboys got up slower than usual and unexpectedly started walking toward the sideline, his right arm dangling in an awkward way. Ian Falconier was sent in at halfback and the game continued on the field. Warboys lay on the sidelines, his arm stretched out uneasily, groaning in pain. Falconier scored a touchdown for the Mustangs, but the cheering was subdued as everyone tried to figure out what was wrong with their star running back and if he would be able to return to play. Finally, Coach Carlson decided Warboys needed to get to the nearest hospital, about forty-five minutes away in Fort Morgan. He had dislocated his right shoulder, and no one wanted to try and reset it on the field. As his mom and dad walked him around the end zone towards the parking lot, Briggsdale scored.

Over the next twelve minutes Prairie persevered. The Mustangs played great defense to hold the Falcons from scoring, and Tyler Carmen managed to bang his way to a touchdown. By halftime it was 22–14, Prairie. As the team took a knee to rest and recharge before the second half, the gravity of the situation was clear. Prairie would be playing on without their star player.

The Mustangs were already missing Godinez, out with the flu, and now with Warboys out too, the tide turned. The second half began with a Prairie punt blocked and a quick Briggsdale touchdown. That turned into two more touchdowns before the game was over, with Prairie only able to answer once. The final score was 46–30, Briggsdale.

On the drive home, word came that Warboys' shoulder had been reset, but it looked like he would be out for the rest of the season. The crossover elimination games began the next week. The Mustangs had ended the regular season ranked fourth in the North Division and would have to face the formidable number-one team from the South, the Hi-Plains Patriots.

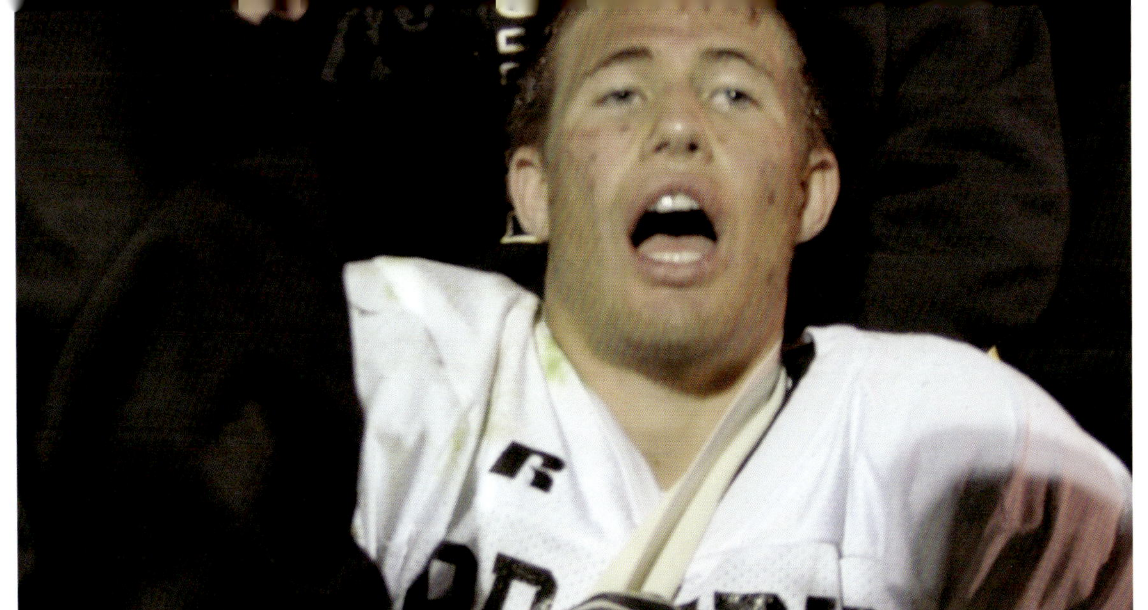

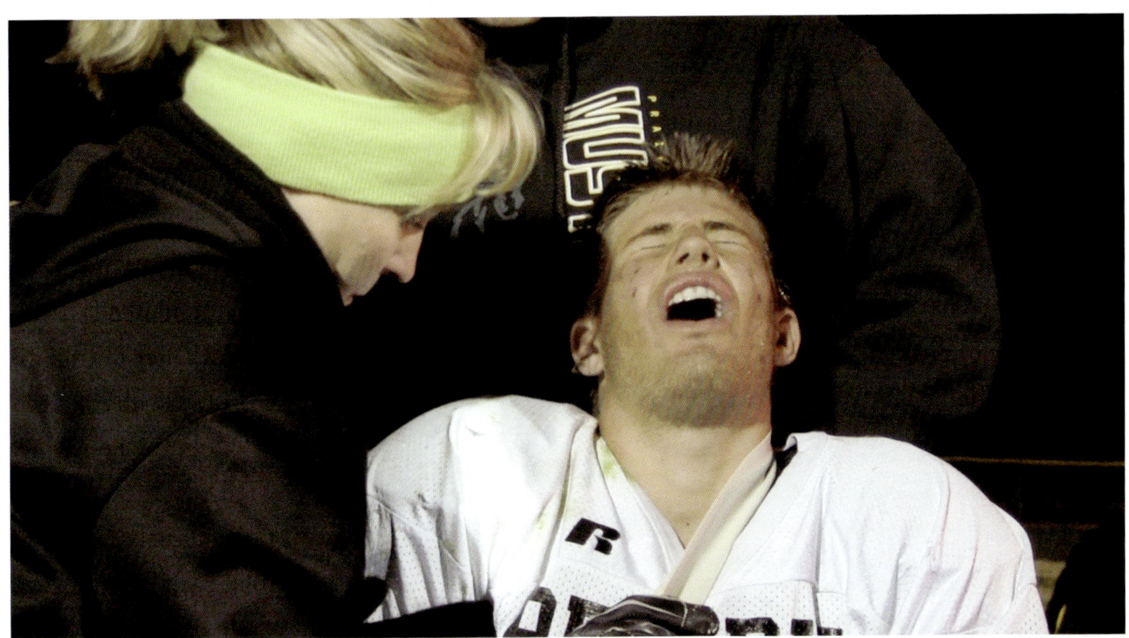

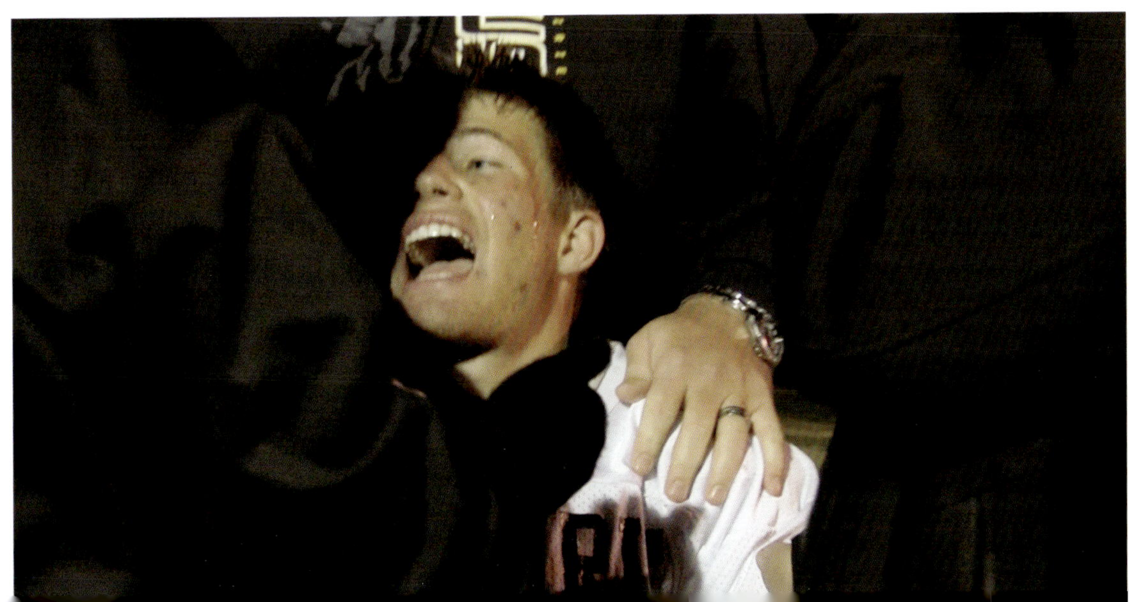

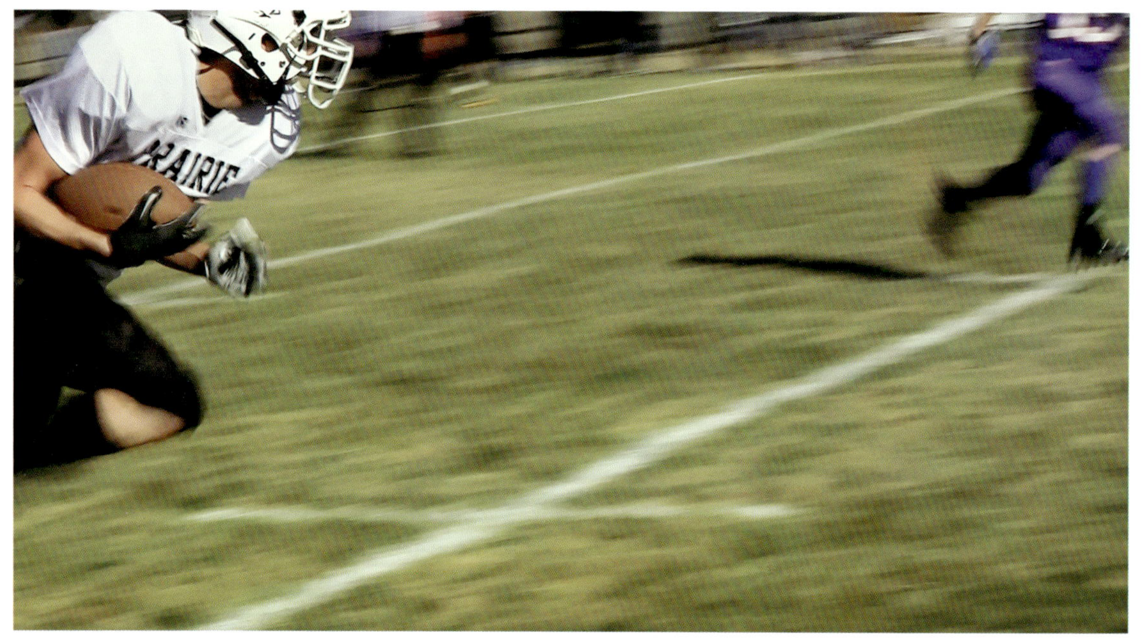

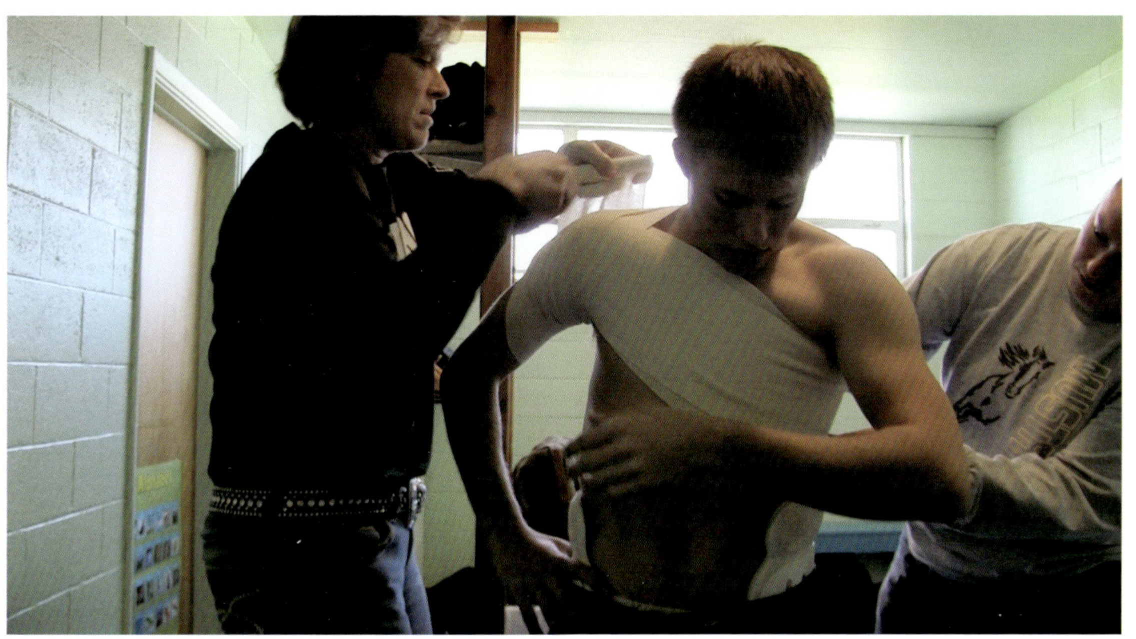

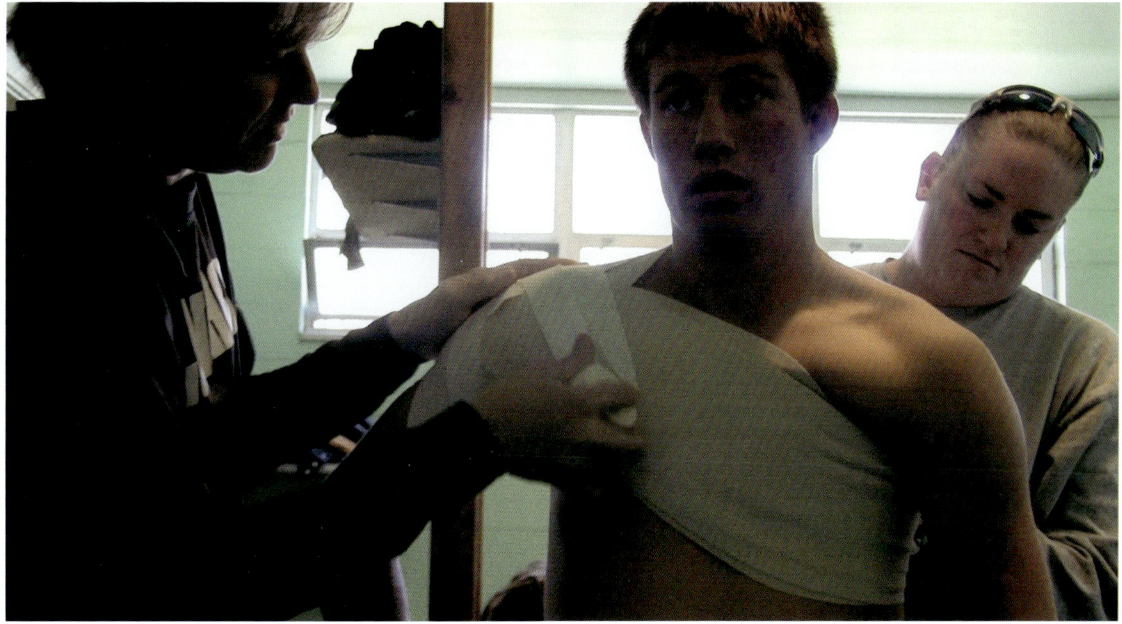

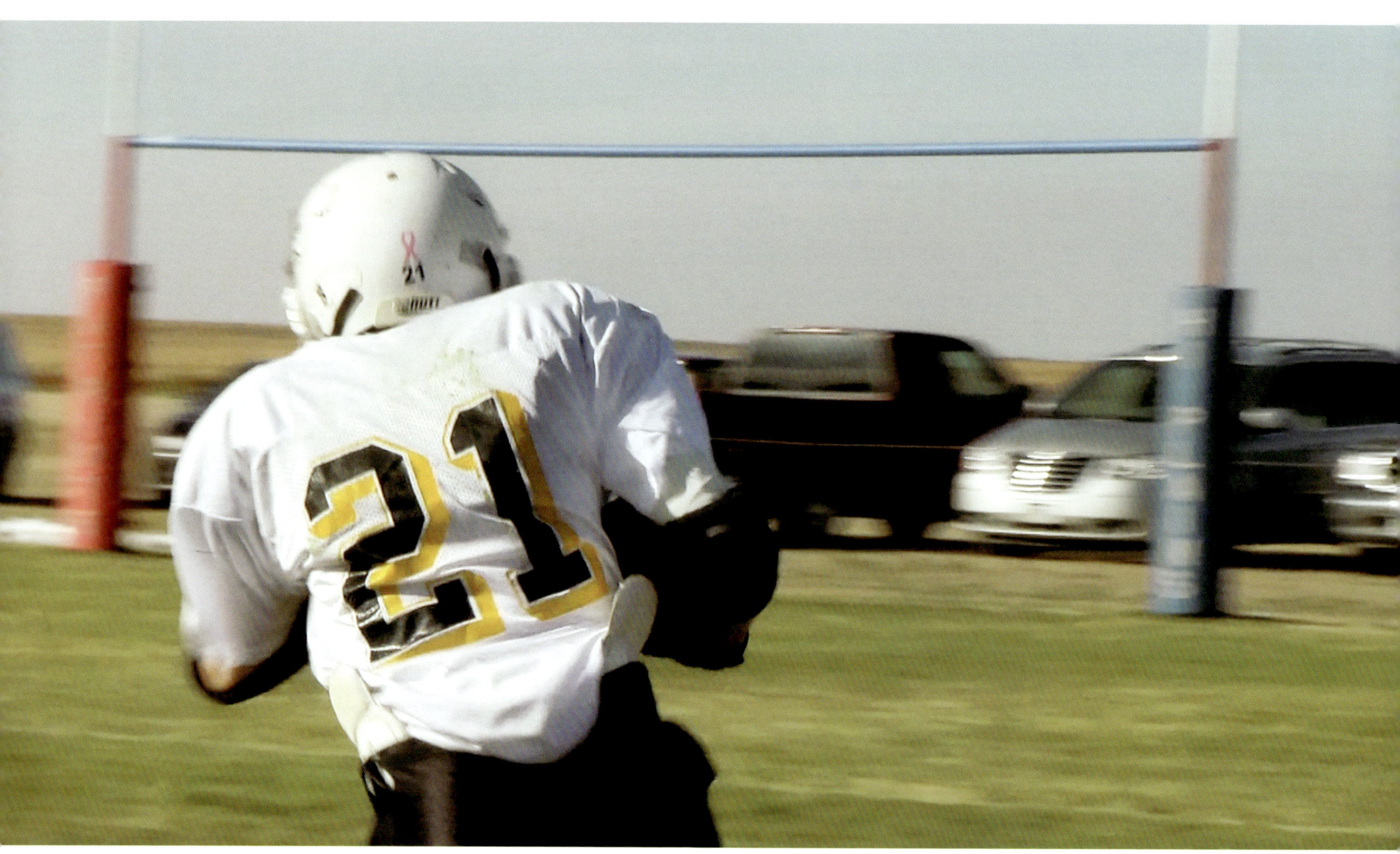

HI-PLAINS PATRIOTS

The Hi-Plains school was situated 150 miles to the south in Kit Carson County in the town of Vona, a semi-ghost town of mostly uninhabited buildings with a population of 106. The Great Depression devastated Vona and towns like it on the eastern plains. Then in 1936, a fire destroyed over half of the business district while the town awaited construction of a new water tower. The place never recovered. On game day, school staff shoveled the snow that had fallen a few days earlier to the edge of the field, leaving a bright white border around the grass.

Surprisingly, the Mustang's trainer had approved Dustin Warboys to play the game. Like the other Prairie players, Warboys had worked hard all season, and he desperately wanted to play. In the middle-school gymnasium that served as the visiting team's locker room, the trainer and her assistant wrapped reams of flexible tape around Warboys' shoulder and chest. In a final stroke of genius, they rigged an elastic strap that enabled him to lift his damaged arm about a foot, just enough to tuck a ball in, but without enough stretch to hurt his shoulder again.

Prairie lost the toss for the first time all season, but Hi-Plains opted to kick off. A stiff wind off the snow-capped peaks to the west chilled the open field and the small set of bleachers set out for fans. Many watched the game from the warmth of their pickup trucks instead, honking their horns to cheer their teams. The Mustangs first possession was met with a tough Hi-Plains defense, and when the Patriots got the ball, they scored quickly. On the next Prairie possession, Warboys swept out to the left, broke two tackles, and ran for a touchdown. The sidelines went crazy, with truck horns honking and the small group of classmates who had made the trip attempting the wave. Hi-Plains had missed their extra point, so when Automatic Austin Littlefield kicked the ball through the uprights, Prairie was momentarily ahead 8–6. Unfortunately, the determined Mustang effort failed to match the power and size of the Patriot players. The half ended 34–16, Hi-Plains.

At halftime, the players huddled together in the end zone to get out of the wind and ate oranges and bananas. A number of players had been sick during the week leading up to the game and their mood seemed low. Warboys was playing well despite the injury, but not surprisingly, he was not at his best.

Hi-Plains put six more points on the scoreboard only a minute into the third quarter. Prairie struggled. The offense had difficulty connecting plays, and the defense grew tired chasing the Patriot running backs. Still, with 2:35 left in the game, the Mustangs rallied. Tyler Carmen, taking the handoff from the quarterback, broke through the line but was immediately locked up by three Patriot defensive players and struggled to stay on his feet. Warboys took the ball out of his hands, broke two tackles, and ran it in for his third touchdown. The truck horns blared approval as the clock ran out with a final score of 48–24, Hi-Plains. Prairie's season was over.

Warboys, Stump, and Johnson, all seniors, had finished their high-school football careers. Parents and friends comforted the players as they headed to the locker room, while the coaches packed up the equipment. Warboys's mom and dad slowly unwound the tape that bound his battered body. By the time they were done, the rest of the team had gone. As Dustin Warboys walked alone across the emptying parking lot, a truck honked its horn in tribute to the effort. He waved in thanks and walked into the setting November sun.

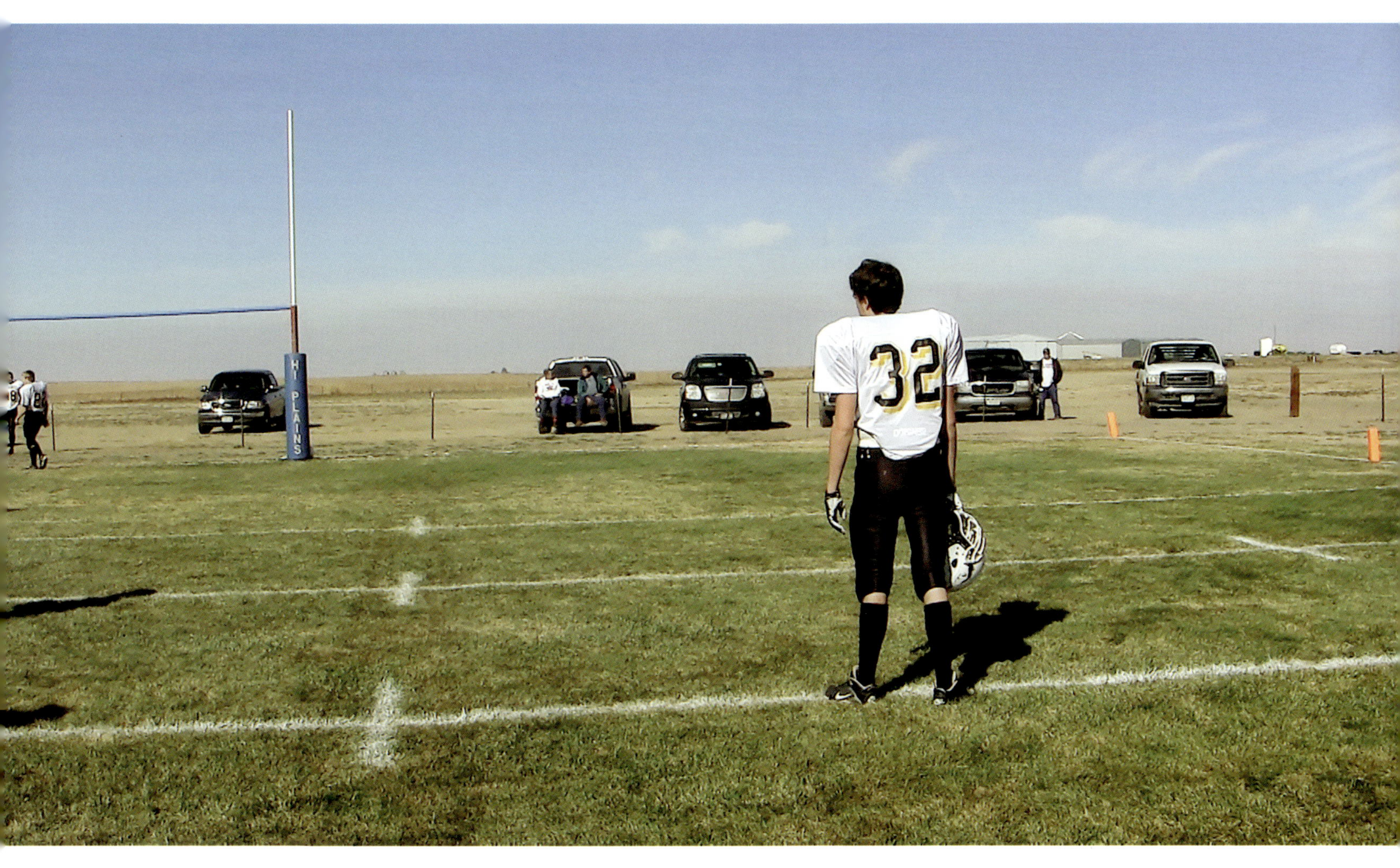

Acknowledgments

The freedom and opportunity to spend three months following the Prairie Mustangs through the 2012 season was a great gift. The immense space of the Pawnee National Grasslands and surrounding prairie never failed to remind me of those I love and those who helped me with this work.

My initial connection with Prairie School was supported by Superintendent Joe Kimmel and Principal Tabitha Piel. Joe put me in contact with football coach Glenn Carlson, who shared my enthusiasm for the project, and helped me get support from the families of the players. Of course, the players on the team deserves my deepest thanks: Tyler Carmen, Ian Fauconier, Brice Funk, Seth Gapter, Mychal Godinez, Zachariah Hastings, T. J. Hubbard, Bill Johnson, Michael Kaiser, Austin Littlefield, Brady Stump, Ross Stump, Dustin Warboys, Trae White, and Eric Williams. Their generosity and willingness to participate allowed me to figure out how to do this work, from the awkward first practice days to the disappointments of the season's ending. I hope this book is a document of a special moment in their lives. Additionally, I want to thank assistant coach Kyle Coles.

Friends and colleagues have always been my greatest resources. Robert Adams, Corey Drieth, Emmet Gowin, and Dave Woody influenced the attitude and method of this work. Their feedback has been significant to the whole endeavor. My colleague and friend Kevin Everson offered technical support and inspiration. Dan Hoogenboom, Mitchell Powers, James Scheuren, and Taka Suzuki each added tech support and ideas. My time away from teaching was sponsored by a sabbatical from the University of Virginia and a grant from the College of Arts and Sciences. Additional financial assistance came from Richard and Jeanne Press, who have never failed to support my work when needed.

As always, my heartfelt thanks go to Devin Johnston, Michael O'Leary, and Jeff Clark at Flood Editions. It has been such a pleasure to work with true professionals and artists who care about how something feels and looks and sounds. Every publisher should be a poet first.

I was thankful to have a few old friends living in Fort Collins when I arrived. Pat and Chip Coronel, Tom Lundberg and Dick Christensen, and Jan DeVore offered breaks from work with wonderful meals and the pleasure of their company. I even got my old teacher Gary Huibgregtse out to do some camera and sound work for games. Deep appreciation goes to Ray Tait. Raybo has been a friend for many years, and that fall on the eastern plains, he worked camera and sound equipment, gave game insight, and offered vision for the entire enterprise. I am grateful for his bottomless friendship.

Finally, Grace Hale, a new love at the time I was making this work, was always there with caring words and encouragement. She is now my wife, and I am thankful to Grace and her daughters, Emma and Sarah, for giving me a home.

This book is dedicated to the memory of Trae White (1996–2013), who tragically died the summer after the 2012 season.

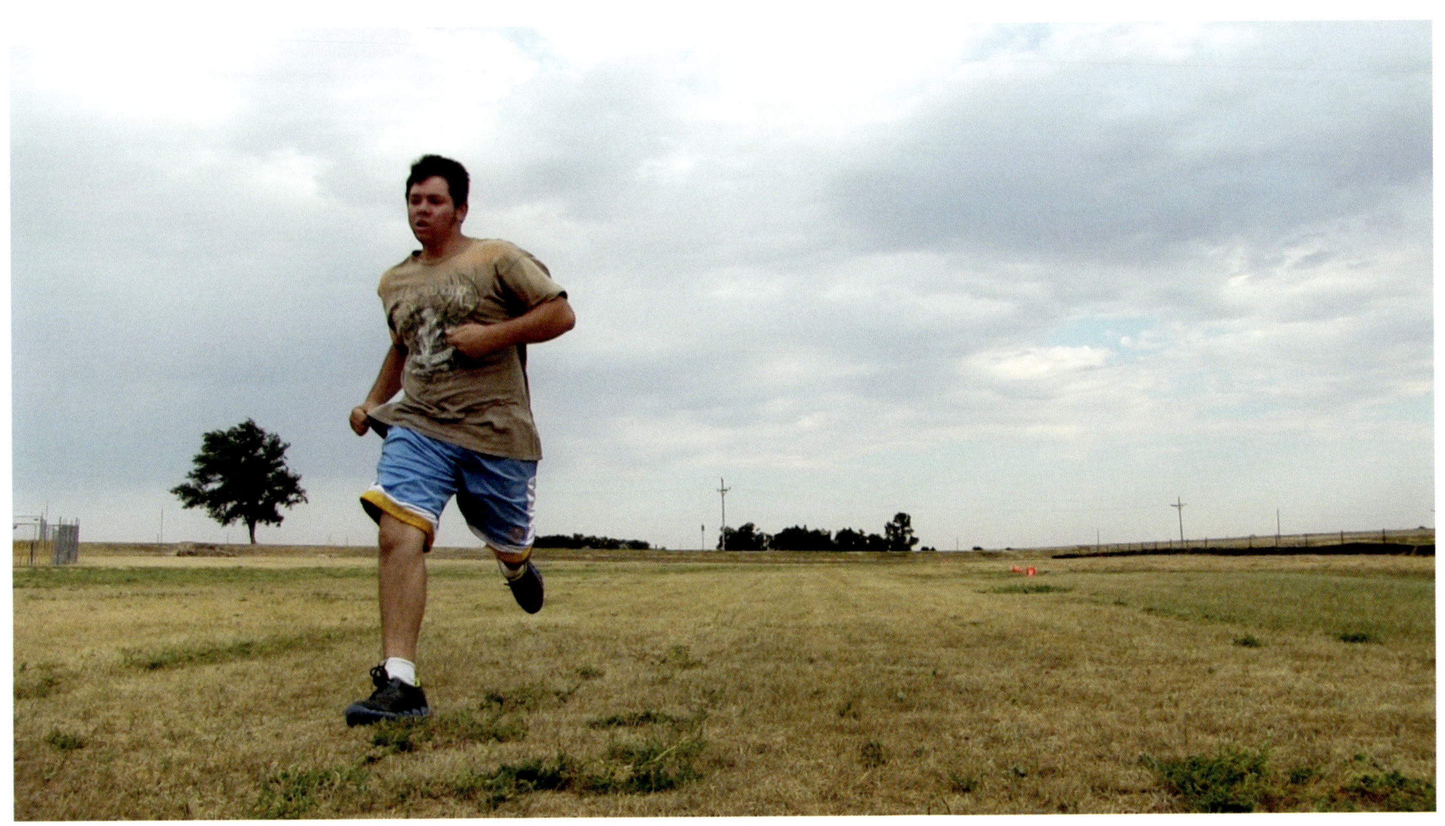

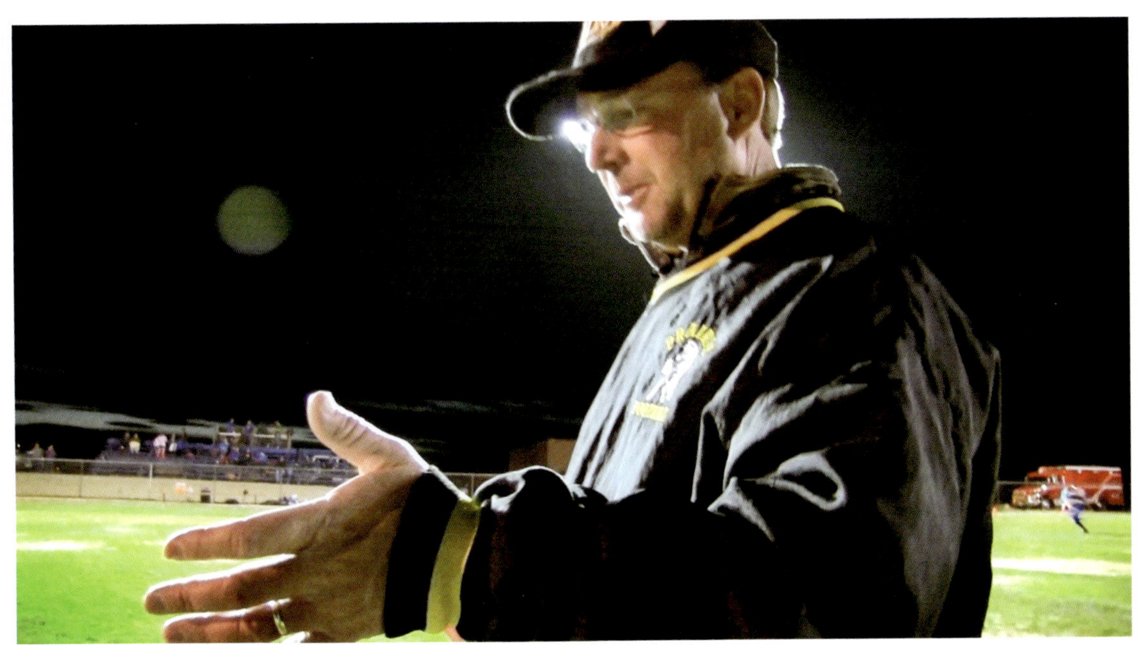

About the Author

For over thirty years, William Wylie's work has focused on the significance of landscape, exploring associations between particular places and their histories. He has published five previous books of photography: *Riverwalk* (2000), *Stillwater* (2002), *Carrara* (2009), *Route 36* (2010), and *Pompeii Archive* (2018). His photographs and short films have been shown internationally and can be found in the permanent collections of the Metropolitan Museum of Art, National Gallery of Art, Smithsonian American Art Museum, and Yale University Art Museum. He lives in Charlottesville and is the Commonwealth Professor of Art at the University of Virginia.

PUBLISHED BY FLOOD EDITIONS

WWW.FLOODEDITIONS.COM

ISBN 978-1-7332734-4-2

DESIGNED BY CRISIS

PRINTED IN CANADA

THIS BOOK WAS MADE POSSIBLE THROUGH

THE GENEROUS SUPPORT OF THE CHAUNCEY

AND MARION D. MCCORMICK FAMILY FOUNDATION,

JEANNE AND RICHARD PRESS, AND THE COLLEGE

OF ARTS AND SCIENCES, UNIVERSITY OF VIRGINIA.

FIRST EDITION